Y0-BPU-945

ANOTHER WINTER, ANOTHER SPRING

A Love Remembered

LOUISE DE KIRILINE LAWRENCE

McGraw-Hill Book Company

New York St. Louis San Francisco
Düsseldorf Mexico Toronto

to Elva

Book design by Milton Jackson.

Printed in the United States of America.

123456789 BPBP 7987

Library of Congress Cataloging in Publication Data

Lawrence, Louise de Kiriline, 1894–
Another winter, another spring.

1. Russia—History—Revolution, 1917–1921—Personal narratives. 2. Lawrence, Louise de Kiriline, 1894– 3. Russia—Social conditions—1917– 4. National characteristics, Russian. I. Title.
DK265.7.L34 947.084'1'0924 76-19094
ISBN 0-07-036722-1

CONTENTS

FOREWORD

THE first draft of this book, spanning some twenty-five years of my life altogether separate from later goals and circumstances, was written when the events described in it were still fresh in memory. Much of it is based on my letters to my mother. For various reasons the manuscript was allowed to rest for more than thirty years. During this time it remained constantly in the back of my mind, ripening, as it were, toward the form it could finally take when I had gained in experience and in vision.

It is not only an account of the life in which I grew up and of which I was a part as a young girl, but an effort to present a historical episode as it is now perceived from a greater distance in time and possibly in a truer perspective.

I wanted too to extract from the impact of politics a more faithful image of a complex, highly emotional, intuitive, and gifted people who inhabit a vast part of the earth. And in so doing, I have endeavored to isolate from the distortions created by political trends and events the essence of the Russian character as it appeared to me in its many phases, altogether devoid of the bias contrived by the preconceived notions of archenemy and communist. Only thus, it is my strong conviction, shall we know and understand each other.

With the exception of the historical figures, some of the Russians in this book appear under fictitious names, either because their real names have slipped my mind or because they are better left unknown.

L. de K. L.

The beauty of life is nothing but this,
that each should act in conformity
with his nature and business.

Fray Luis de Leon

PART 1

CHAPTER 1

VILLA ON THE HILL

ABOUT two hundred miles south of Stockholm, the elongated fjord of Bråviken cuts deeply into the Baltic coastline of Sweden. Its northern shore rises abruptly into the forested mountain region of Kolmården, famous for its awesome beauty, notorious for its lengendary history of hijacking and robbery. In the middle of this range an open marble quarry shines from the distance like a drift of snow, though the marble broken from this northern rock is sea-green, blotched, and veined. Here the fjord widens into the bay of Swinesund. And along its western shore the Svensksund acres stretched far back into the country.

The recorded history of this land dates back to the Vikings. Then the sea covered miles of what are now fields and pastures. Deep in the soil archeologists have unearthed artifacts dating back to the Scandinavian stone and bronze ages.

In the year 1772, during one of the many wars between Sweden and Russia, the enemy overran the Baltic coast, burning and ransacking. The original manor house of Svensksund fell victim to the pillage and was burned to the ground. Only the wide marble stairway remained, descending to an avenue of ancient, immense horse chestnut trees.

Flanking the old manor house were two annexes, and these buildings miraculously escaped the fire. The owners took up residence in the right one, adding new wings as the family expanded. This became known as the Big House, and there, nearly a hundred years later, my father, Sixten Flach, was born.

My mother, Hillevid Neergaard, was Danish. But her mother, Wendela, came from the branch of the Flach family that lived in the western part of Sweden, and in the spring of 1890 she took her debutante daughter on a tour to visit them all.

This was an era of genuine sociability. The country houses, perennially prepared for invasions of house guests winter and summer, were large and comfortable. And thus, on a fine spring day, Hillevid came to Svensksund for the first time. She found a spacious rambling house with many wings, some twenty rooms and attics connected by steps, stairways, and passages. In front of the house was a round flower garden not yet in bloom, with tiny fancy fences surrounding each bed. Beside the glassed-in veranda stood a weeping ash under whose tentlike branches on warm summer days after-dinner coffee was served. A graveled terrace ran to the edge of a steep escarpment more than a hundred feet above the pasturelands below. Beyond, the shoreline of the bay merged into stands of waving reeds. Spruce-clad inlets dotted the bay, and then there was Kolmården, the dark-green backdrop of the silvery fjord, a vast panorama of land and water.

Life at Svensksund was one of ease without elegance, thrift and practicality without fuss. Inside, the house had an air of slight stuffiness with its white-scrubbed plank floors and its white antimacassars adorning every one of the solidly comfortable chairs and sofas. Grandfather Sixten walked with a cane. He had a wart on the side of his nose, and a prominent benign tumor displaced his starched white collar. His white beard waggled when he spoke. Less visible was the high court title bestowed on him by the king, for he bore it without pretention.

Grandmother Augusta was short and roly-poly, almost as broad as she was tall. She wore her gray hair slicked back into a flat pancake on top of which perched a fanciful cap of white lace and black velvet ribbons.

Sixten, the second son, ran the estate while Jana, the only daughter, held the reins of the household in her capable hands. And the old people were left well cared for and free to follow their own whims.

The difference between the solid living at Svensksund and the carefree gaiety of her life in Copenhagen must have struck Hillevid forcefully. Less dramatic were her feelings about Sixten. She liked him well enough, but she was not deeply involved with him. And for a long time the three-week visit to Svensksund remained in her memory as an episode of pleasant but minor interest, suffused with the rise and glow of Sixten's as yet unspoken adoration. But a year later, when my parents became engaged, my mother was in love with another man.

Hillevid was still a small girl when her father died of dysentery while on a holiday with his wife in Italy. The young widow took the loss of her husband with fortitude. She refused to make things easy for herself by selling the estate and going to live with her four sons and Hillevid in the capital. With her means and position it would have been a life of unchallenged ease and security. But Wendela had different notions. With an iron hand and a rich endowment of organizational skill, she proceeded to run the estate, beautiful Faarevejle on Langeland, a small island within Denmark's inland seas, where the castle-like white house stood surrounded by vast lawns and beautiful trees. It was her duty, she felt, to preserve the ancestral home and, when the time was right, hand it on to her eldest son in the same condition in which it had been left to her. And, eventually, she did. To her, duty was the supreme virtue.

Grandmaman Wendela lived up to her idea of *noblesse oblige* with great success. She had character, acumen, and will, but above all she had style. To define her set of values as morality would be to rob them of a certain undefinable quality, a kind of *élan*. She must have been strikingly handsome when the vivid coloring of youth still enhanced her finely molded features. In old age her face had great distinction. As I remember her, she wore her silvery hair artfully arranged in a pompadour with sausages of precise curls built into a tapering tower. Her gray eyes did not always have the warmth that animated them when she was emotionally stirred. A finely curved nose and a haughty mouth always slightly puckered completed the portrait. She never laughed outright from the heart, although she by no means lacked the Flach family's sense of humor. When occasionally she allowed it to shine upon us, she expected us always to laugh heartily while she herself indulged in ladylike chuckles.

No one had so straight a back as Grandmaman. When she prayed she bent only her head; when she cried she sat bolt upright and dabbed her eyes. She smoked—one Havana cigar every day after dinner. Straight as a ramrod, she walked up and down the drawing room, puffing elegantly. She indulged openly only *en famille.* When there was company she withdrew to her own rooms, later to reappear without apology in a highly affable frame of mind.

It was no surprise that Grandmaman was supremely successful in handling both her sons and the estate. All her transactions were conducted with scrupulous honesty, and inexhaustible resourcefulness soon became her trademark. She was inordinately proud of her four sons. Hillevid, the youngest and the only girl, she largely ignored, leaving her in the care of governesses.

When the time came for the eldest son to take over the estate, Grandmaman packed her belongings and with her daughter left Faarevejle to establish residence in Copenhagen. In a large apartment in an elegant neighborhood close to the royal palace she lived and entertained according to her station. She presented her daughter at court, and as a debutante the young girl took a lively part in the social events of the winter season. By contrast to her mother, Hillevid was a mousy-looking young thing with features of no particular distinction and thin straight hair. Indeed, she might easily have been entirely overlooked had it not been for her vivacity. After she left governesses and school discipline behind her, her vitality blossomed, illuminating and enhancing her best features, the sensitive mouth with its even white teeth so frequently shining in laughter, the straight nose, the willowy figure, the firm breasts.

Hillevid's animation and wit soon earned her popularity among the fashionable set, eclipsing even that of her mother. She was eighteen and enjoying life with her whole heart. Copenhagen was a capital renowned for its gay social life, its lighthearted fun and frivolities. She became the intimate friend of Crown Prince Frederik's four daughters, Louise, Ingeborg, Dagmar, and Thyra. An especially warm attachment developed between her and Louise, who eventually became the godmother of Hillevid's first child and endowed the baby, together with her name, with a soft pink-and-white crocheted coverlet, forever considered too precious to be used. Unlike many friendships with persons in high places, this one endured warmly and intimately until the princess's death after too short a life of sadness and disillusionment. Twenty-three years later, the child, by lucky chance coming in contact with many of these same people, was to benefit greatly from the fact that she was Hillevid Neergaard's daughter.

It was at this time that Hillevid met Axel Lerche.

Wendela's announcement of her intention to remarry fell upon Hillevid like a bombshell and brought her the first grave crisis of her life. A former cavalry officer though not of noble birth, Wendela's intended was a man of utmost gentility and distinctly unmartial in appearance with his slight frame, drooping fair moustache, and mild blue eyes. He was also a Catholic.

Hillevid looked upon her mother's betrothal as a personal affront. Never, she vowed, would she sit there and be witness to this preposterous love affair. She must get away. But how? She had no private means; in those days young girls of good family did not work.

In vain she waited for Axel Lerche to declare himself. In the course of the season he had shown himself far from indifferent to her. They had danced together at every ball, he had always claimed the first waltz and the cotillion, and sometimes also a dance in between. They had skated together on the moat, a popular pastime of the young set in those days. They had often met in his sister's apartment, above the one Hillevid shared with her mother. And now, suddenly, she realized she was deeply in love. He, he alone, could save her from the abominable situation in which she found herself. Into every meeting with Axel she poured her most ardent unspoken wish that he propose, now, soon. But he did not. Day followed day and he said nothing—nothing—nothing!

Wendela's wedding was set for September. Meanwhile, there was the wedding of Ebbe, Hillevid's brother. Hillevid was to be one of the bridesmaids. And, suddenly, she thought of Sixten. He would be there, he loved her, he wanted her, but he was so much older than she—fourteen years! Still, Sixten loomed large in her mind as a lifesaver, a protector, an escape.

Too late Axel Lerche spoke. He followed Hillevid to Svensksund, carrying to her his heart, trying to persuade her to change her mind and come to him. Too late. For the sake of her firstborn, Hillevid made the agonizing choice for the three of them.

My father adored my mother, and he built for her a dream house where he planned they would live together in great happiness. He put into it all that his fond heart could devise to please her, all he could design for her comfort and pleasure.

A winding road led from the Big House a mile and half through parklike woodland of spruce and larch and pine trees to the Villa on the hill. At this height the bay and the fjord spread far beneath, unobstructed by trees. Below, the flat hatlike crowns of the Scotch pines that clung to the shelves of the seaward cliff accurately measured the rise of the hill. But on the south and west sides the hill smoothed out into a gradual slope. In the far distance it opened upon a landscape of square fields, with little houses tucked among islands of rock and green growth as far as the eye could see. Thus Father laid at Mother's feet all that he possessed.

On a solid foundation of granite rock Father built the house of dry fragrant wood. Overlapping wooden shingles covered walls and roof. The roof was steep and straddled several gables that jutted upward with wonderful irregularity. The house, all of it stained a deep brown, blended with unobtrusive modesty into its surroundings of tall feathery evergreens.

On a bright cold January day, in a warm room facing south of the Villa on the hill, Mother gave birth to me, and named me for her friend Louise.

Her second pregnancy was difficult, and a toxic condition forced her to spend many months miserably in bed.

Ebba was a small and sickly baby. She was also anemic. While I had reddish-blond hair, hers was dark brown, and so were her eyes. I was hearty and strong, a child, Mother said, perpetually happy for no other reason than that I was born that way. Stubborn and self-willed, I also was given to short-tempered flare-ups sudden thunder and lightning, come and gone, leaving the sky cloudless. Ebba, on the other hand, possessed the power of resistance so often fused into the character of the physically weak.

My memories of our early childhood are like leaves on a tree, each one complete and separate. The Swiss *bonne,* buxom, soft, and loving, who smelled of soap and clean linen, cared for us for two and a half years and spoke with us always in French. Ebba and I cried when she left.

Father appeared to me like a giant, long of leg and strong of body. His image was incomplete without the gold chain draped across his vest, ending at a flat gold watch slipped into his tiny vest pocket.

The pressure of his broad thumbnail on a certain tiny spot on the watch could make the lid spring open. When I became fully aware of him as my father, his reddish hair was already thinning and lines were beginning to dig into his ruddy face. I loved watching him shave with his straight razor, and I was especially intrigued by the application afterward of a transparent harness to train the tips of his full blond moustache at a jaunty upward angle.

Kindness filled his steel-blue, slightly nearsighted eyes. He had inherited his mother's self-reliance and hardihood. Father's voice was strong, and when he was aroused it was heard throughout the house. But his quickly flaring temper flickered out almost as soon as it burst into flame, for he was basically a gentle man. He was plagued by only two major complaints: the pastor, whom he considered a meek fool with an irritating lisp, hardly worth listening to when on rare occasions he found himself obliged to appear with his family in the parish church, and the weather, which God Almighty never regulated exactly as the crops required.

With tact and goodwill my parents pursued their daily duties in the house and in the field. There was no disharmony. Had someone told me then that their marriage had once been shaken by a very grave crisis, I would not have believed it. And this mutually encompassed attitude was important and helpful to them both.

It would not have been compatible with Mother's character to languish in regret over lost dreams. She had inherited Grandmaman Wendela's resolution and pride in sufficient measure to carry her through the difficulty. Whatever she lost in renouncing her first love was restored to her in the love of her daughters. And this love became her life's principal mainstay, sublimated into an emotion into which she injected enough intelligent control to save herself and us from the evils of dotage. Whatever mistakes she may have committed in the name of motherhood, she achieved a rare proportion and perspective in her efforts to bring up her daughters to become self-reliant and independent individuals. And this impulse, shared by my father, became the focal point of their own salvation—although there may have been occasions later when the effectiveness of their efforts took them by surprise.

"Your wills grow in the forest," Mother would tell us when, headstrong and self-willed, we insisted on having our own way.

The idea fascinated me. We clamored for evidence. She took us into the forest and showed us two sapling spruces standing along the path. She named the smaller one Ebba and the larger Louise. Imagine having one's will growing in the forest! Thereafter we never passed those trees without noting how much they had grown.

My lively imagination had no difficulty creating a fanciful world peopled with mythic beings. I named them *Bebborna.* They were black and dressed in pale blue and pink frocks. How this distinction of skin color happened is a mystery, for no countries on earth have less connection with black people than the Scandinavian, either historically or geographically.

Bebborna were an intimate part of the household, the same as I was. I communicated with them by pantomime, which on occasion turned into quite good acting with apt monologue thrown in.

Once or twice a month Mother took us with her to town for shopping by horse-drawn carriage, a trip of ten miles each way. We traveled mostly in the landau, which we liked because the top was nearly always down and we had a free view of all we passed. In bad weather the coupé was used, a tight compartment with light-gray upholstery that smelled musty. It had windows that one pushed down to open and pulled up with straps to close, and they rattled. Best of all we liked to ride in the large open sleigh in the winter, with the coachman perched at the rear of the passengers on a bicycle seat. A large white net was draped over the horses' rumps and on to the front of the sleigh to prevent the hard lumps of snow thrown up by the horses' hoofs from hitting us in the face. We sat covered with robes, our feet tucked warmly into bags of fur. And the bells jingled rhythmically in the frosty air.

Naturally, the *Bebborna* were brought along. In the crowded shops and on the busy streets their invisibility was a decided convenience, and they were a good influence on me. It was clearly up to me, for instance, to show them how one yields the way to grownups, how one opens the door, how one curtsies.

Father insisted that his daughters be brought up hardy and fearless. He scorned effeminate behaviors. Courage and pluck should be natural ingredients in any character. He placed great emphasis on outdoor activities, and so on toboggans, skis, skates, and horses we learned our first lessons of good sportsmanship. We learned to travel cross-country on long slim skis on snow that speedily lost the softness caused by the last snowfall and formed a crust. Upon the clean, clear ice of the bay and the fjord, behind frisky, sharp-shod horses or leaning sideways against a bulging sail, we shot across the gleaming blue-green surface, experiencing the thrills of speed and practicing the skills of balance.

A lively social life was traditional among the people who lived on the estates scattered around the countryside. Mother adored entertaining. She had a flair for running a big country household and for arranging dinner parties. With a masterly hand she trained her help, who recognized her aptitude for guiding them and responded by taking the same pride as she did in a program well executed. Like all people who do well in their chosen work, she delighted in running her house.

Long before Mother's arrival upon the scene, Father had formed a close friendship with Prince Carl, one of the king's sons, primarily developed out of their common interests, the land, agriculture, hunting. Prince Carl was tall and lanky. His chiseled features, the eagle nose, the classic mouth under a well-groomed moustache, were of the kind a sculptor might dream of as a model. A premature deafness may have been the reason for his very soft and peculiarly hollow voice. The prince visited the Villa on two occasions. I can remember no special fuss arising from his presence in the house, nothing beyond the usual entertainments when there was company. The prince was of course given the best guestroom, and his valet lodged next door. While the maid was making up his room one morning, I walked in and noted the large, slightly rumpled pillows where his head had rested. He must have slept very comfortably in that large clean bed on Mother's best sheets. He was taller than Father, and he did not speak like other people, and in my mind all this became synonymous with a king's son.

At night there was a dinner party. Ebba and I, dressed in our best frocks, were ushered into the dining room just after the dessert had been served. The doors opened upon twenty or more people in festive dress seated around the table covered with the gleaming white cloth. Candles glowed all along the center of the table and in the chandelier above, and their light was reflected in the sparkling crystal glasses. People spoke with us, kissed us, fussed over us. But our eyes were fastened upon the beautiful glitter and our ears heard nothing but the music of the many voices.

On a dark October day in 1902, Grandfather Sixten died. For the first time I became conscious of the possibility that somebody who had been there might suddenly not be there any more. This I did not connect with death, although I knew the word. What impressed me were the serious faces, the black clothes, the strong fragrance of freshly cut spruce boughs, and the heavy, almost suffocating redolence of too many strange flowers, wreaths upon wreaths.

Grandfather's death brought great changes into the lives of all of us. Father now became the rightful owner of Svensksund. We moved to the Big House, while Grandmother Augusta and Aunt Jana took up residence in the Villa on the hill.

CHAPTER 2

THE BIG HOUSE

"You could at least have left the aspen where it was," Grandmother Augusta remarked dryly when she saw the great changes that had transformed the Big House after my parents had finished their renovations.

Indeed, the weeping aspen cramped in the corner between the veranda and the house had vanished, and with it the venerable cherry tree. And the flower beds with their fancy fences grouped around the giant pink-flowered hawthorn in the center of the courtyard, they too were gone.

In their place well-trimmed lawns followed the curves of the graveled paths and filled the space between the hawthorn and the circular driveway. Only the Virginia creeper and the caprifolium, hiding every inch of the old house, were left to garland the windows. Tall and deeply recessed into the thick walls, they divided vertically into two sections, both opening inward over the wide sills, allowing the sea-scented air to flow freely through. Inside the house the heavy furniture and the antimacassars were gone. The new look of the rooms was tasteful and elegant. Carefully chosen antique chairs, tables, and sofas were scattered sparingly through the rooms, and in the blue-and-gold drawing room a huge polar bear skin sprawled in front of the fireplace.

Wood fires heated the whole house in winter. Each room was provided with its own heating unit, the *kakelugn,* an enlarged chimney flue of heat-absorbing tiles glazed on the outside, reaching from floor to ceiling. Once or twice daily during the chill winter, fires were lit in the firebox about a foot from the floor. When they burned down, dampers and shutters were tightly closed upon the glowing embers, and the heated tiles released their stored warmth into the room slowly and evenly.

Old Man Eriksson answered for the supply of wood that kept the heating system going. Occupational wear and tear and the passage of the years had bowed and gnarled his bony frame. He spent his days in the woodshed behind the annex, cutting the wood, which he trundled to the house on a squeaky wheelbarrow. Like a bearded faun, he lived among the emblems of his life, his sawhorse, his bucksaw, and his ax, and the smell of sawdust and snuff pervaded his person.

We loved to play around old Eriksson in the woodshed. Occasionally he would allow us to take a pinch of snuff from his ancient silver box, and we would sneeze and giggle at the violent effect. He would regale us with extraordinary tales of fairies and trolls as with slow strokes his knotted arm sent the saw slicing through the wood. And as the sawdust fell from his blade in rhythmic cascades, so his words fell softly upon our ears to the accompaniment of the sounds of saw and ax, words about the things the old man dreamed of.

In the Big House kerosene lamps of all sizes and designs provided the illumination. Mother liked brightness. Small lamps stood on shelves in passages and halls, tall ones lit up dark corners, and large ones hanging from the ceiling on wrought-iron chains shed their glow in places of concentrated activity. Three months of "white nights" is the special gift of the high latitudes in the summer, and while they last, scarcely any other illumination is needed. But when the days shortened and midwinter darkness set in, with less than six hours of daylight, the housemaid would come tiptoeing through the house at dusk to light the lamps. The next morning saw them all lined up in the pantry, like a company on fatigue duty, to be filled and tended, a special art that Mother imparted personally to every new maid.

Squat, tough, and muscle-bound, the drawer of water to the Big House drove his team to the well a mile out in the field. He hand-pumped the water into his large iron-girdled barrel, tapped it into pails carried dangling from a yoke, and poured it into the potbellied storage vats by the kitchen door on the back porch.

Laundry was done at Svensksund every third or fourth month. In the course of three laborious days and one night, a dozen farm women gathered at the laundry house, where they rubbed huge piles of linen, steeped it in boiling lye water, and then rinsed it in the clear water down at the creek. With rubber aprons tightly tied around their middles and tiny puffed sleeves adorning powerful red arms, they worked amid mountains of soapy foam. They made the steeping into a grand night. Young girls came to help, and young boys came to party. And there was dancing on flagstones and cuddling in the corners in the dim light of the lanterns, while the wheezy accordion played folk tunes. Suddenly, the music broke into the wild rhythm of a polka. Feet stomped, skirts swung high, and the air was steamy with sweat, lye water, and coffee. Finally, stretched and mangled, the linen was restored to the shelves of Mother's spacious walk-in closet. And for several days the smell of sweet fresh air lingered around the closet.

Emma Grundelius, short and round, came to Svensksund so long ago that the year had been forgotten. Her voluminous skirts, gathered around her middle, touched the floor with every step she took. Her skin was slightly shriveled like an autumn leaf, and soft blond down covered her upper lip. In the winter Emma set up the loom in the sunniest room of the annex. Ebba and I also took our turns sending the prettily carved shuttle through the warp. At first our feet got badly tangled in the treadles, but soon we learned to do as the other women did and kicked off our shoes to paddle away in our stocking feet, one-tap-tap, two-tap-tap. A piece of red thread marked the end of each person's contribution. This, naturally, promoted competition, but none of us, not even Mother, could match the speed of Emma's shuttle and quick tap-taps, producing yards upon yards of toweling with bright red borders.

Life at the Big House brought us close to the work on the farm and to its people, who, like us, were dependent on its success. A bearded foreman carried out Father's commands, but the large ledgers were Father's personal concern, assignable to no one, every meticulous entry imprinted with a broad gold nib in his own precise hand.

Father was one of those early risers who come quickly awake from deep sleep to meet head on the dawn of the new day. His feet tucked into tall boots, cane in hand, he strode forth before breakfast on his regular first tour of stables and fields to tackle the day's problems, to size up the weather and its probabilities.

The farm was Father's life. From it he drew his inspiration, upon it he based all his ambitions. The welfare of his own family and of the people who worked on it, the soil, the crops, the changing seasons provided the substance of his existence.

When the first Christmas was being celebrated at the Big House, Grandmaman Wendela was with us. Father sat at the end of the dining room table. At his feet stood three large clothesbaskets, all empty. The mounds of parcels they had contained, wrapped in brown paper and adorned with splashes of red sealing wax, had only a few minutes earlier been sent sliding across the table to their excited recipients.

"That's all!" said Father, looking at me. "Now you and Ebba take Grandmaman to the Green Room and stay there till I call you."

This was odd. Was there another surprise? For whom? For Grandmaman?

Finally, in the Green Room, we heard Father's voice echoing through the house. Unable to contain my curiosity, I darted to a side door, but before I could get a glimpse of anything, it was unceremoniously slammed in my face. I raced back to join the others, and at last the door opened. I squeezed through and ran into the dining room. In the middle of the room stood two ponies, one a bay, the other piebald, brown and white. A groom led them by their halters. A maid dutifully collected a small smoking mound in a dustpan.

Impossible to believe! Were they real? For us—were they for us? Imagine being the real owner of a real horse!

The move to the Big House brought a marked improvement in the relationship between Father and Mother. For Mother it inaugurated a complete change in status. Now she was the mistress of Svensksund, a position that carried with it new demands upon her talents of organization and widening responsibilities, and a closer sharing of the work with Father.

Mother recognized the challenge. She quickly accepted it and scored success after success. She showed excellent taste in all that she undertook, from decorating a room to giving parties with elegance and grace. Now her wit and vivacity came into full bloom. Under her skilled management Svensksund acquired a reputation for gaiety and hospitality.

Mother's success put her in an easier frame of mind and she became more appreciative of Father's care and solicitude. Although she may not have been capable of a fully valid response to a love so deep and all-pervasive as Father's, the improved relationship nevertheless created a font from which each drew healing drafts of tolerance and affection.

And so it seemed that these happy years at Svensksund were destined to continue unendingly into the future.

It seemed ridiculous to hire a governess before Ebba was old enough to take lessons, so it was decided that I should acquire my first learning in the parish elementary school. For the first time I was brought together with children outside my own world. A faint odor of unaired rooms foreign to me clung to their clothing. Certainly a meeting of the spirits took place between the tomboy child from Svensksund and the teacher. Miss Björk was a hunchback who breathed with a slightly wheezy sound. Smiling encouragement, she dispensed her teachings of arithmetic, spelling, sewing, and knitting with detached serenity.

When Ebba was old enough for lessons, the search for a suitable governess began, and brought Nanny Nilsson into our lives. Nanny met our ill-concealed curiosity with equanimity and passed Mother's critical linguistic test in French with worldly nonchalance. She was an attractive young woman with large questioning eyes and a finely molded hooked nose. This was her best feature, and she made especially good use of it when enacting dramatic charades. She was unaware of or simply ignored the imperfections of the rest of her figure, which suffered from a body too long and legs too short.

Nanny adapted herself to life at Svensksund with surprising facility. She played up to Mother's wit and to Father's ingrained habits with sympathy and understanding. With a mixture of discipline and camaraderie, she won our obedience. She played with us, and joined with good spirit in our wild rides behind the ponies.

Fortunately, Nanny was still with us when, several years later, Father suddenly became ill with a bleeding ulcer. The family fortune had been in decline for some time, causing him much worry and anxiety. No one knew then that there was any connection between stomach ulcers and nervous stress. The treatment consisted of strict diet and rest. For weeks Father had to lie on his back to be tended like a child and was allowed to drink only milk and water, which he sipped through a glass straw.

A tall, good-looking nurse of undoubted ability took over the reins of the entire household. And in the clash of wills between Mother, outraged at having her authority usurped in her own house, and Sister Esther, whose governing principle—the patient's care and well-being above all—was unassailable, Nanny emerged as the discreet peacemaker and adjuster of countless controversies.

How far the nurse went in alienating Father's affections no one but the three involved ever knew.

As a result of the enforced immobility, Father contracted phlebitis in both legs. Thus Mother's fervent hopes of getting rid of Sister Esther quickly were dashed, and the household was obliged to gird itself for an indeterminate period of tension and anxiety. Father lay helpless, weak and worried. Perhaps it would have been impossible for him to do anything but submit to Sister Esther's skillful ministrations and to accept meekly her insistence upon his rigid isolation.

When, after three months, Father at last got back on his feet, the progress of our education had reached a point requiring a decision that was to bring about significant changes in our family life. Nanny had reached the limit of her teaching capacity. Losing her was a blow. When the holidays were over, in her stead came a middle-aged spinster with frizzy blond hair and a pointed nose, who was to coach us for entry the next fall into a finishing school in Stockholm.

Whether by intuition or by deduction, Miss Palmquist soon sized up the situation. Sister Esther was gone and Father was not happy. Miss Palmquist made the inexcusable error of showing too plainly her pity for Father and her disapproval of Mother. Moreover, she entertained certain unconventional social ideas that she impressed upon me with convincing logic during special lessons. Liberty, equality, and brotherhood—these were stirring words. The contrast between these notions and the traditional patriarchism in which I had been raised seemed strangely seductive. My parents' constant warning against snobbish and condescending behavior only supported my receptiveness.

Miss Palmquist's teachings, along with the metamorphosis I was experiencing with the onset of puberty, resulted in my first violent crush. The object was a fair stalwart young farmhand with a glint in his blue eyes. I wrote impassioned messages never meant for delivery and hid them among the flowers on my balcony, never dreaming they would fall into Mother's hands.

The flabbergasting discovery of the notes took my parents off balance. The simple explanation of the natural biological drive escaped them, and their rejection of the shocking infatuation explained nothing. To be thought bad was a new and dreadful experience that weighed heavily upon my spirit. Yet this first serious controversy between us plainly proved that the rarer the errors, the less grievous and sustained the aftereffects.

The event spelled the end of Miss Palmquist. Possibly Mother was influenced by her own unhappy experiences with governesses when, in a moment of exaggerated ire, she labeled her "the socialistic vampire." The dismissal took the poor woman by surprise and she left under a cloud of ill-concealed hostility.

In the autumn Mother established herself in a small apartment in Stockholm and Ebba and I went to school. Two years later I successfully passed my final examinations. In the autumn Mother and Ebba returned to Stockholm without me.

I was delighted to be home with Father, proud to be the grown-up daughter of the house. I was thrilled to take Mother's place at the dining room table opposite Father. Every morning throughout their married life Mother had tossed across the table to Father his soft-boiled egg, and with virtuoso agility he caught it whole. I did not care to trespass, however, on this parental ritual.

While summer lingered through the golden days of September, Father showed his delight at having me with him in a thousand ways. We went together on extensive tours across the fields. He tried haltingly, for he did not easily reveal his inner thoughts and feelings, to explain to me the bond that tied him so closely to this land. He spoke of the importance of proper fertilization, of the farmer's gold embedded in the huge pile of strong-smelling manure outside the stables, of the rotation of the crops and what it meant to growth. And thus he tacitly imparted to me his hopes that I would be his successor. But there was lots of time. . . .

One evening we were sitting together in the Green Room when the question that I had been thinking about, of going to Stockholm for the winter months, suddenly popped out.

Father looked at me and a deep sadness clouded his eyes. The shock of guilt made me obstinate. "But I'll be back with you again in the spring," I told him quickly, and the smile with which I tried to soften my words must have been a bleak imitation.

"You don't want to stay with me any longer." It was a statement, not a question. He had difficulty with the words.

"Yes, but . . ." I could not finish the stupid sentence.

For a long time Father hid his face behind the newspaper. He shifted his long legs and turned the page. Finally he said, and his speech was slow and deliberate, "Of course—of course you must go—if you wish. . . ."

My haste to pack was almost obscene. But all I felt was relief at not having to stay at Svensksund all through the long winter, grateful for the freedom gained. I would go back into the big world, have fun, and then return for good. There was lots of time.

As the carriage taking me to the train began to move I waved gaily to father. I heard him say, "Good-bye, my girl!"

I saw that his cheeks were wet. With his hand raised, he stood there motionless, until finally the turn of the road hid him from view.

A month later Father came to Stockholm to visit us and to see to business. His train came in late and he had some meetings to attend, so he decided to stay the night at a downtown hotel. Early in the morning he suffered a massive stomach hemorrhage. The night clerk found him sprawled on his bed unconscious, his hand fallen from the bell, his dark blood soaked into the white sheets.

Desperate efforts were made over him, but the doctors were unable to stop the bleeding. They decided on an operation as a last resort. After a hushed and unbearable wait, we saw Father, gasping for breath, being wheeled out of the operating room. Early the next morning my Father died.

Mother, Ebba, and I returned to a dark and empty Svensksund. Once again funeral flowers and freshly cut spruce boughs spread their heavy fragrance through the house. The people came and stood silently. They followed him to the grave. Afterward they dispersed in small straggling groups and went away, and we were left to meet the great change.

In Father's room off the hall a faint scent of *eau de quinine* and tobacco still lingered. His large desk stood there, a relic from a closed episode. Once the head with the plans and the perspective was gone, the people and the beasts of Svensksund labored without coordination. Father's name no longer stood as the necessary guarantee for the purposeful planning and execution of the tasks. The resources of Svensksund dwindled, the foundation gave way.

Father's will contained a touching personal message to Mother, no binding demand, but a last plea reflecting his concern about his daughters' future and about the preservation of Svensksund: "Don't sell!" And the document, written in his strong clear hand, remains in mute evidence of all his dashed hopes, his unfulfilled dreams.

Whatever great capacities Mother possessed, she was not the type of person to accept a challenge of this kind and create out of it a life's work, exulting in its great odds. Out of the debris of Svensksund she pieced together a sufficient amount of money and household goods to establish for us a new home in a small flat on a back street in a residential area of Stockholm. And may this be her monument.

CHAPTER 3

SOCIAL LIFE AND A VOCATION

AUNT JANA was one of those rare individuals who humbly accepts whatever life brings without complaint and then sets about making the best of it.

The example of Aunt Jana dispensing devoted care upon the crippled, the sick, and the old among the people of Svensksund first put into my head the idea of becoming a nurse. She taught me to roll bandages and dress wounds. It pleased her to find I was not squeamish about blood and injuries. The challenge of an emergency appealed to me. I began to dream of romantic adventures in a great hospital. But I could not apply for admittance to the Red Cross School of Nursing until I was twenty-one—three years hence.

The great opening event of the winter social season was at hand, the ball at the royal palace to present the year's debutantes at court. Excited and nervous, I stood before the looking glass in Mother's room. In the brilliant light of many lamps, Mother, Ebba, and the maid hovered around me, critically inspecting every detail of my attire.

I felt stiff and breathless in my new stays. The deep décolletage of my trainless white satin gown was edged with paillettes of mother-of-pearl. The silk of my puffed sleeves, obligatory for all ladies attending formal court functions and passed from mother to daughter, was yellowed with age. The long white gloves refused to slip on easily. I was flushed and hot.

The doorbell rang. My escort for the occasion, the son of one of our former neighbors, stood before me boyishly round-faced and tall in his resplendent dress uniform, tasseled sword at his side, beplumed hat under his arm. His manners were impeccable; all former teasing was now forgotten. Followed by the fond gaze of three pairs of eyes from the open window, we drove off in a landau hired for the occasion.

The function took place in the enormous ballroom of the royal palace known as the White Sea, and the gathering spread into the adjacent festival apartments. There was continuous measured movement to the softly murmurous sound of many voices. A glimpse of tall, bearded King Gustav in gold-braided uniform opening the ball with the crown princess was followed by waves of resplendent dancers swinging onto the soon crowded dance floor. Thanks to my dutiful escort's attention, my dance program with the royal crest and the small pink pencil dangling from a tassel was quickly scribbled full. Soon word came for the debutantes to assemble in a certain anteroom, where I was handed over to the lady who was to present me.

All this was entirely Mother's idea. "I'm arranging this for you as part of your education and training, not for fun." Her tone was firm. "It's an experience you ought to have."

Experience! I had not seen it in that light before, and my protests evaporated.

For reasons of economy, Mother decided to forgo the rather costly exercise of taking me to court herself. She entrusted me to her good friend Dagmar Swartz, whose husband was the finance minister. And now, here we were in the foremost section of the long line of presenting ladies and debutantes.

The door opened and the queue began to move. Suddenly I found myself on the threshold of a large reception room. Before me a vision of gold, a shiny parquet floor, gilded chairs along the walls not intended for anyone to sit on, mirrors reflecting the occupants of the room. Diagonally across the room, so that we who were to make our bows could pass from one to the other and out through the double doors at the other end without turning our backs on any of them, the three receiving royal ladies stood at a certain distance from each other. High court officials and ladies-in-waiting provided them with a discreetly withdrawn background.

My own name smote my ears with intimidating force. Before the extended hand of the crown princess I performed my first deep curtsy. I saw a round smiling full face, extremely blue eyes, luscious dark wavy hair. The former Margaret of Connaught, crown princess of Sweden, had on this occasion taken over the duties of the ailing Queen Victoria. Her sweet temperament, her warm concern about people, especially the young ones, her women's field hockey teams had made her famous.

The slight frou-frou of Tante Dagmar's train sweeping upon the shiny floor urged me on. I found myself before a vision in opalescence. Much had already been written and rumored about the Grand Duchess Marie of Russia, whom Wilhelm, the talented Bernadotte poet and writer, the brother of Crown Prince Gustav Adolf, had married not long ago. One thought of the nunlike strictness with which she had been brought up at the St. Petersburg court. One whispered of the playful, irresponsible escapades in which she had indulged after her marriage, a bird let out of a cage, of her boredom with her new, somewhat stilted entourage, of her impetuosity. One jealously remarked about her priceless gems and her remarkable beauty. For a brief instant I stood face to face with her, a dazzling creature as if just escaped out of the pages of a colorful fairy tale. A diadem shaped in the Russian style crowned her small regal head, and its magnificent opals enhanced the luster of her black hair and the ivory of her skin. Her train of rich lamé fell from her shoulders, clung briefly to her slender waist, and then descended in shimmering folds to the floor. Her face, surrounded by all this stiff splendor, was that of a child, rounded, pouting, eager to have all this fuss and protocol over with soon so that she could escape, have fun, dance.

"Glad to see you here with us today!"

The informal pronoun with which I was addressed, the friendly, slightly familiar voice jolted me away from the fascinating exotic image. Princess Ingeborg's smiling eyes met mine. The sister of my godmother Louise, the wife of Prince Carl, Father's friend, she was not a stranger. Suddenly relaxed, I basked in the royal sunshine and my last curtsy went off smoothly. Known for an occasional display of airs even toward her close friends, today the princess, slender and elegant in a clinging sheath of silver brocade, was pure affability toward Hillevid's daughter. Her words and the expression on her face radiated spontaneous warmth, rare in these exalted circles. And I left her to mingle once again with the resplendent throngs, moving, swirling to the rhythms of the orchestras in the great ballroom with an agreeable feeling of belonging.

The night was chilly and dark when, three days after New Year 1914, I arrived at Egeskov in Denmark for the first time for an extended visit with my second godmother, Tante Jessy Ahlefeldt-Laurvig-Bille. I had never met her before. The liveried footman, carrying my suitcase and the carriage plaid, ushered me into the spacious hall. A warm smell of wood smoke greeted me, mingled with the faint odor of burning candles in massive candelabra, flickering lightly in the air from the opened oak doors. Out of the blue drawing room Tante Jessy came stepping quickly, her arms spread wide to embrace me. I dropped her a respectful curtsy. I had to bend to return her welcoming kiss, for she was short.

"So this is Hillevid's daughter!" she exclaimed, holding me at arms' length. "Yes, you do look like her—but you also look like your father."

Tante Jessy must have been over sixty at this time. Her plump figure was bound by Parisian stays that effectively prevented any bending at the waist. Upon her ample bosom nestled several rows of Oriental pearls. Innocent of cosmetics, her smooth face framed by soft brown curls looked almost girlish. Any suspicion that her wonderful coiffure was in fact a wig was based on no evidence other than the youthful color.

Tante Jessy ruled her vast estates with the softest of kid gloves. Characteristically, she affected a shy pose at total variance with her authority. With swimming eyes, softly batting lids, girlish blushes, and fluttering hands she gave orders that were obeyed, expressed opinions that were not disputed. Demurely she prevailed.

Having kissed me once again, Tante Jessy turned and with a small gesture dismissed the servants standing around. She preceded me into a cozy room comfortably overfurnished in Victorian style. By the love seat a low tea wagon stood with the silver teakettle whispering over a spirit-burning lamp. An Irish terrier, stiff-legged and irate, leaped from the basket in the corner, yapping until she hushed him. By the heavily draped window a canary in a gilded cage flitted axiously from perch to perch. Tante Jessy covered the cage with a green cloth.

A few days later, wrapped warmly in buffalo robes, Tante Jessy and I started out in her brass-fitted Daimler town car, chauffeur and butler in front, on our way to Copenhagen.

Life with Tante Jessy in the capital turned out to be an interlude of extravagant opulence. The atmosphere of the house was one of softened footfalls upon carpets of luxurious thickness. My room was on the top floor under the roof, deep and low-ceilinged. Late mornings, sumptuous meals, drives in the afternoon with Tante Jessy to air the terrier or call on hawk-nosed ladies of distinction alternated with receptions and balls in the evenings.

To find that Mother was still well remembered in Copenhagen, after so many years since her departure to Sweden was an agreeable discovery. When Prince Gustav, the portly brother of Godmother Louise, led me onto the dance floor, he spoke of my mother as the charming young girl he had known in his youth. The blue eyes in his still young-looking face lit up with pleasant memories. "Hillevid's daughter" became a designation I bore with much pride and gratitude. And, like a charm, it opened all doors.

I regret to say that Tante Jessy never got her money's worth of pleasure and companionship out of me. But she never complained, nor did she demand the impossible. When I finally asked to be relieved of the obligation to be a drawing room entertainer, she acquiesced readily and happily. I felt uncomfortably ungrateful and tried to explain the reasons, my inadequacies. Tante Jessy only waved her hands airily, smiled sweetly, and batted her eyelids.

Life in glamorous idleness began to pall. The eternal striving to fill each hour with purposeless preoccupations, with talk only to produce sounds to fill the silence, dancing, flitting from ball to ball, every day and night the same, soon created feelings of futility and boredom. In this world of soft carpets and cultivated gaiety there was too much of everything—too much service, too much food, too many people concentrating on doing nothing. The artificiality gorged and progressively destroyed the appetite. I left the table of opulence and went back to Sweden hungry for something I could not identify or name, an opportunity to feel passion, a chance to spend energy and heart recklessly.

July 1914. Who among those of us living at a safe distance from the holocaust could talk of sacrifice? Inconvenience, rationing of goods and food, yes. But these were no sacrifices to be compared with those demanded of the people whose lives were in danger every day, every hour. Nation set against nation, families torn apart, the mental and physical abuse of individuals, and the effects of all this on their sensitivities and their outlook—we only heard about these things. Yet the tremors of the violent explosion spread like the tremors of an earthquake, and no one alive at that time could escape its influence, devastating to most, stimulating to some. In my case, it was like a clarion call.

Now, suddenly, where confusion had befogged the wits before, purpose emerged. In a flash the meandering path I had pursued changed into a wide open road leading toward a specific goal. One point was particularly clear in my mind: There was to be no headlong rush to reach the goal now being formulated as a result of the outbreak of the war, no playing at learning first aid, rolling bandages, and helping out in a hospital as a nurse's aide. I wanted to get thorough training in the professional skills of nursing, no matter how long it took.

Of the available nursing schools, the one operated by the Red Cross was of especially high repute. The requirements emphasized dedication. The applicant paid, in fact, a sizable sum for the privilege of training there. If the student was found unsuited for the work, she was asked to leave. If she survived the two-year course, she was required to remain for a year and a half after graduation at the disposal of the registry for private or other duties. Previous experience in the care of the sick was desirable before admission. For this reason I entered the General Hospital of Norrköping, the city close to Svensksund, as a probationer. The hospital was run by deaconesses in caps edged with frilly lace and angelic smiles on their faces. The physician in charge, a wonderful man with thick gray hair, whom I had known all my life, opened the doors for me. Thus occupied, I awaited my twenty-first birthday.

To describe exactly the traumatic effect of my first year in nursing is not a matter of great pride. I was overwhelmed by the sheer physical exertion. I never dreamed anyone could be expected to work so hard and for such long hours. And it was somewhat disconcerting to find that it was actually within one's capacity. In those days, day duty began at 6:00 A.M. and ended at 8:00 P.M. If the work on the ward permitted, a break of two hours was allowed at the discretion of the head nurse. Every fourth night, sometimes every third, the student went on night duty. At eight the next morning she was relieved and thereafter remained off duty for the next twenty-four hours.

I yearned for the day when at last, dressed in the gray uniform of the Red Cross and with the white cap on my head, I would be called Sister Louise. But where was the glamour so easily surmised, the glory so fondly imagined? Certainly not in these exhausting daily and nightly chores, running with bedpans, scrubbing, polishing, bedmaking, rushing through the wards upon aching feet and never getting enough sleep. And those dark, hateful, lonely nights! Often I caught myself weeping from sheer fatigue, soft bitter tears, wishing for a miracle to take me out of this misery, even to become ill, to lie down and rest forever.

Then with dramatic impact came the awareness of the smells, of the awful pathological abnormalities, the pitiful morbidity in nearly every hospital scene. A fierce unreasoning fear of death, an abhorrence of decay overwhelmed me. Disease seemed to blight the world. It gripped, distorted, inexorably poisoned people's bodies in untold invidious ways. No one could escape.

By degrees time dispelled this sense of overwhelming disaster. Slowly, partly from habituation and partly from increasing absorption in the work, another mood replaced it. Recognition came of the masterly skills and organization required to care for sick people in a large general hospital, and with it a sneaking exultation. I grew increasingly aware of the remarkable refinement of the techniques being taught me, remarkable indeed in their absolute economy of movement and purposive execution. Skill became my fetish. My hands grew adept in the administration of treatments, in the dressing of a wound, in the art of making a bed under a gravely ill patient. The approach to excellence was a stimulating experience. Without ado, without any great effort, the starched, soft-spoken head nurse subdued the rebellious, immature girl that I was and extracted from her efficiency of performance. And when for the first time a patient's eyes took on a look of relief at my approach, of confidence that he could entrust his aching body to my ministrations, then the realization dawned that the strict discipline and the meticulous teaching were imparting to me not only a vocation but an art.

The emergency department of one of the great city hospitals was the place above all others where I achieved a complete sense of personal fulfillment. Here, in competition with fellow students, I learned presence of mind, how to handle the mangled body of a woman run down by a car, how to cut the charred clothes from a badly burned child, how to deal with an attempted suicide coughing up parts of his insides seared by sulphuric acid.

Every night when my turn came to be on duty, the shrill ringing of the bell brought me out of bed and down the stairs eagerly, tense and prepared to deal with whatever awaited me on the stretcher. Night after night the bell rang into my body renewed energy and developing skill. Shortness of staff often forced a sharing of responsibility between the doctor and the nurse. This called on all the competence of both of them and enhanced the nurse's contribution to the saving of lives. As case followed case, the work of helping them became a privilege demanding no reward beyond that of being allowed to remain there undisturbed to continue the work.

When graduation day came, so eagerly anticipated, so long awaited, I felt no great elation. Neither the uplifting speeches, the bouquets of flowers, nor even the pin and the diploma seemed any longer of such immense significance. One thing only appeared important: to be placed in the kind of work entirely suited to one's temperament and ability, challenging work that compelled the giving of oneself wholly.

CHAPTER 4

AN UNBIDDEN MEETING

THE narrow hall was stuffy, permeated with the odors of cheap cooking and unwashed clothes. The door closed like the lid of a coffin upon the stairway, cold as a cellar. Impenetrable darkness. Heavy draperies parted, letting in a strip of dim light, and a hand beckoned me into the presence. Somebody had told me that the lady was good at telling fortunes.

Why this unseemly haste to have done with the present, this irresistible longing to delve into the future? The encounter with the tall, fair young man had been a summer's dream. His kisses made me fling myself again into his arms; it had been heaven. The warm days, flowers, walks in the evenings under the gnarled old trees of the parks around Stockholm, where for ages past young people had met to make love. And the summer had opened visions of wedded bliss. But he had not meant it to become a reality.

The brusque awakening had been a shock. Why did he reject this beautiful thing? The idea of being undesirable was new and appalling, and left me with a feeling of utter emptiness. Now the days seemed to join together to form a never ending tunnel. Tearful and outraged, I fought the finality that I could neither imagine nor admit.

My zest for work disappeared. I found it boring, excruciatingly boring, every minute of it a burden. I hated the uniform. The registry sent me to work in homes to look after convalescents who needed companionship and indulgence but not expert nursing care. They sent me to look after spoiled children of rich people, who needed a nanny but not a skilled nurse. Vehemently I rebelled against the demands placed upon me by people who were not ill, but whose pocketbooks allowed them to hire well-trained servants. This, certainly, was no part of the vocation I had imagined and worked so hard to achieve.

My record suffered from these repeated misplacements. I tried— No, I did not try, for it was impossible to submit with grace to things like these. I asked to be moved, to be placed somewhere else where the work would be challenging, as it had been in the emergency department of the great city hospital. This seemed to me a reasonable request. The superintendent looked at me with sublime patience. This, she told me, was my duty. But in the end my rebellious determination proved to be stronger than her authority.

Now here I was, full of impatience and discontent, in this cluttered, unpleasant room. The obese fortune-teller turned her pale face upon me. A pack of worn, soiled cards adorned with mystifying green figures lay beside her pudgy hand. On a small stand between us a crystal ball stared balefully like a giant fish eye into the ceiling. Why had I come? How foolish, how utterly stupid!

I let her talk. And all I remember from the session was something about remarkable gray eyes and a man, tall and fair. And that, of course, could never be. I came out angry with myself. Circumstances combine to create logical consequences whereof future events are shaped. Had the woman said so, I wouldn't have believed her.

The war was still going on with all its miseries and horrors and somewhere, surely, there must be a place for me. At this time an exchange of invalided prisoners of war had begun through the International Red Cross. These men now useless for combat were evacuated from enemy prison camps and taken to a neutral land for the exchange, a head for a head. Camps had been built and outfitted for this purpose in Denmark, one for Russian prisoners and another for German.

My thoughts raced to Agnete Brockenhuus-Schack, Tante Jessy's improbable daughter, known everywhere, who spoke with a voice raspy from smoking cigarettes and who moved with the assurance of a man. She had introduced me into Copenhagen's high society and now she was a Red Cross worker. She had not only the means and the time at her disposal, but a determination to do something useful with her life. Besides being a good organizer and administrator, she carried to the task good connections, and they were important. I wrote to her. "Yes, of course," came her answer, "we have a place for you. We need another nurse to take charge of one of the barracks of tubercular Russian soldiers at Horserød."

Russians! The old enmities imprinted into my mind by hearsay and history lessons were not so easily eradicated. Russia, the massive land in the east, always in search of outlets to the sea, of land and more land to satisfy its gluttonous cravings for its own purported security, a ruthless giant dangerously dwarfing its smaller neighbors.

Nonetheless, soon after New Year I took the train south and on a dull wintry afternoon arrived at Horserød, the camp for Russian prisoners of war.

Zinaida Andreyevna, the Russian nurse in charge of another barracks of sixty sick soldiers, came into my office at Barracks 42. She was a stately woman with a Slavic face, rosy cheeks, high cheekbones, and a full red mouth. Her white veil was fastened under her chin. Her soft brown eyes suggested compassion and empathy.

"But you must come!" Her voice was low, throaty, pleading as she spoke in French, and each word was pronounced deliberately and slowly. That evening the soldiers were giving a concert in celebration of the Russian Christmas.

It was the end of my third day in camp and I was tired. Everything took a little getting accustomed to and I was still confused by a mass of strange impressions. It had been a long day among the sixty human wrecks that had been entrusted to my care. Most of them were only boys, curiously naive. Some of them would never again see their homeland, their health gone, their strength undermined or destroyed by tuberculosis.

Zinaida Andreyevna looked at me and smiled. "You must not refuse," she said quietly. "They like us to join in their fun."

She extended her hand to me, and I took it. This was the beginning of an alliance and a friendship many times interrupted by events but never broken. They called her a sister of mercy, and that's what she was. She was here now not only to mend bodies but to try to erase, or at least to help these men to bear, the deep agonies caused by war and revolution.

A few minutes later we entered together the barracks where the concert was being held. A strong smell of fresh lumber and tar paper assailed my nostrils the first moment I set foot within the barbed enclosure. When reveille sounded at six every morning from the Danish administration buildings, I awoke to it in my small room in the Danish nurses' residence. It mixed with the odors of food in the dining hall and with the strong disinfectant the orderlies used to wash the floors of Barracks 42. And from that time on, whenever encountered, it never failed to bring back to my mind vivid pictures of Horserød.

Rows of stools filled the center of the hall. A few lanterns hung from the beams in the ceiling and provided the illumination. The place was hazy with tobacco smoke that made it difficult to discern the faces and figures of the men in scattered groups in the dim light. Here and there the starched white veils of the nurses produced bright spots that relieved the monotony of the dark scene.

After a slight delay the concert began. The program included music and singing, the recital of poetry, a short play. How naively amateurish these soldiers were in their clumsy masculinity! With irresistible enthusiasm they abandoned themselves to their various roles. And the appreciative audience applauded, laughed, and shouted at the tops of their voices: *"Bis! Bis!"*

I could not understand a word. But what I heard seemed to me enchanting, like cadences of music composed mostly of *sch* sounds, rising and falling. And as the performance warmed up and drifted into the rousing rhythms of Russian and gipsy folk songs accompanied on balalaikas twanged at incredible speed, when the performers flung themselves with acrobatic verve into their *Rousskaia,* then these men, these half invalids, were no longer amateurs. They had become perfectionists in an art for the art's own sake, betraying the beat of the Russian heart.

My attention was suddenly diverted from the performance. From the row of stools behind us the steady stare of a pair of gray eyes met mine. The young man, his face somewhat drawn as if from recent illness, continued to stare, not the least abashed at having been caught.

Zinaida Andreyevna laughed heartily at some joke I could not understand, and I laughed with her. I drew her attention to the man behind us. She turned and nodded with a smile. The ghost of a smile flitted across the young man's face.

The performance on the stage ended and we stood up and joined in the boisterous applause. The man behind us left his seat and stood leaning against the wall. Tall and lanky, slightly stooped, he wore his officer's cap at a rakish angle. A white Maltese cross gleamed on his left breast pocket. He acknowledged Zinaida Andreyevna's friendly greeting with a salute, a curious mixture of respect and nonchalance.

A few days later, on the eve of the Russian New Year, a dance was held in the Russian officers' mess. The roomy lounge was set with armchairs and bridge tables that gave the place a homelike atmosphere. The dining hall was cleared for dancing.

Zinaida Andreyevna and I were late, and when we arrived the dance was already in full swing. A few couples were on the floor, Danish nurses and their friends. By tacit consent the Russian nurses did not dance, because some of them mourned men lost in the war and all of them felt that the political situation in their homeland did not warrant any merrymaking. In their becoming uniforms they became the centers of several groups of officers engaged in serious discussion.

A gathering of friends immediately surrounded Zinaida Andreyevna.

"Your small hand, please, Zinaida Andreyevna, so glad you came!" And she surrendered her hand to each one to be kissed.

"And how did your walk turn out today, Aleksandr Mikhailovich?" she inquired in her husky voice. The officer's adventures, always related upon his return from his daily walk, had become topics of good-humored derision among his friends.

"And how are you, Konstantin Grigorievich? May I introduce you to Mademoiselle Flach, a friend of Countess Schack. She's a nursing sister in the soldiers' camp."

Among the officers was Zinaida Andreyevna's husband in his general's uniform. Noticeably shorter than his wife, he was many years her senior. A well-trimmed pointed beard outlined a fretful mouth in partial contradiction to the expression of sad resignation in his eyes. Though they were seemingly so badly matched, the quick look of affection that passed between these two was unmistakable. Rumors circulated that at one time during the war, General Kliuev had betrayed his trust. Whether it was true or untrue, the look of proud sadness that occasionally came into Zinaida Andreyevna's eyes as she glanced at her husband suggested that the bitter edge of the accusation had not escaped her. But the knowledge only bound her with unfaltering loyalty still closer to him.

Apart from that one glance, her graciousness and sympathy encompassed all of these men equally, some of them hobbling on crutches, some with empty sleeves, others with that vague shell-shocked look on their faces, and some, too, showing encouraging signs of returning strength and mending bodies. They were all her children. Before a future so uncertain, they were like chips cast upon the stormy seas, all equally in need of her compassion and love.

Colonel Trebinsky bowed over my hand. As one of the official hosts, he displayed a most gallant, most elegant demeanor. Of slight build with a wasplike waist, he sported a well-groomed moustache over a somewhat sensuous mouth. His hooked nose was too large; his brown eyes, often with a surprised look, were pleading. His tunic was of faultless fit; his breeches, forming two half balloons, clung tightly to each slender knee. Konstantin Pavlovich was complaisance personified. I could have imagined him as a master of ceremonies, as a maître d'hôtel, but never as a soldier in the grime of battle.

"*Ah, mademoiselle, permettez-moi de vous souhaiter la bienvenue dans notre petite compagnie!* Would you care to dance, sisteritsa? In that case, let me introduce some of our best dancers to you."

"Make sure that they speak either French or English," I reminded him, laughing as he hastened away to carry out his errand.

He returned accompanied by a tall officer who dragged his left leg slightly as he walked; it was hardly a limp.

"May I—Lieutenant Kirilin—Mademoiselle Flach. Gleb Nikolayevich, our new sisteritsa. You must speak French with her."

A faint smile played around the lieutenant's sensitive mouth as he acknowledged the introduction. The white Maltese cross on his breast pocket shone. Those steel-blue—no, gray—eyes glittered. A slightly mocking expression spread over his face and settled in his eyes, a look of frank mischief.

"We've met before," he said in a low voice after Trebinsky left. "Does it matter? Do they need to know? Will you dance?"

The faint mockery, the insinuation of conspiracy, the nonchalance of his manner—was it all a piece of insufferable arrogance? No, I didn't think so. Then was it just a pose? A shield? Had life taught him bitterness too early? All these Russians were immersed in personal histories of such tragedy that no outsider could measure it.

We danced a swinging waltz. Despite the slight limp, he danced well. The rhythm of the balalaikas was seductive. If his behavior had aroused in my mind any annoyance or suspicions, now suddenly I was inclined to forgive the mockery of his smile, the impudence in his eyes, and to fall in with his game that we were old friends who had met before.

"You dance well," he said.

I let the remark pass. From the wings Trebinsky was watching us—with approval, I thought.

The white Maltese cross aroused my curiosity.

"My military school," he explained. "Corps des Pages Impérial."

The pride in his voice could not be missed, but apart from that, the information did not convey much to me. And we danced.

Suddenly: "Why don't you wear a *kosenko,* a veil, like the other nurses?" His tone was challenging, the question impertinent. "The contraption you're wearing on your head, tied under your chin like that, looks perfectly ridiculous!"

How dared he make fun of the cap I wore so proudly, the badge of my school of nursing? Under their smooth surface, these Russians certainly were a tactless and cloddish lot. My explanation that Swedish Red Cross nurses never wore veils did not seem to interest him.

Our conversation slipped into less controversial channels. No need for the dapper Trebinsky to go in search of other partners for me. Lieutenant Kirilin must have overcome his dislike of my cap, and I forgot everything that was not entirely pleasant and agreeable.

The Danish captain, a man of muscular build with a square, young-looking face, came into the office of Barracks 42 on his morning tour of inspection. His shock of white hair accentuated his smooth ruddy skin. I liked his visits; he always had a pleasant word, a joke to tell. And his advice on any point of administration was sound and well considered. As he stood talking pleasantly across the table, he had a habit of slapping his boots with his riding crop.

"You're Hillevid Neergaard's daughter, aren't you?"

In these surroundings the question surprised me. Why had I not met him before in Copenhagen? He spoke with enthusiasm of my mother, how well he remembered her as one of the most charming girls, bright, witty, and they had danced. This surprised me still more, for he seemed too young to have been at the dancing age when my mother was.

"Do you play bridge?" When I said I did, he invited me to a party he was planning for the next evening.

"Any of the Russians you would like me to invite?"

I hesitated, then: "Yes, Kirilin."

"But he doesn't play bridge. Oh, never mind, at eight, then, tomorrow night, Barracks Four—you know, across the road from the camp." He saluted, and the soft click of his spurs followed him out as he closed the door.

I decided not to wear a uniform. The soft pink crepe-de-Chine blouse went well with my purple tweed skirt. I dressed with care. It was past eight when I finally found Barracks 4, outside the barbed-wire enclosure. A soldier showed me to the captain's sitting room. A delicate scent of fine tobacco pleasantly suppressed the smell of tar paper and new lumber. The door opened on an animated babble of Danish voices.

The captain immediately disengaged himself and came toward me. "So glad you're here!" He introduced several people whom I had not met.

My roving glance quickly established the fact that Kirilin was not present. Well, what of it? The captain took me by surprise:

"Kirilin will be around later. Some camp business to attend to. Will you play bridge?"

My first thought was: How awful to be caught in the midst of a boring game of bridge when he comes! But the captain insisted.

I was not a good bridge player that night, I even had trouble counting the trumps. And as the evening wore on, hope dwindled. Interest in the game also dwindled, and at the end of the rubber I asked to be allowed to watch.

Finding an armchair in a dim corner, I sat down. Suddenly I heard footsteps. One, two, one, two—the corridor outside the captain's sitting room was a long one. Strange how mesmerizing loud rhythmic sounds can be! The steps stopped outside the door. Pause. A resolute tap.

There was a confusion of greetings. Kirilin knew most of the guests. He bowed over my hand, but did not kiss it.

"Sorry I couldn't come earlier. Certain duties in the officers' mess kept me late."

Why should he think it mattered to me? The captain had invited him, not I. It took me some time to relax sufficiently to become carried away, like the others, by the rising animation of the party.

Gleb Nikolayevich was in high spirits. His boyish face glowed, the blue-gray eyes shone. His rich voice rang with warmth and enthusiasm as he began telling of wild adventures. The other Russians in the room turned away from their cards, joined the group in the corner, laughed, listened, making their own contributions.

"Recite something, Gleb Nikolayevich—go on!" someone urged him.

Then he fell to reciting in French—for my benefit—beautiful poems about *l'amour,* classics by the great French poets. Some I knew from the classroom and theater, but I had never fully understood them as I did now when I heard them spoken with the poetic passion of his voice. Then, abruptly, he switched to Russian for Pushkin's famous epic "Poltava."

It was like the wind in the pines, like a roaring torrent, like the reverberating harmonies of an organ, the crash of a storm. The glorification of victory, the defeat of the Swedes, the heroes of the battle of Narva, disdain for the conquered, the rising passion, all emphasized by the rhythm—and I didn't understand a word!

A roar of applause broke out when Gleb Nikolayevich finished and sat back, cheeks flushed, eyes flashing, challenging, riveted on my face. My ears filled with the babble of voices. I leaned forward.

"Will you teach me Russian?" I asked in a small voice.

"Why should *you* want to learn Russian?" he countered sharply. It was as if no one but the two of us had been in the room.

I searched in vain for a plausible reason.

"Very well." He bit off the words. "I will teach you Russian. The day after tomorrow at half past eight I shall come to your room for the first lesson."

CHAPTER 5

REVOLUTION

THE green-shaded lamp threw a soft light over books and blotting paper as I sat with my Russian teacher at the desk in my tiny room in the Danish nurses' barracks. Through the thin walls came voices, some high-pitched with the softly slurred Danish accent mingled with deeper masculine tones. All struggled with the same perplexing task of teaching and learning Russian.

A soft tongue of a thousand nuances, the Russian language lends itself equally well to high forms of poetry and to abusive utterances. Its syntax baffled me, vastly different from any of the other languages I had studied. Its lack of articles puzzled me. I was amazed to find that when I wanted to say, "I have a chair," I had to say in Russian, "By me chair." And there were the many long words full of *sh* and *shch* sounds, and the pronunciation was very hard.

I tried again: *"Oo menya yest stol."*

"No, can't you hear? The *l* should be hard—*stoll*—not soft."

"Stol."

"God, you have no ear!" He threw up his hands in despair.

Gleb Nikolayevich was by no means a patient teacher, though an utterly painstaking one. He would not let me off until I had mastered the evil word to his satisfaction. Once I realized this, my aptitude for mimicry came to my aid and, surprisingly, I eventually acquired the "ear."

The hours we spent together in the evenings soon were extended to my official hours of free time after lunch. We went for long walks in the winter-bound beech forests that surrounded the camp. The officers were allowed outside the camp. There they felt free. There they were simply invalids under the bond of their word of honor to their neutral hosts. And the relationship between hosts and bonded was one of mutual trust.

Gleb's two best friends also became my friends. We called Konstantin Pavlovich Trebinsky "Ptichka," meaning "little bird," because he looked like one with his pinched face, hawk nose, and slightly bulging eyes. The name did not offend him; on the contrary, it flattered and pleased him.

Stanislav Stanislavovich Vronsky was Gleb's roommate. He was Polish by birth. His pleasant, somewhat coarse face expressed an abundance of goodwill. The war had robbed him of his right leg, and he named his artificial leg Marie. He accused her of fickleness, a disinclination to obey orders. He left her for the most part standing at attention by his cot, while he gaily hopped around on his crutches.

On my day off the four of us undertook excursions on rented bicycles to various places of interest in the neighborhood. Vronsky usually led the way, his crutches lashed to the crossbar, his one leg pedaling at double speed, always tactfully refraining from glancing back at Gleb and me as we lagged a bit behind.

We visited Helsingør, the Elsinore made famous in Shakespeare's *Hamlet,* not far from the camp. A charming town even in winter, full of stately trees, parks, old houses, and quaint streets, it sprawled along the narrowest part of the sound linking the Baltic with the Kattegat, the arm of the North Sea that separates Denmark from Sweden. Under the elms that stood guard around Hamlet's empty sarcophagus, as if insisting upon the reality of the character supposed to be entombed there, we spent hours. Here, with his hand clasping mine, he spoke to me of his literary aspirations and ideas, thoughts never before expressed—Shakespeare, Ibsen, Tolstoi. And at these moments of close confidence, I felt the shy, uncertain groping for love and trust, his need for an anchor.

Together we explored the famous fortress Kronborg with its green copper roof, erected in 1425 at the edge of the sound and serving as a bastion during periods of war between the two close neighbors. High up on the bulwarks, with the fresh sea air upon our faces, we sat close together on the old canon and gazed across the water to Sweden, my land with its low contour outlined in the hazy distance. I looked up at him and there was a smile of deep understanding on the boyish face.

Desperately I wanted to talk with him of the war, to penetrate the things that touched him and his life most deeply, to share his pain and make it mine. Love is sometimes guilty of monumental indiscretions. But the hard look that on these occasions came into his eyes, the curt severity that immediately put its stamp on his whole attitude, warned me not to trespass. I thought on these occasions that he felt no love, that he would not let me in. There was nothing for me, nothing but the slight limp, the dark-brown stain of blood on his torn and war-worn greatcoat.

Strange moods possessed him, moods of teasing mockery or of perverse bitterness. To hell with what's to happen next! This attitude sometimes alternated with an overly sensitive and prideful withdrawal at the least suggestion of sympathy or affection. This constant swinging between emotional extremes I found very difficult to understand, to gauge, and to parry.

Zinaida Andreyevna realized my difficulties.

"Gleb Nikolayevich needs very careful handling," she explained as we were talking in her room. "All these men live on a volcano of nerves, resulting partly from the suffering of their bodies, partly from the war, the risks, the imprisonment. They are hypersensitive. Too much pain, mental and physical, becomes unbearable. So they hide their thoughts and feelings under various pretexts. And this relieves them."

She sat for a while without moving, her hands resting in her lap.

"Gleb Nikolayevich's story is unusual. He's probably told you that his home is in Tsarskoe Selo. His father, a general and a lawyer, was a fine man. Gleb and his two brothers, Vladimir and Boris, were educated in the Corps des Pages. Most of our grand dukes received their education there. Gleb's class was the last one to graduate before the war. Their graduation was hastened because of the war, so that these young officers, few older than nineteen, could be posted to the regiments of the Imperial Guards at once. These were our best troops, reliable, skilled, and by tradition the most courageous. They were immediately assigned to the forward positions in Galicia and Poland. 'First to attack, last to retreat' was their motto. And among these troops, at the very beginning of the war, we suffered our most grievous losses."

She smoothed her apron with her hand. Her voice was full of emotion.

"What horrible waste that was!" she continued. "The cream of Russia's manhood sacrificed rashly in a mad flurry of premature advances. The result was inevitable—overextended lines, poor support, followed by a disastrous retreat. While their regiments on the same battlefield covered the retreat, Vladimir was killed and Gleb seriously wounded and taken prisoner. And this was the beginning of the great Russian disaster."

She paused. When she took up her story once again, her voice was infinitely sad.

"Communications with the front were poor. Finally word came to Tsarskoe Selo that both Vladimir and Gleb had been killed in battle. The blow was too much for their mother. She threw herself out of the window and died on the way to the hospital. Two years later, Boris was killed in battle too."

Again she paused, but her tale was not yet finished.

"My husband was at the same prisoner-of-war camp as Gleb. He saw how badly he was wounded, how his hip had been shattered by shrapnel, the bones splintered. For a long time he was not expected to pull through. And the suffering—who can tell the extent of it? His recovery was very slow, it took years, and they dared not tell him about his mother and brothers. He was told here only a short time before you came."

For a long time we both sat very still and silent.

All the Russians in the camp, men and women, officers and soldiers, followed with intense interest and apprehension the portentous events that were currently taking place in their homeland. Vladimir Ilitch Ulyanov, who called himself Lenin now, had emerged from obscurity to direct events since the October uprising when the Bolsheviks came to power. Lenin's political skill and daring were uncanny. He knew how to turn every event, every circumstance to his own advantage. During his years of exile he had prepared himself well for the critical historical moment that he knew was coming. The century-long oppression to which the lower classes of the Russian people had been subjected was the source from which the great revolutionaries like Lenin drew personal strength. In February 1917, while Lenin was in Switzerland, his great moment finally arrived. His train rolled across Germany to Petrograd and he became the head of the Bolshevik Revolution.

Even in a place like Horserød, far removed from the epicenter of the Russian earthquake, its repercussions were keenly felt. With every dispatch of fresh news the nervous tensions between officers and soldiers increased. The February events, now that the new regime had become firmly established, had a profound effect upon the political climate in the camp. There were explosive outbreaks of hostility and insubordination.

The officers reacted strongly. Their committee, which heretofore had been responsible for the maintenance of order within the barbed-wire enclosure, emphatically rejected any departure from accepted military discipline. This, they considered, would be unseemly so long as they remained the guests of their neutral hosts. But, as further news came through, the situation gradually worsened. Like a treacherous undercurrent that could be neither damned nor ignored, subversion seeped in and spread into one barracks after another in the soldiers' camp. Small groups sitting together on the beds held surreptitious meetings to discuss the situation. The atmosphere in the formerly peaceful camp became reticent, divided, oppressive. The Danish administration kept strictly aloof. The maintenance of outward discipline and order was their business. With authoritative discretion they avoided all meddling in the camp's inner political affairs.

And then, early one afternoon, a seething, grumbling mob of soldiers assembled outside the officers' committee room. Quite obviously many of them considered this demonstration an act of excessive daring. It was to them too abrupt a breech of ingrained discipline. And they hesitated. But bold agitators arose in their midst and with their strident eloquence soon cast timidity and hesitancy to the winds. The soldiers demanded the immediate dissolution of the officers' committee and the surrender of all authority. The Revolution had caught fire in the Horserød camp.

After a brief and fainthearted palaver, the officers' committee, to which Gleb and Trebinsky belonged, ingloriously capitulated. It was immediately replaced by the soldiers' soviet. An ambitious sergeant from Barracks 42, a keen student of self-promoting schemes, was chosen as chairman of this self-appointed body. And that night the soldiers' camp reverberated with boisterous celebrations of the new regime, of the quick victory won with such ease. Now freedom was theirs, and an intoxicating new power.

The officers' barracks were plunged into gloom. When the tsar had been deposed, the situation of these men had not appeared to be threatened. Almost all of them had recognized the necessity of a democratic revolution in Russia, and they had pledged it their support. But now, suddenly, storm clouds had overtaken them and threatened to unleash upon their heads unknown violence. Their first reaction was an overwhelming resentment against fate and heartbreaking disillusionment. They had endured the deadly dangers and the nerve-racking experiences of the war, they had wasted the best years of their young lives in enemy prison camps. Was all this in vain? Were they to return home to total upheaval and devastation? It was staggering. They couldn't believe it. Doomed by the epaulets on their shoulders, they belonged to the now outlawed ruling class, looked upon with indiscriminate hatred that was impervious to reason. Revenge, blood, executions—these were the new order of the day in Russia. The passionately longed-for, the endlessly anticipated day of homecoming had turned into an event of paralyzing disenchantment. They were caught in a hideous trap.

The effect of the shock varied with character and personality. A surprisingly small number of the officers started to cut their epaulets from their tunics. The next morning they went over to the soldiers' camp and attempted to exact from the hard new masters a promise of at least tolerable acceptance in return for their offer of fealty.

To another group the mere thought of returning home under these evil circumstances was intolerable. General Kliuev and Trebinsky were among these. They applied to the Danes for political asylum and it was granted. And they began the tedious, often humiliating business of trying to adjust to their new existence as refugees in a foreign land. Some of these, the luckier and more adaptable ones, were eventually able to blend successfully into the new life and environment, by means of talent and ambition to carve for themselves places of personal fulfillment. But many, frustrated and discouraged by their dependence upon charity, remained irrevocably torn from their roots, racked by nostalgia for a land they could neither return to nor forget.

Through Gleb's and my meetings ran an undercurrent of immense sadness, a sense of impending disaster that we could not shake and that affected every word uttered, every thought cherished and hidden. As the events pressed in upon us, I imagined that the cynical bravado that had so disturbed me had left him forever. But no, it was creeping back, poisoning his thoughts.

"Lisinka, listen, listen to me!" His voice was impatient, low, his lips taut. "In two days I'm leaving to go back home."

I stood speechless.

"Listen!" I did not realize it was his voice I heard. But his words formed into sentences, like building blocks, one laid upon the other. "Lisa, I must go back to Russia!" Now his voice was pleading. "I have to see for myself what's going on there. I must know." The clipped sentences followed in rapid succession. "My father, my sister Marie, the only ones left of my family, are there alone. The thought is unbearable. You understand? Don't you, Lisa?" At long last he was talking to me of the things that concerned him most deeply. If I smiled, it was quite unconsciously.

"I can no longer bear to sit here in idle safety like a coward while they are perhaps in danger. You understand? I'm free to go." He put strong emphasis on every word, and I wondered dully, What was he trying to convince me of?

Now softly: "It's not only my family—what is left of them—it's Russia. This, perhaps, you cannot understand?" He hesitated, as if he had asked too much. "For better or for worse my destiny is tied with Russia. Lisa, I cannot stay away."

All my arguments against his leaving me lay shattered, like a card house collapsed by a puff of wind, unuttered. The shadow of this monster Russia, too distant and unreal to comprehend, demolished in that instant every claim upon him I might ever have insisted upon.

Two days later firm decisive footsteps resounded in the long corridor outside my door in the Danish nurses' barracks, steps indicating a slight limp. It was early morning, just after breakfast. Without knocking, Gleb entered. In his hand was his faded and worn peaked cap with the officer's badge. He had always worn it rakishly cocked over one ear.

"Lisa, I brought you this. It's the only thing of value I have."

I was in his arms. A few moments later he was gone, and I stood with his cap in my hand. All the way down the long passageway his steps reechoed loudly. A door opened and slammed shut. And it was the end.

CHAPTER 6

WITHIN RANGE OF THE POSSIBLE

EARLY in 1918, to the dismay of Russia's allies, the Bolsheviks concluded with the Germans a separate preliminary cease-fire. The soldiers at the front, who had staged their own local revolutions, like those at Horserød, identified the cease-fire as a bona fide end of the war and simply went home.

Under the heavy loads the transportation systems broke down all over the country. The movement of people and goods created grave food shortages, especially in the cities. Moreover, in a country that covered more than a third of the earth's land area, attempts at reconstruction according to a new and untried political schema presented monumental difficulties.

With the cease-fire agreement, the speedy repatriation of the prisoners of war became a burning question. For the Germans it was easy enough, just a crossing of the border, and their camp soon stood empty. For the Russians, however, it was a different matter. How were they to get from Denmark to Russia? To transport them through a Germany still at war was impossible. In Finland, Baron von Mannerheim with his intrepid freedom fighters was carrying on a bitter struggle for liberty and independence, and for a time this conflict closed the direct route across the Baltic to Petrograd. Only one way remained open, through Sweden around the top of Norway to Murmansk. But to move a large contingent of invalid prisoners of war home to Russia by this roundabout way was impractical. This was nonetheless the route that Gleb and two fellow officers, traveling on their own, had decided to take, in the hope of eventually reaching Petrograd by train or on foot along the railroad tracks.

After they left, the camp slipped into a state of dissolution. Evacuation was everywhere and on all occasions the main topic of conversation. Departure—how, when, and by what means—occupied the minds of the officers, the soldiers, and the nurses alike. It was rumored that the Soviet government had promised to dispatch ships to Denmark for their repatriation as soon as the situation in Finland made this possible. Was it true? Disbelief aggravated the endless waiting. Meanwhile, another group of officers, fired by Gleb's and his companions' example and too impatient to await word of their success or failure, procured enough money and the necessary visas to start out on the long journey.

As time dragged on, one noticed small gatherings of two or three men detaching themselves from the rest. Most of these were officers, but some also were enlisted men, all of them frightened. Suddenly they could not bear the thought of returning to Russia under the present conditions. They were ignorant of life there under the red banner, they heard only rumors, and hope lingered that a strong counterrevolutionary movement would eventually be organized. The executions, the constant nagging fear of being arrested, the Cheka—the disreputable security police—all loomed large. Russia's reputation for harsh treament of her undesirables had for centuries run like poison through all her political life. The salt mines of Siberia, unimaginable degradation and suffering meted out to rebellious lower classes . . . Now, incredibly, the roles of the classes were reversed. Primitive self-preservation bade them choose with prudence any alternative to repatriation while it was still available. To remain in Denmark, to wait and see, might at least offer them temporary safety from violence, a certain security. Was that not what they were seeking and what they needed so desperately? And for the moment this offer of refuge obscured to them the tragedy of the refugee, the humiliating poverty, the dependence on doles, the bitterness of a futile homesickness, and the isolation through deadly indifference in a strange land and society.

For me there was nothing but blank loneliness. My memories from this period are little more than a blur, all except the tense listening to the resounding footsteps upon the wooden sidewalks and the pain in realizing with a start that they could never be his. My tiny room with its bed, desk, and washstand was a prison cell. Reveille, which used to make me leap from bed, sounded the start of only another long day of emptiness.

Zinaida Andreyevna continued to walk among her invalids, dispensing support and encouragement. Now her face was always serious and brooding. She carried the burden of Russia's torment and defeat upon her shoulders. The choice of staying or returning to Russia was not hers, but her husband's. And for him there was only one choice. But the soldiers were hers, her Russia, her compatriots, in great need of sympathy and compassion as they had always been, no matter what they did or thought, one class, she and they together. And they gave her in return their respect.

She spoke to me of this relationship, and I tried to emulate her thoughts and actions in my own relationship with my tubercular patients. I realized my inadequacy. I lacked the sensitivity of the Russian.

Trebinsky and Vronsky made touching attempts to substitute for the companionship I had lost. They took me out for walks and made me go with them on excursions, but to revisit these places of recent happiness only sharpened the pain of the memory. They tried to make me laugh, but their efforts often fell through awkwardly. I should of course have laughed if for no other reason than to reward their chivalry and devotion. What Gleb had not even attempted—my adoption into the Russian clan—they accorded me spontaneously and unconditionally.

Spring burst upon the landscape. Overnight the beech trees' tender leaves miraculously unfolded and formed a green-shimmering veil around each tree. The heady aromas of the new leaves and the spring-blooming plants spread beyond the edge of the forest, too potent to be contained within the limited area of their own community.

It was heartbreaking to be unable to share with Gleb the joy I remembered from the springtimes at Svensksund. To me there could be no greater happiness than to experience a springtime with him and to make him realize the promise of it. But he had gone away.

And so this springtime at Horserød passed, wasted as far as I was concerned. I left before the final evacuation of the camp took place, and by then summer had already reached full bloom.

Again an invitation from Tante Jessy arrived at a critical point in my life. Mother and Ebba were also to spend the summer at Egeskov.

Horserød and Egeskov were poles apart. At Horserød I had been forced to face the uncompromising and shocking realities of life. At Egeskov I was offered an overabundance of luxury and security. Smooth service anticipated every move, every requirement not yet felt, and the day's monotonous rounds of effortless activities were often too boringly pleasant even to stir an objection.

How charming this time at Egeskov might have been had my mind been fully open to its lavish tranquillity, its vegetative pleasures! The sun was soft upon the creeping gray and yellow algae that mottled the walls of the castle. Sharply drawn shadows outlined the massive contours of turrets and the angling walls, and the entire scene was reflected in the still black water of the moat. A beautiful, an enchanting place!

My sister and I shared an apartment in the east wing. We liked to dawdle in the mornings, the only undisturbed time of the day we had to ourselves, a time that seemed curiously inadequate to contain all the reading, chatting, and playful activities—such as spitting into the moat to make the carp rise—that we tried to crowd into it. For this reason we chronically appeared too late for the breakfasts rich in cream and honey in the company of Tante Jessy and Mother.

Following his departure from Horserød, Gleb had sent me a postcard from Stockholm, then another from Narvik, and another from Vardø, the last outpost before he entered the unknown, the danger zone across the border of Russia. They had contained only brief messages hurriedly written with a purple indelible pencil, half in French, half in Russian. They had told me little of his feelings, his thoughts, and his experiences as he made his way toward home. They had been, nevertheless, proof of a sustained contact between us, however fragile, however thinly extended across the great distance, a hope, perhaps a promise.

After that he had been swallowed by the great unknown. There was nothing but impenetrable silence. Day after day I looked for a letter with a persistence, a last hope that would not die. The postman in his navy-blue uniform would come bicycling up the drive, and I would waylay him before he reached the large entrance doors under the archway, before he could enter the hall to lay the mail on the table.

"Anything for me today?"

"No, miss, sorry, not today."

One day, half on purpose, I missed the postman. What was the use? Everything contradicted my fast shrinking hope that I would ever again hear from Gleb. He had held me in his arms, there had been a love; a need for each other developed between us. It had been not just a dream but a reality. Then why, why had he left me to go straight into the jaws of the Revolution? And he one of the most vulnerable to its deadly dangers.

From habit I drifted into the hall. No one was there. The light summer breeze wafted through the open doors the fragrance of the large flowering rhododendron outside. The day's mail lay on the table in the center of the room already sorted.

There was a letter for me. The strange-looking envelope addressed in a strange hand was soiled from much handling. Then I knew in a flash. I grasped it and ran to my room.

A letter was inside in Gleb's handwriting. I tore it open. At first I could not understand the meaning of the words scrawled on that piece of paper. Suddenly to realize that the fragile thread spun between us held overwhelmed me. The rest came in a rush, as when in a blush the blood returns to a deadly pale face. Breathlessly I grasped the full meaning of the words. At last I understood the feelings they conveyed. They changed my whole world. And I knew that life was glorious, that he and I were young and in love, that no distance existed wide enough to separate us, that there were no difficulties we could not overcome. No circumstances, no considerations could come between us, no wars, no revolutions, for at long last he had expressed the words I had longed to hear.

I kept my secret all that day, and then at night, when the house had grown quiet after all had gone to their rooms, I went up to mother's round chamber in the east turret. She was in bed reading. She smiled a welcome. But as I began telling her of Gleb and Russia and my happiness, the smile slowly drained from her face. And the telling plunged me precipitously from the heights of bliss into a disconcerting reality.

"But, child!" she said gently with masterly self-restraint. "But, child . . ."

Gradually, as I talked, the difficulties of my plans emerged in a more glaring light. To her they were insurmountable. To me they were simply hurdles that courage and resourcefulness could overcome. I wanted to join Gleb in Russia. The problems of getting into Russia in the midst of a revolution, of procuring a visa and funds to travel were all solvable. There were many ways to get in and out of Russia—false passports, bought visas, marriage by proxy. The conversations at Horserød had centered around these things. And my imagination performed somersaults in order to convince Mother that I could do anything I wanted, that I could sweep away any difficulties. Love could move mountains. Hadn't she heard? Didn't she know?

But I could not convince her. Didn't she see that times had changed, that other values existed besides financial security, position, home, servants, children? The war had changed all that. And I wanted to face it and to be part of it. I wanted to accept the difficulties as they arose. My place was with Gleb and not here in an almost shameful security. Mother's view was old-fashioned, archaic, timid. Mine was new, enterprising, courageous. Now the time had come when my nursing skills would really become a great asset, when the hard training would pay dividends. Over there, in a country ravished by war and revolution, there must be a tremendous need for good nurses. And when there was less to eat, one ate less, it was quite simple.

Mother looked at me and her eyes were very serious.

"Isn't there a possibility that you might add to his troubles and dangers by joining him now?" she said softly. "I shouldn't imagine a man would feel happy having his wife exposed to dangers and perhaps suffering for his sake."

That silenced me for the moment as I remembered Gleb's strict sense of duty. Mother had scored a point.

Yet it was not so. Now it was my sacred right to share the dangers and the hardships with him. I refused to believe that he would be better off without me. Not now—for he had written, he wanted me. That was enough. Across closed borders and open seas we had come together again. Wasn't that sign enough? And this coming together was meant for life. Our love would triumphantly carry us over everything, poverty, hunger, dangers, even death.

I said, "Mother, you don't understand," as if she had never been young, as if she had never known idealism, enthusiasm. Gleb and I would find a way. We were not afraid.

Mother did not argue the point. Perhaps she realized the futility of battling the tidal wave of change. The whole thing had crept upon her imperceptibly, and she was taken by surprise.

There was a long silence. The night watchman came to the drawbridge below the open window. His voice drifted slowly through the night: "Twelve o'clock—and all is well!"

Mother lay with her head propped against the white pillow, and the blue room was warm and pleasant. And as I looked at her, it seemed to me that her mind had gone wandering somewhere where I could not follow.

To stay at Egeskov was impossible. And finally Mother gave in to my stormy entreaties to let me return to Stockholm, where her apartment stood temporarily empty. I would be more than a hundred miles closer to Gleb, and for a time I needed to be alone.

Tante Jessy, hearing of the reason for my departure, batted her eyelashes furiously. "Nonsense! Psht—psht—never heard of such foolishness!" And with an impatient gesture of her hand she dismissed the whole idea of this ludicrous marriage. "No one marries a Russian nowadays. No financial security—no position—refugees without nationality—psht—psht—impossible!"

Having accepted without question her noble family's choice of a husband befitting her station and with the accumulation of worldly goods and financial security to back her, Tante Jessy could not be expected to sanction such wild marriage plans as mine.

Before Gleb left Horserød, thinking that the contact might prove useful to him one day, I had given him a letter to deliver personally to my cousin Elsa Brändström. Her father was Sweden's ambassador to Russia, and the embassy in Petrograd was still functioning. When Gleb's letter came, I knew that he had met Elsa.

She was a remarkable woman. She looked like a modern Valkyrie, tall and fair. Her blond hair was a soft translucent aura around her face, and her intense blue eyes her most memorable features. Her fearlessness was legendary. During the war she had gone to Siberia as a Red Cross delegate to ameliorate the hard lot of the German and Czech prisoners of war who were held there under appalling conditions. Her remarkable organizing skill and her sense of fairness won for her advantages and improvements for them that saved many a prisoner's life and sanity. In constant contact with lice and disease, Elsa eventually had contracted typhus and nearly died, and the soldiers gave her the name of "the Angel of Siberia."

Now, by putting our letters in envelopes addressed to her, Gleb and I were able to correspond with each other. My letters to Gleb crossed the closed border in the Swedish diplomatic courier's bag; she sent his letters to me in the same way. And the brief interviews she granted him when he came to deliver his closely scribbled messages soon became the only encouragement left to him.

My impetuous proposal to join Gleb in Russia at once met with his instant disapproval. His letter to this effect was tenderly persuasive. Under no circumstances should I come. To tell me all the reasons why such a thing could not be contemplated would serve no useful purpose, he wrote. What he needed most was faith in his good judgment. He talked of the "inside" and the "outside." No one "outside" could even remotely realize the risks such an undertaking would entail for both of us.

"But," he wrote, "to have you as my link with the outside is of utmost importance." This was talking in riddles, but a sunrise of hope dawned within me. Was he actually talking of coming here? The thought brought an almost painful feeling of joy.

"Do you think you could obtain for me a Swedish visa?" the letter continued. "If the worse comes to the worst . . ."

It was said. It was meant. To be thrown into action was a great relief. Full of eager confidence, I arranged for an interview with Mr. Sager of the visa department in the Foreign Office. I had met him, danced with him, and he was a nice man. He greeted me by expressing encouraging interest in whatever small matter I might have to discuss with him. A handsome, well-groomed man, he had the courteous manner of a rising young diplomat.

My errand was simply stated.

"So you're engaged!" His eyebrows lifted slightly. "My best felicitations, Miss Flach!" A short pause. "But—why a Russian?" His hand made a small deprecatory gesture. "Frankly, I don't approve of the idea of surrendering any of our charming young ladies to our estimable neighbor in the east."

I sat stiff and silent, feeling suddenly inexplicably culpable.

Observing my consternation, he said softly, "But who am I to reproach you? My wife—as you know . . ." and he smiled broadly.

Then I remembered the beautiful Mrs. Sager—a Russian. And

wasn't there something about her having been a ballerina whom he had met while on diplomatic service in Petrograd? He smiled again, and the coincidence, I felt, made things somewhat easier.

But I was mistaken.

"At present the Foreign Office issues no visas to foreigners." Sager went into a long explanation about the refugee problem. A lump rose in my throat and I didn't know how to get rid of it. "We're becoming very selective. And a Russian refugee . . . Forgive me for saying so, but for obvious reasons they're not among the most desirable."

Hope sank. The pride, the happiness in being engaged to Gleb dimmed strangely.

Mr. Sager went on to explain that I would have to provide a promise, a guarantee that Gleb would not stay in Sweden more than three months.

Hope bounced back. That would be easy, and at that moment three months seemed time unlimited. I promised, I bonded the faith of myself and all my family.

"But even so," Mr. Sager warned as he bowed me out, "your request is not likely to go through except as a special concession."

Out in the street, in the sunshine, I happily jumped at conclusions. The visa seemed to be as good as granted, and my next letter to Gleb was full of exuberant plans.

By the time a week had passed, the waiting became tedious. When several more weeks passed, I was in a state of feverish anxiety. What if "the worse came to the worst" tomorrow for Gleb? What this actually meant I could only conjecture. Arrest? Imprisonment? I learned what total helplessness meant.

The summons to Sager's office came as an anticlimax. "The Foreign Office has granted a visa to Lieutenant Kirilin—with reservations. The police commissioner must first approve his entry." Mr. Sager laid his hand on a sheaf of papers on his desk. "I thought your fiancé would stand a better chance if you yourself took the papers to the commissioner."

"Who is this man?" The question was abrupt. The commissioner's voice was harsh. He smacked the papers I had given him with the back of his hand.

Hope fluttered uneasily. I told him that Gleb was a former officer of the Imperial Guard, that he had been badly wounded early in the war and taken prisoner, that he had returned home an invalid. "And now his life may be in danger."

"There are many like him," the commissioner observed. A protracted pause. "We're overrun with Russian refugees. Besides, they cannot be trusted."

I was outraged. Gleb was honest, trustworthy, and wonderful and charming besides. But I found it hard to plead with this Swede for my Russian, for I was fighting the distrust of centuries.

Finally he spoke again. "A visa will be granted this man on one condition: that he is out of this country within three months." For a second he fastened his piercing eyes upon my face. "Good day."

Gleb's letter telling me of the death of his father contained few details. Apparently it had been written in a hurry. I had known that his father was failing. Now there was only his sister Marie, the youngest of the family. He was arranging for her to go to their aunt, who lived in Petrograd. He was pleased with this arrangement. The aunt was running a Soviet eating place, and Marie could work there and be comparatively safe. His own need to leave Tsarskoe Selo was becoming more and more pressing, and he planned to do so shortly.

This came as a shock to me. What did it mean? Not to know where he was, to lose contact with him, this seemed to me worse than anything that could happen. How I hoped he had got the visa from Elsa! But there was no word. Again and again I reread his last letter to find a hint about the visa, but there was none.

No letter came from Gleb the following week. It could mean only one thing: that he had left Tsarskoe Selo. Had he been forced to leave? Or worse? And this awful silence dragged on, week after week.

The accounts of the red terror that was sweeping across the unfortunate country, of the persecutions suffered by the bourgeoisie, among whom former officers figured most prominently, were at this time becoming highly intensified. Simultaneously, the counterrevolutionary activities in the south, east, and north, aided and supported by the Allies, were gaining in strength and momentum. Russian leaders emerged, General Anton Denikin in the south, later succeeded by General Baron Piotr Wrangel, Admiral Aleksandr Kolchak in the east, and General Evgeny Miller in the north, and in the course of their initial successes they became almost legendary figures. The rumors about these White armies aroused in the anticommunists inside Russia desperate hopes of deliverance at the same time that the menace to their safety and to their lives became greatly increased. And they awakened in those on the outside a hope of a Bolshevik defeat and of a return to the political power they had lost. Most important to most of them was the fact that these men were providing a concerted effort to replace both the old regime and the Communists with something far better, a democracy that would be just and viable.

The gruesome tales that came from inside Russia were no longer at such a great distance from me that they could not touch me. They had become a reality converging upon me with nightmarish insistence. And my question: God, what has happened to him? remained unanswered.

Only one gleam of light penetrated the darkness: Gleb must have got the visa by now, and he must have had some plan in mind when he asked me to get it for him. People were escaping from Red Russia into Finland. The flight across the Siestra Rieka, the tiny creek separating Russia from Finland, was speedily becoming an organized business with guides and disguises that could be hired for a price. I began scanning the papers for the arrival time of the next boat from Finland.

Well ahead of the scheduled time I was at the quay. The darkening days of October lay wet and gray and foggy over the familiar outlines of land and water. Black-headed gulls on black-tipped wings wheeled over the water among the ships, uttering their mournful cries. Winches rattled loudly and the air smelled of fish and waterlogged timbers.

It was a long wait. But finally the gleaming white Finnish boat came into view. Slowly it glided toward the quay. People, gray people crowded its railings. I strained to find among them the well-known face. The Russian refugees were clearly recognizable. Their worn clothing, unmistakably Russian, their hesitating walk down the gangplank, their anxious glances gave them away. Gingerly, hesitating to the last, they stepped off the ship without assurance into the elusive freedom of poverty-stricken exile. And their eyes reflected the conflict between relief from danger and the overwhelming gloom caused by the loss of home and country. Day after day I returned to the quay to witness the same scenes, straining for the miracle that never happened. And I returned home each time more discouraged, more doubtful of a hope ever less likely to become a reality.

No matter how that incredible telegram I held in my hand might have been worded, the shock could hardly have been more severe. Great sorrow and great joy are emotions lying very close to each other. The prospect that I would see Gleb once again, tomorrow, seemed unreal. There was no explanation apart from the terse announcement that he would be in Stockholm the next day. I needed none. Where he came from, why he came, nothing mattered. He was safe, he was alive. Somehow he had managed to escape an environment where the impact of explosive events destroyed all attempts at forecasting and planning. And suddenly I was struck by the amazing significance attached to so trivial a matter as the ability to plan activities and to foresee events with more or less assurance.

The early northern twilight was just about to descend when once again I stood on the now familiar quay. The water in the harbor reflected the lingering glow of the sun upon the narrow gabled houses of the Old City along the waterfront. It illuminated also the masts, the riggings of the moored ships, the dirty sheds and scattered cargo. The place had never looked so bright and so attractive to me. I waited, and even though I knew exactly what would eventually happen, how the trim bow of the white ship would glide into view, when it finally did come it seemed to me a breathtaking surprise. My eyes strained across the diminishing distance to the solid mass of gray-brown people at the railings. I saw a hand waving above the heads of the gray mass. It was Gleb.

The white hull of the ship ground lightly against the wet timbers, the gangplank clattered. Uniformed men ran singly down the gangplank and into the customs shed. Presently, in a flood, the passengers poured down and into the shed. I had eyes only for one. Tall, gaunt, hollow-eyed he came, wearing no overcoat, in the frayed brown tunic I knew so well, military breeches, high Russian boots.

Gleb stood before me and I heard one word: "Lisa!"

CHAPTER 7

THE DECISION

At this time it happened that I had to move out of the apartment that Mother had sublet. This lack of a home of our own was soon to pose unexpected problems for us.

When Mother heard of Gleb's arrival, she came to Stockholm and she and I moved in with an aunt. In her small flat there was no room for Gleb. In a city overcrowded with refugees, all I had been able to get for him on such short notice was a miserable room on a noisy downtown street.

The joy of being together again, the love and the trust that had brought him miraculously through deathly dangers back to me and tenderly expressed in every glance and word, were soon to be severely tested. His position as a penniless refugee and yet my fiancé profoundly disturbed him. He realized my relatives' unuttered disapproval of the rash engagement; he felt frustrated by his inability to fulfill the demands placed upon him, not only by them but by his own standards of pride and honor, based on family tradition and his military education. The relatives' invitations to lunches and dinners to celebrate the occasion intensified his discomfort by focusing on the incongruities of the present state of affairs. And my efforts to shield him, to withdraw him from these well-meant social obligations proved futile and ineffective. If we could only be left alone!

In an effort to escape during the early part of the day, we went for long walks in the parks surrounding the city, where there was peace and privacy and we could be ourselves. On the leaf-strewn paths ripe with the pungent autumn fragrances we found a measure of solitude and a blessed chance of intimate communion. There where the sun broke through the clouds and played upon the frosty dew gathered on the dead grasses, making them glitter like a thousand stars, we found a bench. In disjointed fragments, piecemeal, Gleb laid down before me the entire story of his past life, that in my keeping it might find its continuance.

The exclusive town of Tsarskoe Selo, the tsar's village, once full of happy homes and young laughter, of bright uniforms and shining horses pulling dashing troikas in winter, had centered around the resplendent court of the tsar. For centuries it had been the cherished place of leisure, recreation, and retirement of the Russian rulers, with their crowds of courtiers and attendants and hangers-on moving like kaleidoscopic figures around its tree-lined streets and in its picturesque parks. Here the famous palace of Catherine the Great stretched its elongated yellow façade amid gardens with artificial lakes and sparkling fountains, a gorgeous monument to Russia's most prominent empress. Its architecture, its priceless paintings and interior decorations bore witness to the old imperial splendor. Not far from it, and surrounded by another immense park, Nikolai II's favorite palace raised its columned front, its white walls shining even on days when the sun was concealed. Its simplicity gave it an air of severe dignity.

Elsewhere scattered around the town were the spacious barracks of the famed regiments of the Imperial Guards, into whose safekeeping the lives of the tsar and his family were entrusted. Most of the men living in the town belonged to these regiments, as did the men of the Kirilin family. Their whole existence was steeped in regimental traditions, in the life of splendor and gaiety of the imperial garrison with its jingling spurs, its resplendent military trappings, and its inevitable entourage of feminine flutter.

Now the barracks lay deserted. The portals of their once sacred military citadel stood unguarded. The colorful historical traditions of the regiments were lost in a vast oppressive emptiness. Gone the echoes of sharply shouted commands, the songs of the soldiers full of dashing rhythm and wistful sadness. Gone all the evidence of the disciplined Russian soldiers' amiable subservience to their keen and pleasure-loving officers and to their "little father," the tsar.

In the white palace a captive dethroned ruler had lived with his frightened family not so long ago, an imperial prisoner accepting the adverse turn of his fortunes with the nobility of a gentleman and the temperance of a martyr. In his magnificent palace park he had moved with tranquil dignity surrounded and guarded by disrespectful and uncouth soldiers. And his fate, like that of so many of his officers, had hung precariously in the balance of the capricious power of the populace. Then he, too, was gone, sent into exile with his family, as had so many exiles before him been sent by a stroke of his own unwilling pen.

When Gleb returned home, the face of Tsarskoe Selo was gray and lifeless. Not even the loveliness of the advancing springtime could hide the disfigurement of the neglected parks, the grass worn by the footprints of the liberated people, and the gutters filled with dead leaves unswept from past autumns. In the all but empty street a man hurried furtively past him. He peered into the drawn face marked with the refinement that no poverty, no humiliation or beggar's clothes could erase entirely, but he did not recognize it. And then he came to the corner of the wide avenue, and with a pang of excitement he saw once again the stone wall that still kept futile guard around his once graceful home. He opened the unhinged gate and went in.

The meeting between the aged father and the lost son was filled with tremendous shock for both of them. Standing aside, awaiting their turn, his sister Marie, a very shy young girl, and their faithful nanny cried softly.

For the past year these three had lived here together in one room to conserve heat. The rest of the house stood empty. Except for the few pieces they had crowded into the one room to make it more livable, most of the furniture was gone. Gone were all the pictures and the bibelots, objects tied by memory and affection to the entire history of the family. Gleb found the few things that still remained piled into a corner of the bare and cold dining room, like goods in a junk shop awaiting disposal. And soon they too would be gone, one by one, in a forlorn effort to keep scanty meals on the table.

Gleb had had no illusions about his homecoming. The hardships of the war and the three years in German prison camps had prepared him for a blighted world. He had returned to this new life fully aware of the irrelevancy of former comfort. He deplored the change, but he did not permit himself the luxury of nostalgia.

With two empty hands he set about to support his reduced family amid the ruins of what once had been.

"If I could only tell you, Lisa, how I felt! If I could only explain my hopes, my conclusions, my understanding of these events! I see the revolution as a logical, an unavoidable sequence of all that had taken place before. The decay of the old! I see it now so clearly. It had gone too far, much too far. The injustices, the oppression . . . It's now up to us to adapt to the change, to work with it, not against it. When a great revolution meets a rigid resistance, a violent rebound and corrupting excess is a logical result."

He paused. "At least that's the way I look at it. And I also know that to become involved in politics in Russia is and always has been extremely dangerous. What I want to do is take a nonpartisan stand on the side of justice and work for the creation of a true democracy, for something that is right and totally beneficial and well balanced. Surely, after the tearing down, after all that is finished with, the restoration of a new social order should become possible."

I knew that Gleb was not alone in his attitude. A great many young people like Gleb, who belonged to the former privileged classes, who had not yet been touched by the poisons of a divided allegiance, were only too willing to share with the less privileged the personal discomforts and hardships that were unavoidable in the violent clash between two sharply diverging social ideas striving for dominance for the sake of a fair solution of the problem. But the irresistible momentum of the revolutionary forces that strove to sweep away the old was impossible to stop, and it destroyed them.

Gleb was unable at this time to assess the violence of the Russian Revolution. Besides, his first concern was to find some rational means of making a living. He met with little success. Meanwhile, he sold some of the remaining pieces of furniture. With this money he would walk miles into the countryside to buy a bag of potatoes and carry it home on his back. He went days without food himself that the others might eat. Finally, by sheer luck, he ran into an old friend who secured for him work with an organization caring for repatriated prisoners of war. This meant that he was now in possession of an invaluable worker's certificate that entitled him to rations. And he stayed with the work patiently for as long as it lasted.

Then, without warning, the organization was dissolved. Gleb

sold some more precious possessions, a few pieces of good clothing he had found in a cupboard; none of it brought much. Gradually he became aware of a menacing change in the attitude of the authorities. The protection given returned veterans was eroding fast. Cuts in rations, enforced registration undermined the already precarious position of anybody belonging to the intelligentsia, regardless of war service. Sudden alarming disappearances became the order of the day. People were arrested by the secret police at night; the wait for the awful nocturnal rap on the door turned life into a nightmare. Without work, Gleb, as a former officer, became markedly vulnerable. But he refused to hide his true identity, nor would he wave a convenient red flag.

Ever since the day of Gleb's homecoming, his father had not been well. The return of the only remaining son had been a shock as well as a great joy. It had freed him from the responsibility of the family. And suddenly age descended upon the old man and bowed his erect soldierly figure. Deep lines of sadness furrowed his face. His eyes, filled with a faraway dreamy light, looked upon the ruins of his world without bitterness. He had begun to withdraw from it three years earlier, when his wife had killed herself. He no longer belonged to this harsh world. He was ill only a week. Gleb and Marie buried him beside his wife and his two sons under the simple white headstone of the Kirilins in the once well-kept Tsarskoe Selo cemetery. After the funeral Gleb found tucked under his father's pillow one of his mother's bloodstained stockings, taken from her injured foot as she lay dying

Now that their father was gone, there was no reason for the brother and sister to stay in the old home. Gleb was rapidly becoming convinced that the new regime had no room for people like himself. He felt the network of relentless terror closing in upon him. And his presence jeopardized Marie's safety. So they arranged for her to go and live with their aunt, an unpretentious and very kind person who lived on a side street behind the Kazan Cathedral in Petrograd. She was fond of Marie and heartily welcomed her. There, Gleb felt, the young girl would be safe and at least have enough to eat.

As for himself, he was young, and the hope of the young is not easily killed. He wanted to live and to live without shame. Rumors kept circulating about significant events taking place in the south.

The name of Denikin had sprung into prominence, a leader fighting not for the revival of the old regime with all its deplorable mistakes, but for a people's democratic government in opposition to the Bolsheviks' bloody dictatorship with its class hatred and its brutalities, and this appealed to him. And finally he reached the portentous decision of which he had written in his last letter. Cautiously and surreptitiously he began to search for a way to get to the south. Underground activities were rapidly becoming organized. He needed help. One of the men with whom he had worked procured for him a travel permit as a war invalid going to a convalescent hospital south of Moscow.

For the last time Gleb replaced with fresh flowers the wilted ones on the four graves. For the last time the old nanny prepared for him a scanty meal in his childhood home. And as he left her, with tears running down her withered cheeks, she touched with her lips the shoulder of the tall man she had nursed as a child in her arms. The house was hers, he had given it to her; belonging to the proletariat, she would be safe there.

At the dirty, crowded railroad station in Moscow Gleb boarded the train for the last and most dangerous part of the journey. He took his place in a coach with other invalids southward bound. The air was heavy with odors of sweaty clothes and tobacco. The men sat tightly wedged side by side on the hard wooden seats. Nobody spoke. Tension was in many faces, mistrust and fear. Suddenly loud voices broke the silence of the crowded coach. Like lightning word spread that Red soldiers were coming aboard in search of deserters. The counterrevolutionary activities in the south had sharpened the vigilance of the Reds. A small detachment of khaki-clad police burst noisily into the coach. Their ruddy faces shone under helmets made from rough fabric with a large red star splashed in front. Long greatcoats flapped against their booted legs. Revolvers hung in holsters from black leather belts.

Gleb's papers were not accepted. With several others under suspicion he was arrested and taken to the Cheka prison hospital for further investigation.

The dingy dormitory reeked of disinfectants, stale tobacco, and sick humans. On a low cot pushed against the wall Gleb faced the end of his trail. "It had to come," he muttered. He turned against the wall, found his knife, and bared his wrist.

But he could not do it.

He rose from his cot and glanced around. Taking nothing with him, he slowly walked out of the suffocating dormitory, down the corridor, into the unswept vestibule. Hands in his pockets, he walked past the sentry, down the front steps, out into the crowded street. Nobody stopped him.

Tense with excitement, he kept on walking down the street. A plan of escape began to take shape in his mind. Back to Petrograd—somehow. Back to get the visa for Sweden. Across the Siestra Rieka into Finland. Oh, God, would it be possible to get as far as that?

He walked down the long Miasnitskaya Street to the Nicolayevsky Station. He hid until the train for Petrograd was due. Without any papers or ticket, just as the train began to move out, he leaped on behind the back of a soldier guard. Throughout the whole of that nightmarish journey he dodged the men of the Cheka. He sneaked behind their backs, clung to the rods, crawled under the benches, hid in the toilet. As the train, with brakes screaming, steamed into stations, he jumped off and caught it again as it laboriously gathered speed beyond. He never missed, never made a miscalculated move. When the train slowing down on a curve clattered into the outskirts of Petrograd, he jumped off, rolled into a deep ditch, and fell asleep, exhausted.

When he awoke it was night. He rose stiffly and walked cautiously into the city. For several days he hid with friends, moving constantly, carefully preparing for the escape into Finland. He did not dare get in touch with Marie. But somehow he had to get the visa. He prayed for his luck to hold. He crept along the narrow street behind the Swedish embassy and finally slipped through the door when the janitor opened it. Elsa gave him the visa.

At last, in the darkness of a moonless November night, creeping from one bush to another, Gleb reached the famous Siestra Rieka. Red soldiers were on guard continually along the creek. He hid, watching, preparing himself for the last precarious dash.

Cautiously he crawled closer to the water's edge. Slowly, so as not to make a splash, he waded into the open stream, until only his head was above water. Under his cap he carried his wallet with a little money, his cherished Maltese cross, and the Swedish visa. He prayed his foot would not slip.

At last, with his heart pounding against his ribs, he reached the other shore. Slowly, deliberately, stopping every so often to flatten himself against the brown earth, he crept up the low bank. He reached cover and flopped panting into the sanctuary of a fragrant yew, his teeth chattering from cold and nerves.

He lay there for a long time unable to move. On the Russian side he heard the twitterings of a small flock of birds and an aching nostalgia clutched at his heart, tears rose in his throat. And then—Finland! And the thought of the alien land was sweet.

Gleb's tale held me spellbound. His hairbreadth escapes, the awful risks seemed logical and natural. His presence made it seem a normal, inevitable sequence of events. The single thought that he was alive overwhelmed me—the full meaning of the nerve-racking suspense he had undergone, the cost of his daring, of his courageous and single-minded effort to extricate himself from the dragnet that had threatened to destroy him, was elusive. I found it strange that the relief of his being safe in Sweden, instead of giving him peace of mind, should so soon affect him with a distressing restlessness.

Gleb had tasted life in the raw. Trivialities, commonplaces had no further hold on him. Only one significant decision remained: What role should he play in the civil war now tearing Russia apart? But to realize fully what these experiences had done to him, where they were leading him, how drastically his values had changed under the pressure of these extraordinary events, was very difficult for me to comprehend—as difficult as it was for my mildly scandalized relatives to accept him willingly, immediately, without question, as my future husband.

When I ventured to suggest to him that it might be better to change his half-military attire for civilian clothes while he was in Sweden, he took it as an insult. His frayed tunic was a garment he wore proudly, for it represented his profession, and because it attested to the hardships he had endured. But finally, to satisfy my relatives' ideas of propriety, he let himself be persuaded to change into civilian clothes. He accompanied me to the family parties that uncles and aunts arranged for us. We danced, and they said we looked nice together. When Mother offered a toast to our future happiness, he kissed her hand that held the glass of red wine with a natural grace. And they all smiled.

Gleb's heart was torn by conflict. He hated being a fugitive, presuming to talk of marriage with no security to offer his bride, and clung tenaciously to the hope that there would be a solution containing both the love that had come to him and the fulfillment of his duty to his country. His trust, his tenderness told me his needs and gave me the assurance necessary to help and support him. Often he was tormented by guilt. He had left Marie, the beloved sister. Somehow the authorities might link his name with hers and endanger her security. He was secure, eating and drinking in plenty while she might be starving. Where would he go? What should he do? He was homesick, and he had closed the doors of his homeland behind him, perhaps forever.

Meanwhile, he paid frequent visits to the Russian consul, and I gladly accompanied him. The courteous man with the sad brooding face in the shabby consular office had by his own request been officially deposed by the Soviets, while he surreptitiously continued to serve the Russian refugees in the name of the old regime. And here Gleb hopefully reached for the one straw upon which he felt he could build an honorable future. He could not accept the sterile lot of the refugee. With his nightmare escape from Moscow he had bought a new lease on life at the price of continued service to Russia in whatever capacity remained open to him. Russia was his mother; he could not abandon her.

Eagerly Gleb watched the development of the White armies and waited for a call to arms. He had heeded the battle cry from the south not so long ago. Now the circle around the Bolshevik citadel appeared to be slowly closing. With the help of the Allied Forces, General Miller had occupied the important northern ports of Archangel and Murmansk and was pushing south toward the heart of Russia and east to Siberia. In Estonia, General Nikolai Yudenich, the hero of Erzerum, was calling upon exiled Russians to create a front aimed at Petrograd.

For a short while Gleb hesitated between joining the northern White Army and joining Yudenich's forces in Estonia. The idea of marching to the immediate deliverance of Tsarskoe Selo was tempting. The aura of heroism and military skill surrounding Yudenich's name seemed to forecast a speedy success for the general's enterprise. Finally, however, taking into consideration the better organization of the northern Russian fronts and the sustained support of the Allies, he decided to apply for a commission there.

This decision wrought a complete change in Gleb's world. At last he had a foothold in the one direction in which he wished to go. Soon he would have a place of his own and an engrossing task to perform. He was no longer a refugee. And beyond this, he envisioned the creation of a true democratic rule of Russia and all her peoples.

We were to be married as soon as Gleb got his papers. If circumstances permitted, I would join him later in Archangel. So we arranged for the banns to be read on the next three consecutive Sundays in Mother's parish church. Meanwhile, during the time of waiting, we decided to spend Christmas with Mother and Ebba in Copenhagen.

We set out in a happy holiday mood. On the way south we stopped over in Helsingborg, across from Helsingør, where Grandmaman Wendela had gone to live after her husband's death. She received Gleb with spontaneous warmth and unquestioning acceptance. The easy simplicity with which she adopted him made him feel for the first time completely at home. We spent two wonderfully relaxed and happy days with her in her beautiful penthouse apartment with its lovely view over the treetops across the water of the sound.

But in Copenhagen, with nothing to do but wait, the old anxieties assailed Gleb again. The prospect of marriage was no palliative whatsoever, rather the contrary. Fears of all kinds invaded his mind. The limit set upon his stay in Sweden worried him. What was he to do if the papers from Archangel did not come in time?

One day we visited some of Gleb's old friends from Horserød. When the camp had been closed they had remained in Denmark, and they were now living meagerly in a dismal room in the east end of the city. They talked, and very soon the loneliness and hopelessness that possessed these lost men imparted themselves to Gleb. After we left them, he stopped beside the canal, gripped the balustrade with his hands so that his knuckles shone white. Sick at heart, he looked down into the murky water. "I should never have left Russia."

Feeling desperately guilty and unnecessary, I could only protest weakly, "But Gleb, you'd have been shot! You didn't leave of your own free will."

"That would have been better than this!"

I tried to cover his nervous hand with mine, but he wrenched it free and faced me, eyes blazing.

"Can't you understand, Lisa? Can't you see? Not here—but over there in my own land in its hour of torment—that's where I should be! And Marie, she may be in danger at this very moment—how do I know? She may be starving. What do *you* know about hunger and hardship?" He said this as if that experience were of priceless merit.

"And I hate these damned clothes." Strained and intense, his voice rose. "I don't recognize myself in them. This is not me." His hand traveled over the gray coat. "I'm a soldier—I've been a soldier all my life. I should be in uniform—over there—fighting. . . ." His voice trailed off into a hoarse whisper. "Imagine if something happened to prevent me from going to Archangel." He looked at me accusingly. "Lisa, you understand then I couldn't marry you, a man without home or future, without means of support. I couldn't drag you into that kind of life. I couldn't live on charity—my wife's least of all. I'd rather be dead, drown myself in these waters."

By this time I too was shaking with emotion. This was something far more devastating than I had ever faced before. Fear mingled with my heartache, my feelings of jealousy and compassion. Then suddenly I said, and I shall never know how I uttered the words, "Let's stop the marriage banns, let's send a wire to the pastor now, at once! There's a telegraph office over there."

The relief on Gleb's face, shocking as it was, gave me wings. And quickly so that I would not falter I took him by the hand. We ran.

In the drab telegraph office we wrote our message to the pastor with blue ink on yellow paper. And the act relieved some of our tension.

A few days later the pastor's reply came. The banns could not be interrupted. They would be in effect for three months, after which, should no marriage take place, they would be canceled automatically.

Just before Christmas Gleb received his papers from Archangel. He was now recruited into the White Army of Northern Russia with the rank of lieutenant. His orders were to proceed to Archangel as soon as he obtained a visa that would permit him to travel through Norway. At last he had the assurance of action, of a future, a course to pursue. He crushed me to his heart. For the solution contained not only a way to fulfill a duty but the prerogative of a love to cherish and maintain.

At noon on the third day after Christmas we were married in the Swedish Church in Copenhagen. Although our marriage opened the last gates through which Gleb would enter the unknown without me, in my heart there was room for nothing but happiness.

Far out on Langelinie, past the Mermaid resting on her gray rock washed by the sea, we drove to the modest church. There were no flowers and no elegant guests. No bridesmaids in pretty gowns preceded me to the altar, no best man stood up for the groom. I walked up the aisle on Gleb's arm in the simple mauve suit I had worn to the captain's party at Horserød. To witness the ceremony only the old gray beadle stood beside my handsome, tall, white-haired uncle. My mother's tearful eyes followed me.

On either side of the choir two Christmas trees illuminated the young pastor, splendidly arrayed in the full vestments of the Lutheran church, very rarely worn. With tactful deference to the rituals of Gleb's Orthodox faith, the pastor had seen fit to don them today. For all its frugal simplicity, our wedding thus had a singular aura of solemnity.

The next evening Gleb and I left for Stockholm. There was to be another ceremony in the Russian Orthodox church to satisfy the Orthodox requirements, but a fasting period caused a delay of two weeks. Out of these days of grace we stole our honeymoon. We stayed at a small cheap hotel on a narrow street. Starched lace curtains fell across the windows of our room. Yellow antimacassars adorned the red plush chairs crowded into the small space left by the ample iron twin beds with their shiny brass knobs.

Time was pitifully short. The minutes fled desperately fast and became days, and each day ended was a day less. We clung with greedy determination to our small measure of bliss, which was to strengthen the tie between us, carry us over the immediate inevitable parting, and endure into the uncertain future.

When the day of the Orthodox wedding came, the deposed Russian ambassador sent a bouquet of fragrant white lilacs and asked me to carry them. Gleb, having forever shed the detested civilian clothes, was comfortable and relaxed. He stood there before me in our small room elegant in his new well-tailored breeches, polished military boots, and his old beloved tunic, dry-cleaned and pressed, with the white Maltese cross shining on the left breast pocket. His eyes gleamed mischievously.

"Just imagine, Lisa," his arms were tight around me, "if suddenly I were to fly like a bird out the church window! Can you imagine the looks on the faces of your disapproving aunts and cousins, the ambassadors and the consuls?"

Gleefully I followed his flight of fancy. Amid bursts of merriment he continued: "Oh, Lisa, can you see them bursting through the doors, running down the street in frantic pursuit after the disappearing bridegroom, skirts flying, ties flying, holding on to their hats—aunts, ambassadors . . ." His imagination knew no bounds. We rocked with laughter.

At the church the fragrant bouquet was taken from my hand and replaced by a lighted candle decorated with orange blossoms and flowing white ribbons. Above our heads, held in turn by our four groomsmen, hovered two enormous golden crowns. The prolonged ritual left nothing undone that could have cast doubt upon its binding solidity. Our rings on a small tray were blessed at the altar and my ring was placed on Gleb's finger and his on mine, and then reversed. We drank wine from the same goblet. And when the priest with his gray beard halfway down his chest at last gave us his stole to hold, and led us around the altar three times, symbolizing our way together through life in marriage, I clung tightly to the hand of my twice-wedded husband, lest he might, like the bird of his fantasy, fly out the window never to return.

CHAPTER 8

THE JOURNEY

THREE short days after the wedding I stood on the dreary station platform, watching the red taillight of Gleb's train growing smaller and smaller until finally it disappeared in the darkness. And suddenly my heart contracted with the pain of losing him. A scream welled into my throat and stuck there like a cramp. A feeling of bitter animosity, almost hatred, overwhelmed me against relatives and friends, against all those who had been for or against my marriage to Gleb, who had held an opinion on it tacitly or verbally, as if the fault were theirs that it was turning out this way. My own mother, her heart full of love and with no other desire than to make this moment easier for me, walking there beside me—even she irked me with her unuttered solicitude.

With a thousand finespun threads of family, home, and country, with all that was familiar and safe, these people held me fast against my desperate urge to go with Gleb. I wanted no protection, no safety. I wanted only to share all my life with him, whatever there was to share in that distant unimaginable northern region of Russia. I hated them because at this moment I had not been strong enough to break away. And the feeling of hate gave me a sense of relief.

I became a wife without the prerogatives of a married woman, a flower without petals, a lamp without oil. Indeed, might I not actually have married a condemned man on the eve of his execution? Yet I carried his name, my passport proclaimed me to be of his nationality, a Russian.

A long dreary month went by. I waited for Gleb to send for me.

I could not work. The waiting absorbed me, it robbed me of faith, of confidence in myself, in Gleb, in the future. And then another month. Torn between intolerable irritation and anxiety, I waited. I waited as if in the whole world there were nothing else to do.

When the unbelievable happened, when the telegram came from Archangel, when the sudden burst of light broke through the dark clouds, it shocked me into a frenzy of activity.

Gleb wanted me. He wanted me to be with him, the words sang in my heart. The thought elated me. Once again the ground was firm under my feet. My position as wife became full of meaning, full of plans, full of future.

With trembling haste I tackled the preparations for the long journey north, to Gleb. Trunk after trunk I packed with things I thought I might need to establish my new home. Eagerly I secured the papers, tickets, visas, credentials that would transplant my whole life into the unknown soil of Russia, my husband's country.

Mother was silent. Each preparation was a labor of sorrow for her. Often tears dropped on her busy hands as she sewed for me and helped me to pack. I turned away not to see them. My whole world centered on Gleb, my tall fair warrior, and this extraordinary chance to go to him and be with him. The thought transcended and engulfed every other consideration. He, the husband, beckoned with all the magnetism of love. And there was no other will, no other desire, no other possibility but to travel to the end of the earth to join him.

On April Fool's Day of 1919 I found myself leaning out of the window of the train, waving away all that I was leaving behind, family, home, safety. I saw the scarlet band around the stationmaster's cap and then the white fluttering square of Mother's handkerchief, an insistent white dot following the train as it picked up speed. It reached the end of the long platform and there for an instant it stayed poised motionless in the air, before the increasing distance finally obliterated it.

A sudden feeling of panic brought tears to my eyes. Where was I going? For what was I about to exchange all that I had known of home and family in a safe, peaceful land? Was I destined never to return? Was the fluttering handkerchief the last I would ever see of my mother?

And then my thoughts flew to my dead father and to the lost home of my childhood. Memories sprang forth—the sweet fragrance of a thousand white anemones crowding upon the carpet of dead needle-narrow leaves under the larches, the first skylark's loud song as it lifted on the wings of its own rapture over the fields waterlogged from the winter's snows, the strong feeling of partnership with nature.

Was I bent upon a fool's errand? No, no, following Gleb into war, wherever the road led, was natural and justified. Thousands of women before me had done the same thing, were doing so now. This was my wedding trip. Thus, on All Fool's Day, at the age of twenty-four, I came to a crossroad and took a left turn in an entirely new direction.

The journey through Sweden lasted a day and two nights. It led farther and farther northward through great forests intersected by great rivers. The train began to climb the slowly rising eastern slope of the ancient Scandinavian mountain range.

In a driving snowstorm the train swept up to Riksgränsen, the lonely last outpost of the Swedish railway within the Arctic Circle. Gathering speed, it droned through the snow tunnel along the mountainside, and in a cloud of snow it dropped zigzagging down into Norway. With each lap the mountain walls rose higher and higher, darkened by the humidity fanned by the milder winds from the Atlantic Ocean. On the other side I gazed dizzily into the deep chasm of a Norwegian fjord; a short while later, the train slid smoothly into the immaculate railway station of Narvik.

The town is an important port of export for the lumber trade. Heavy wet snow was falling as I got off the train. Slush covered the streets. The modest hotel shone with cleanness. The wooden floors, innocent of wax, were scrubbed white. My room was plain. It was warm and smelled pleasantly of wood smoke.

The next day a small tug took me and my seven trunks to Lofoten, the rocky islands jutting out into the sea, famous for their scenic beauty. A gray swell heaved under the boat, reflecting the gray mist that swathed the islands and then lost itself into the overcast above.

We hove to at a small fishing village. Its houses clung precariously to the steep slope down to the water. A row of well-built boathouses on stilts provided them with a bulwark of safety.

The master of the tugboat, hard-fisted, crisp of speech, got his crew and two or three people who had come down to the landing place to unload my trunks. The coastal steamer was due within the hour.

Aboard ship I found myself in a small world of comfort and luxury. The stateroom was elegant and the table excellent. The beauty of this land and sea fascinated me. It filled every nautical mile with variations of mood and illumination of a magnificence I had never dreamed existed. Pierced by deep dark fjords, this coast of Norway shattered into innumerable islands, into steep cliffs topped with snow, rough pyramids of rock that plunged abruptly into the sea. When occasionally the sun's slanting rays penetrated the shredded gray clouds and the mists lifted, the effect of sudden illumination upon this landscape of mountains, sea, and snow was indescribably enchanting.

Slowly the ship steamed into the harbor of Tromsø. There was a forest of mastheads along the quay. Squat, broad-beamed fishing boats rolled into port with their decks slippery with herring scales. Countless gulls wheeled overhead, sounding their petulant cries. In the center of the town the cathedral reached its spire high above the roofs of the neat and modest houses. A wall of snow-capped mountains sheltered them against the biting northerly winds.

A lively place bustling with activity, Tromsø possessed the atmosphere of freshness and energy that belongs to places where people live in constant struggle with the elements. It was the gateway to the far Arctic, opening upon little-traveled latitudes. As we steamed out of the harbor, a cascade of silvery sunbeams broke through the fog and for a few minutes played upon the swell of the sea and the snowy mountainsides, exploding a profusion of stars.

Twice more we made port, at Hammerfest, the town that still today claims to be the most northerly in the world, and Honningsvåg, a fishing village tucked into a sheltered spot at the south end of Nord Kapp. Then the ship plowed through the choppy, frigid Barents Sea, until in the gathering dusk of the early afternoon of another day it tied up at the makeshift quay at Vardø.

Upon arrival we were told that the boat to Murmansk had just left. It would be at least a week before it returned.

Vardø's unassuming hostelry housed and catered to the constant stream of travelers that passed to and from Russia. Few women journeyed in my direction. Most of them traveled the opposite way, out of Russia, away from the war zone, to seek safety in foreign lands.

A group of refugee women and children was just being picked up by the coastal ship that had brought me here.

The table d'hôte, this shrewd arrangement practiced by most Scandinavian out-of-the-way hostelries, placed me between two men, one Russian and the other French. We passed each other the salt, the pepper, the bread.

Aleksandr Ivanovich had arrived by steerage on the coastal steamer. His round head was close-cropped; his face was sallow, with the high cheekbones of the Slav. One might have called him ugly had it not been for the luminous expression in his light-gray eyes. He gave the impression of being one of those old-style officers of the Russian army who, lacking enough food, equipment, and ammunition, became legendary during the First World War for their dogged, uncomplaining pursuit of the war until there was no front left to hold.

The fellow on my left, Count Claude de Montrichard, was in sharp contrast to Aleksandr Ivanovich. His urbane manners, the easy shrug of the shoulders immediately proclaimed his French origin. Handsomely turned out in sky-blue tunic and scarlet breeches and with a tiny black moustache adding to the dapper appearance, he looked exotic in these drab arctic surroundings. He had served with the French Air Force during the war, he said, and he was now traveling from Paris to Archangel as a diplomatic courier.

The three of us became constant companions. Together we explored Vardø, the small town perched upon the northwestern headland that forms a part of the Vardanger Fjord coast. There were no sidewalks. Low, dark, weathered houses lay scattered about on the bare tundra, wherever the wall of a cleft or a shallow ravine afforded some protection against the polar winds, all facing south in search of warmth and light. Silhouetted against the gray stormy sky high on the barren hills, frozen codfish hung to dry flapped in the wind, producing loud eerie clapping noises.

The town was blessed with a picture show. The dingy, smelly room had hard wooden seats and an out-of-tune upright piano. One evening a spotty, jumpy Charlie Chaplin film transported its audience into paroxysms of hilarity. The children in their fur-lined parkas shook with laughter, and drowned out the tinny music of the piano with their screams of delight.

When the audience burst forth from the cramped theater into the frosty night, the sky was ablaze with a magnificent display of the aurora borealis. Huge iridescent curtains of light waved overhead, the glow reflected upon our upturned faces. A faint crackling sound seemed to come from the sparkling multicolored draperies, like static electricity crackling under a hand stroking lightly the back of a cat.

"The Murmansk boat just docked!"

The news caused a stir of excitement. The waiting was at an end. A throng of passengers inundated the hotel. Men in the uniforms of the Allied Forces mingled with the civilians. Some wore the bored expressions of those who had to pass through this confounded place yet another time. Others, their eyes fearful and questioning, gave evidence of uneasiness at their abrupt arrival into the frightening, free "outside" world.

A Russian woman with two small children could not get a room. An awful dread of the future gleamed in her eyes. I offered her my room, and the act put me in a heroic mood. Gleb had so often said I did not understand his and Russia's troubles, but I would prove him wrong. That night I went to sleep on the floor of the hotel's palm-filled parlor. The doors did not close, so I placed my trunks in a protecting circle around me.

The next day we boarded the boat. I was sitting on the deck on one of my trunks, waiting to be assigned to a cabin, when a tall, lanky man pushed through the throng of people on the quay. Slowly and deliberately he made his way up the gangplank; I recognized the British consul, whom Montrichard and I had visited a few days before to make sure our papers were in order.

"Hello," he called. "Bad news!"

My heart gave a jolt, my thoughts raced to Gleb. "Nothing to do with me, I hope?"

"Orders just came through for this ship to go into Pechenga to take on British troops for Murmansk," he said crisply. "Women are not allowed on board troopships."

I was the only woman aboard. I sat tense waiting for his next word:

"If anybody asks any questions, just say you didn't see me." A fleeting smile and he was gone.

Tears filled my eyes and I dived precipitately belowdecks.

The stench down there was staggering. Never had I dreamed air could be so befouled. An unholy mixture of odors of ancient timbers, drains, stale water, greasy cooking, lavatory, and seasickness made my stomach heave. I reached for the companionway and got up on deck before being sick.

After a frantic search I found Aleksandr Ivanovich and Montrichard in the smoking room aft, busily making themselves comfortable in the airy, half-circular place. Had they been below? I told them of the smell down there in the horrible cubbyholes they called cabins. I would be sick if I had to stay there. Had they seen the consul? What did he say? They laughed uproariously at my woebegone face.

"Never mind, don't worry. Here," Montrichard said with a sweeping gesture of his hand. "We invite you to share this salon with us. We'll look after you. See," he indicated the red plush settee behind the floor-fast table, "there you can make your bed, and there's plenty of room here for both you and us and your baggage too."

His tone was frank and courteous, reassuring, with the comradeship common among travelers. Relieved, I accepted their invitation, and I was soon to learn in what good company I was, how lucky I was that they had come to Vardø at the same time I did, and that the table d'hôte arrangement had placed me between them.

A small icebreaker met the ship at the mouth of the Pechenga Fjord, and in its wake we steamed slowly through the opened channel, full of broken ice that scraped and bounced against the hull.

Some twenty miles farther on the isolated Finnmarken village of Pechenga was situated, and forty miles or so beyond it the borders of three countries, Russia, Norway, and Finland, met. A cold wintry sun shone bleakly upon the rolling hills of the snow-covered landscape.

As we approached our destination my anxiety increased. There the troops would board the ship. With dismay I thought of the possibility of being put ashore in this dismal place. How would I live? How would I ever be able to get out of here again to travel to Gleb across hundreds of miles of tundra and wilderness? Would I be permitted to board another ship if it chanced to call? What an ill-contrived ending to an enterprising journey! And in spite of my companions' assurance of protection, I was afraid.

About two miles off Pechenga the two ships made fast at the edge of the ice. Soon long trains of reindeer surrounded us, each animal tied to the preceding *akja,* the boatlike sledge used by the Lapps. At the head of the train the owner ran easily on long slender cross-country skies. Some of these trains consisted of as many as eight or ten reindeer sleds loaded with furs and other trade goods. Unhurriedly the caravans milled around the ships. Trading was a slow process; the men were chary, halting, like their harsh, abrupt speech.

Montrichard lent me his binoculars, and I saw the scattered tiny houses of the village nestled under the still deep cover of snow. Beyond them the glitter of gold broke from the onion domes of the famous Boris i Gleb Monastery, where holy men of the Orthodox faith hid away in Arctic isolation for prayer and penance. The place had an austere charm and beauty. Only once in a lifetime destiny might take the traveler to such a far place. My curiosity and the fascination of its utter remoteness aroused a desire to see more, to explore the deeper meaning of this land and the people that inhabited it. This was my first meeting with Russia.

In the afternoon the troops invaded the ship, khaki-clad men with ruddy faces under enormous wolfskin hats, with clumsy white Shackleton boots on their feet and dry jokes on their lips. They stomped down belowdecks, and I marveled at their immunity to the stench.

Suddenly the door of our salon was flung open and a tall, boyish-looking British officer entered, obviously the commander of the troops.

"Hello," he said pleasantly and, sitting down on Aleksandr Ivanovich's bed, he pulled out his cigarettes and lit one. I shrank into the farthest corner of my couch in a forlorn attempt to remain unnoticed. Surely the dreaded moment had arrived.

"How long have you been here?" Montrichard spoke English with hardly a trace of an accent. He threw a glance of quiet encouragement in my direction.

"Oh, about two months. Rotten place—absolutely rotten, nothing to do. Bad spot for spies, though. A weak spot in the armor, so to speak, one has to be on the alert. However, nice to get back into circulation again. You going to Archangel, I s'ppose?"

Montrichard nodded. By this time the rattling of chains and shouts of command reached my unbelieving ears. A hope flickered ever so faintly.

"We're due at Murmansk tomorrow, I understand," Montrichard went on. "Have a cup of tea?"

Aleksandr Ivanovich caught up the empty teakettle, dived down into the galley for boiling water, and was back again in a moment.

He threw a handful of tea leaves into the kettle, shook it, stirred it, then poured the dark-brown brew into three mugs and a glass.

"At this time of the year you'll have some difficulty reaching Archangel," the officer warned. The mention of new difficulties made me almost forget the present threat of being left in Pechenga. But the young man still seemed to be unaware of my presence. Desperately I thought: When will this ship begin to move?

"The breakup, you mean?" I blessed Montrichard for keeping the conversation going.

"More than likely the last icebreaker—your last chance—will have left for Archangel by the time we dock tomorrow," the officer explained. "Overland the railway takes you only as far as Kem. The rest of the four hundred–odd miles must be traveled by sleigh over endless swamps. They're frozen hard in winter, but by April they're impassable, and the breakup lasts two months." He took a few puffs on his cigarette. "Going by sea is no better; icebreakers can't get through the narrow gorge of the White Sea when it's choked with ice."

The young man took a sip of tea. The blue smoke of his cigarette dissipated in the air, leaving a smell of good tobacco.

And then, through the conversation, I heard the peremptory tinkle of the bell in the engineroom. At last—at long last! The ship lurched, the hull ground against the ice. I was the only one who seemed to take any notice of what was happening. In a few moments the engines droned evenly, reassuringly. I felt marvelously relaxed.

Happy to have somebody to talk with, the young officer went on: "Just heard Shackleton got through overland, in the nick of time, one might say. The route goes through no man's land. They'd had a few scraps with the Bolos, it seems."

One difficulty safely overcome, others loomed ahead. Gleb must have had sublime confidence in my ability to conquer the unimaginable when he called me to come to Archangel.

"Well, cheerio, must get down to my men."

I had to ask the question: "Have you been below?"

"Yes, why?"

"You don't mind the dreadful stench?"

"Hardly noticed." And he was gone.

I was abashed. Hard wars make hardened men. I was glad that

Gleb was not there—he would have laughed at a soldier's wife complaining of a bad smell.

The blue-gray sea was like a looking glass as our ship steamed slowly into the wide mouth of the Tuloma River, breaking the gleaming surface. I had by this time acquired a strong feeling of affection for this Russian ship that pursued whatever useful service was demanded from her with dogged perseverance, carrying on board an indifferent crowd today, gone tomorrow. She slid over the magnetic pole with no other signs of the event than the dizzy dance of the compass in its box on the bridge. Through a haze of flattened motionless smoke I discerned in the distance an array of masts. It was Murmansk, the northernmost end of the Murman railway, Russia's one icefree port bearing upon the Atlantic, where the whiplash current of the Gulf Stream warmed the Arctic waters.

Detaching itself slowly from the haze, a steamer forged toward us, black smoke belching from her funnels, a collar of white foam at her bow. As we met, flags dipped into the backwash in mutual salute. I saw the name *Canada* in large black lettering on her curved bow. Greetings roared from ship to ship. White handkerchiefs fluttered in the wind from crowded decks.

"There she goes!" The exclamation came from behind me.

"Who? What d'you mean?"

"The last icebreaker to Archangel."

There she goes! Couldn't she have waited just one more hour for us? What now? How long, for how many days and weeks, perhaps, would we have to wait for the next chance to continue the long journey? A chill wind curling the top of the water made me shudder.

CHAPTER 9

THE STOWAWAY

THE smell of tar and fresh lumber filled the air, and instantly my mind went back to Horserød, with its smell of tar warming in the April sunshine, the scent of fresh lumber from the rows of barracks, the wooden walks built on stilts above the mud and creaking under the weight of passing men, resounding to their footfalls. But this was nothing like Horserød.

Murmansk, at the rear of the active front against the Bolsheviks, was warlike, heterogeneous under the intervention of the Allied Forces. It was the main reserve depot of men and supplies, serving the whole northern front. Across wide gaps of no man's land, the front stretched from the Finnish border to the Pechora River in the east, where attempts were repeatedly being made to reach the Ural mountain range to form an effective encircling movement with Kolchak's White armies in Siberia.

The gigantic task of constructing this icefree port some 150 miles within the Arctic Circle had been completed a few years ago. Having mushroomed too fast to carry an imprint of permanence, the town of Murmansk was raw. Everything except the harbor seemed to be improvised. Only the piers stretching their long arms far out into the deep river, beckoning to oceangoing ships, were built to last. And the entire port had the sweeping lines, the impression of immense space that I later came to identify with Russia.

The spring thaw was just beginning. Lumbering mule-drawn wagons and rattling trucks made deep ruts in the slush and splashed mud on the black tar-paper walls of the barracks, which dried white.

Soldiers came and went, almost all of them in British uniforms. Hands opened and closed doors, leaving circles of greasy grime around the knobs. A group of Chinese laborers was working in the street, their unintelligible conversation and slanting eyes and long pigtails providing a touch of the Orient to the outlandish character of the place.

Beyond the waterfront, the settlement crept up a gently rising slope. Overlooking the river, the administrative barracks of the Allied Forces' headquarters, British, American, French, and Russian, crowded together, each within its compound crisscrossed by paths and sidewalks centered around its flagpole.

Immediately upon landing, Montrichard had gone to report at the French headquarters, and for a time we did not see him. With silent insistence Aleksandr Ivanovich attached himself to me, and under his protection I undertook my first steps upon Russian soil.

Our first duty was to report to the officer commanding the Russian Army. With an odd sense of awe I observed the flag with its simple design of white, blue, and red horizontal stripes flying atop its slender pole, the symbol of old Russia. And although my feelings were still too nebulous to allow me a sense of national pride and affection, this was the premise with which I now tried to adopt her as my own country.

After dealing with Aleksandr Ivanovich, the Russian commander, a tall man with impeccable manners, told me there was no place for women in Murmansk. Oh, yes, of course, he remembered Kirilin, who had passed through on his way to Archangel. As for me, regrettably, he could do nothing, except perhaps offer a cot in a corner of his office.

That night Aleksandr Ivanovich stayed with me on board the Russian steamer berthed in the harbor. For supper we drank tea and ate bully beef out of a can.

The next morning we called at the Embarkation Office in the wooden shack down by the quay. A young British naval officer of massive bulk occupied the chair behind the counter. His rosy, babylike face protruded above a tight collar. He looked more like a landlubber clerk than a fresh-weather sailor.

"No ships for Archangel within the next three or four weeks," he said in that tone of finality so often adopted by civil servants in positions of importance. "That's to say, none for lady passengers." He leaned back comfortably in his chair.

In my naiveté I ventured to suggest that a troopship might take on an army nurse going there on duty.

"Sorry, ma'am, hospital ships take nurses, not troopships. But you, sir, better look in now and again. I may be able to arrange your passage quite soon."

Fortunately, I had no difficulty obtaining an interview with Colonel Moss of the Royal Army Medical Corps. A short, dapper man of fair complexion, he looked like an Irishman. His manner was crisp, pleasantly so.

I presented my papers and asked him to help me. He looked them over with care. Finally, having turned over the last page, he said as if speaking to himself, "Of course, of course, the wife of a Russian officer fighting with us in Archangel. A graduate nurse. Of course." He picked up the receiver of the telephone at his elbow. "Put me through to the matron of the *Braemer Castle,* will you?" He turned to me. "I'm going to put you up on one of our hospital ships. I think you'll be comfortable there. The matron is a very fine woman, served with us all through the war. By the way, do you speak Russian?"

My affirmative answer pleased him. A young doctor on the *Braemer Castle,* it appeared, was studying scurvy. Would I, as a favor, act as his interpreter for a few hours every morning?

I was delighted. Suddenly my luck had changed and I was given lodging, board, and interesting work.

At the *Braemer Castle,* many willing hands took charge of me and my luggage. I hardly had time to say good-bye to Aleksandr Ivanovich, who promised he would be back with shipping news every day, before I was whisked up the gangplank into the presence of the beautifully starched and welcoming matron. She took me into a large stateroom and left me there.

The hospital ship represented that other world of civilized order and amenities. The luster of the brass and mahogany, the soft carpet gave me a sense of luxury. I felt like a lost pup having suddenly and mysteriously gained the lapdog's satin cushion.

I sent Gleb a wire about my good luck. It would please him. Being no longer homeless, I saw the path ahead smooth. My one remaining fear was that Gleb might have been sent to the front and that he would not be in Archangel when I arrived.

I became absorbed in the work with the young doctor, and in his discussions and treatment of the anemic patients who came to him with their faces drawn from the pain and the weakening effects of their spongy bleeding gums and other affected membranes.

And so one day passed after the other. Aleksandr Ivanovich called every evening, but there was never good news about our chances for an early departure. In spite of the comfort and felicity of the situation, I began to grow restless.

More than a week later Aleksandr Ivanovich appeared early one afternoon to tell me that two large icebreakers were loading supplies in preparation for leaving for Archangel shortly. Exciting news, to be sure, but what good would it do me?

"I don't know anything for certain," he said, "but I'll be back again tonight. Get ready, Luisa Oskarovna!" At Horserød, when deciding on a patronymic according to Russian usage, I had chosen Father's second name instead of Sixten.

Alone, I did not want to entertain false hopes, but I felt myself trembling with anticipation and excitement. I packed my things, then walked around aimlessly with my heart beating in my throat.

About half an hour after Aleksandr Ivanovich left I had a surprise visit from Montrichard, accompanied by two French naval officers.

"I see you're very comfortable aboard this English ship," he said after introductions were over. "Have you made any arrangements for continuing your journey to Archangel?"

My negative answer made him smile. "*Bon,* that's just why we came to see you this afternoon. Would you object to becoming a stowaway?"

"That's a bad joke, Count Claude," I said reprovingly. The proposition seemed too fantastic.

"No, no, madame, I'm quite serious. The *Mikula* is an icebreaker under the French flag, and these friends of mine are two of her officers. They invite you to make the trip to Archangel with them on two conditions: you must keep it a strict secret, and you must promise not to show yourself on deck until we give you leave. The *Mikula* is to carry British troops. *Que dites-vous, madame?*" he added triumphantly.

It was fantastic. A thousand questions: Could it really be done?

How do you get smuggled on board a ship? What about an embarkation permit? Was there no risk?

He brushed aside my questions. "Will you do it?"

"Yes, of course!" I answered quickly.

"C'est entendu, alors!" said the tallest of the two French officers. "Can you be ready with your things tonight at eight? We'll be here then with the launch." But what about Aleksandr Ivanovich? I asked. "Don't worry, he's coming too," he assured me.

I could only say, "Thank you," I could hardly think. What incredible luck that I should have fallen in with two such traveling companions as Aleksandr Ivanovich and Montrichard!

Embarkation permit—now I didn't need one. But a landing permit for Archangel? "Get one if you can," said one of the officers. They took their leave.

My first thought was to send another telegram to Gleb. I wrote: "April twenty-second." That was all; anything more would have given the secret away. He would surely understand and be there to meet me.

With my heart pounding I entered the Embarkation Office.

"What's on your mind today?" drawled the portly officer, leaning back in his chair.

Looking him straight in the eye, I asked for a landing permit for Archangel. The quizzical smile on his face faded.

"Just like that?" he asked, fiddling with a pencil.

"Just like that." I tried to smile.

There was a minute of silence.

"Let's see your passport," he demanded. In a matter-of-fact way he began filling out forms. He gave them to me. "Good luck!"

We shook hands across the counter.

"Thank you!" I flew out of his office.

The only thought that bothered me now was the matron. I could not say good-bye to her because of my promise of secrecy. I could only write to her later.

Just before dusk the *Mikula* launch made fast alongside the *Braemer Castle.* Quickly my trunks were transferred to it, no questions asked, no explanations offered.

The boat shot across the black surface of the water around piers and ships, and then out toward two large vessels riding at anchor on the broad river. Expertly I and my seven trunks were handed up a rope ladder to the deck and I was ushered down into the officers' quarters. With the discreet courtesy characteristic of the French, a few sailors hovered around us. If once I thought that French sailors looked silly with their bright-red pompons atop their flat caps, I no longer thought so.

I was shown into a marvelously spacious and well-appointed stateroom, one of several opening upon a narrow white passageway. Later I was told it belonged to the second mate. To accommodate the special guest he had willingly doubled up with the first engineer. This turned out to be only one minor aspect of the courtesy and consideration I was to enjoy aboard the *Mikula.* Indeed, no stowaway before or after me ever crossed the seas in so royal a style as I was to do in the course of the coming exciting week.

The next day the British troops took possession of their forward quarters. Toward evening the deafening clangor of the ship weighing anchor filled our ears. At last we were on our way. I peered through the porthole and without regret watched the profusion of twinkling lights along the piers of Murmansk, their reflections trembling in the swell, gradually becoming obliterated in the distance.

Well out on the Tuloma River a fierce gale from the north plunged our ship into heavy seas, and soon the convoy was obliged to seek shelter in the lee of a small group of islands. Dimly, through the porthole, I could see the hulls of two other ships. Riding their anchors, they looked ghostly in the half-light. And the gale, deviated by the barrier of the islands, howled overhead.

One of these ships was the *War Grange,* a freighter with a cargo of airplanes. The other was the *Svietagor.* Originally a Russian icebreaker, now under British command, it was said to be the most powerful then in existence. Its flat bottom slanting upward, both fore and aft, indicated its capacity of breaking the ice going either forward or in reverse, a feat the *Mikula* could not perform.

Late the next afternoon the convoy struck ice. Through the porthole I saw white ice floes floating here and there upon the black swell. Now and again a floe collided with the ship's hull and the crushed ice dissolved in the foamy wake.

During the night we encountered thick ice. The noise awakened me. I could feel the ship being slammed sideways as it settled into the broken ice, shuddering and shaking. The roar was deafening. How long could the hull withstand the enormous pressure of the elements? I asked myself. And in the midst of it, I fell asleep again.

When the cabin boy, red pompon atop his sailor's hat, brought my hot water in the morning and announced, *"Le déjeuner est servi,"* I realized with a start that the *Mikula*'s engines were silent.

"What's happening? Why are we stopped?"

"We're in the middle of the ice, madame. We'll soon be moving again," he assured me.

I dressed quickly and went into the wardroom. The chief engineer was having breakfast. He explained the situation.

"The *Mikula* is taking it easy, *voyons,* while the *Svietagor* crushes the ice around the *War Grange.* May be quite a problem to get that big hulk through the ice. But no, we haven't reached the worst yet. We're just at the mouth of the White Sea—we still have to negotiate the narrow gorge. And the ice looks thick, *sapristi,* but it does! Madame is allowed on deck today. They told you, didn't they? Quite a sight up there."

The engineer was right. Bright sunshine, not the kind of bleak illumination offered by the pale sun of Vardø and Pechenga, but a strong white glow blazed upon a fantastic icescape. Shimmering ripples of warming air ascended from the surface of ice and snow, reflecting the intense heat of the sunshine and presaging the approach of spring. As if in a monster's building game, huge blocks of ice were pushed on top of one another, creating towers of sparkling bluish crystal twenty to forty feet high. Vast and dazzling, the ice fields encompassed the whole visible world, and the glare forced me to close my eyes.

At a short distance the *War Grange* lay immobilized as the *Svietagor* broke the ice around the helpless ship. Black smoke poured from the icebreaker's funnels and raced its own shadow across the ice fields. The commander's crisp orders came distinctly through the cold air.

Finally the job was done and the engines of the *Mikula* resumed their droning murmur. With the two icebreakers abreast crushing open a wide channel, the *War Grange* followed awkwardly. I stood in the prow and watched as the *Mikula,* with a mighty effort, heaved itself out of the water and slid far up on a huge floe on its flat bottom. Under its weight black cracks zigzagged like bolts of lightning across the ice and the icebreaker crashed down into the opening channel.

With loud crunching noises, pushed and rocked by the ice, the ships repeated the maneuver over and over, laboriously forcing their way through the dazzling subpolar world of sun and ice.

Suddenly I sensed I was not alone. Turning, I saw one of the British officers standing close behind me. Broad red braids adorned his cap and sleeves. His short swagger stick rested in the crotch of his arm.

"Marvelous, this, eh?" he said, gazing into the sun and gripping the railing as if intending to break it down. He eyed me up and down. "Didn't know there were any ladies aboard." A small mocking smile played upon his lips. "Where have you been hiding all this time?"

I told him I was the guest of the French officers. I owed him no further explanation.

"Oh?" The officer's eyebrows lifted. "Why don't you come and stay with us instead? You'd be far more comfortable, I'm sure."

When I related the incident to my friends in the wardroom, they chortled heartily. But the next time I encountered the officer his manner was distant and his tone irreproachable.

For three more days the convoy continued to crash through the ice. The going was very slow. Day and night the thick floes thundered against the hull. On the fourth day the convoy picked up a distress signal. A few hours later a small icebound ship out of Malyye Karmakuly on the Novaya Zemlya Islands, with supplies running short and children aboard, was freed and joined the convoy.

Late on the afternoon of the fifth day four ships with the disabled *War Grange* in tow entered the wide mouth of the North Dvina. Emerging from under a patchy cover of snow, low desolate shorelines etched in brown lined our path. As we slipped into the river, the ice became thinner and the two icebreakers were able to push it aside with greater ease.

This was Russia, this bare expressionless shore, the vast unknown. My heart filled with a kind of fearful anticipation, a feeling of powerful predestination. Would Gleb be there at the end of this fantastic journey to welcome me? His presence would redeem the bleak picture before me and make it appear less foreign, less enigmatic. He had said that I would never understand Russia, never fully realize her essence, and I had refused to believe him. He must be there to greet me, to put animation and beauty and warmth into these first impressions, to explain to me the secret of this land and to make me love it.

The sun set and left behind an evening sky drenched in flamboyant orange hues that sent fiery reflections across the dusky ice and then lost itself in the outline of the low riverbanks, now turned purple. On the shore two lone pines lifted their dark gnarled silhouettes against the glowing sky.

The river narrowed and along the shores tiny houses came into view. Presently the banks increased in height, becoming steep cliffs. There was now more open water in the river, the current was stronger. Broken pieces of ice raced madly downstream on the rising spring flood.

The houses on the shore gathered closer to one another, and presently Archangel spread itself atop the cliffs along the eastern bank, a spectacle of white colonnades. In their midst, like a magnificent golden crown, the cathedral's four onion-shaped domes shone softly in the fading light of the sunset sky. Under its shadow the *Mikula* slowly edged alongside the quay.

PART 2

CHAPTER 10

ARCHANGEL

THE *Mikula's* scarred hull nudged creaking against the dock. At first the gathering of people on the quay was small, but as word of the ship's arrival spread, the crowd increased. I stood at the ship's rail and stared at the moving figures, looking for the one I yearned to see. But he was not there. Attracted by the excitement, more people came running down the riverbank. They came in small groups, officials, soldiers. I scrutinized each face and with each new group my hope rose afresh.

Standing beside me, Montrichard asked, "He isn't here?"

I could not trust myself to speak.

Behind me I heard Aleksandr Ivanovich's low voice: "Well, we didn't exactly keep to the regular timetable, did we?" I couldn't help smiling.

Both of them stood there ready to help me over this last obstacle. But I told them I was going ashore and that the time had come to say good-bye. We shook hands, and they must have seen in my eyes my special feeling for them, my appreciation of their kindness, my deep gratitude for their help and protection throughout this extraordinary journey.

The air was crisp and clear above the sixty-fourth parallel. Strange odors, strange sounds, broken sentences of Russian dialects surrounded me. Men in fur caps, turned sideways across their heads; men in long fur coats, tanned side out, pinched at the waist and the bottom slapping against high boots. Uniformed officials. A few women, dark kerchiefs framing round faces.

Hesitantly I made my way up the steep hill to the street above. Rounded cobblestones underneath the hard snow made the walking rough. To the left the cathedral with its gleaming golden roof and domes dominated all that could be seen. A broad thoroughfare ran parallel with the river. Footsteps were hollow and distinct against its raised wooden sidewalks. But unmet and alone, I could not form any coherent impression of this strange place. My long-anticipated arrival was a desolate anticlimax.

"Luisa Oskarovna!"

I looked up, amazed, and recognized one of Gleb's friends from Horserød, Lieutenant Smith. Breathlessly, I asked for Gleb. "Is he at the front?"

"Well, I think he's at the front—at least I heard he was going."

So Gleb was gone. Why couldn't he have waited for me, asked for compassionate leave, something—anything—so he could be here when I arrived? He knew I was coming. Wasn't the arrival of his wife after such a long and difficult journey important enough for a few days' delay? Was I not, after all, as important to him as he was to me?

He saw my distress, and took my arm. "Don't worry, Luisa Oskarovna, we'll soon find out. I'll take you to Gleb's friends the Kovalevskys. They'll know where he is."

We turned off the main thoroughfare into a spacious side street. We came to a yellow frame house with white-painted corners set in a grove of trees.

There was no bell or knocker at the door; we just walked in. We found ourselves in a large disorderly room. Many people were obviously using it as a living room, dining room, and work room, with never enough time to tidy it. A large table was pushed against a wall with many windows. On it stood a brass samovar that had long since stopped simmering. Glasses and cups were scattered on the table, some of them still filled with clear tea.

Natalia Ivanovna Kovalevskaya came toward us. Of all the large group of people in that house, I remember only her very clearly. Neither her figure nor her dress was remarkable. She was short and thin and her old gray frock was worn and shabby, but her face was arresting. Perhaps it was only the expression on her face that was striking, for feature by feature she was neither unusual nor beautiful.

Her large brown eyes had remarkable depth, hinting at the detached, compassionate patience of one who has achieved comprehension through the chastening effects of deep sorrow.

"So you've arrived." Her voice was strangely toneless. She merely stated a fact.

The smile that lit her face briefly gave the impression of being a rare thing. "Gleb Nikolayevich will be glad."

Her words softened the edge of my feelings. "Where is he? Is he at the front?"

"No, he's here."

My relief was unspeakable. Natalia Ivanovna disappeared into the hallway. We heard her speaking on the telephone.

"He's been so worried something would happen to the ship in the ice. He expected you much sooner."

A fleeting thought of the ship the *Mikula* had rescued and what might have happened to its passengers and crew crossed my mind. Nothing more was said, and the silence was pleasant and tranquil.

A car roared down the street, then stopped. The front steps creaked under long leaps. Gleb stood in the doorway, tall and tanned. His cap was in his hand, and his hair was smooth on his well-shaped head. His eyes shone with a strange wild happiness. He strode over to Natalia Ivanovna, kissed her hand, then turned to me. And I could no longer doubt that with the coming of his wife his happiness was complete.

When at last I could speak again, I asked Gleb to take us to our room.

"No, Lisa, I have a room but it's not fit for you, and there's no room in it for both of us. You'll have to stay here tonight, but tomorrow we'll find a place where we can be together."

I looked at him incredulously, and he must have realized my unhappiness, for his eyes became troubled.

"Lisa, please, don't forget, this is wartime," he pleaded quietly. "It's difficult to find rooms in Archangel. I wanted us to look for one together."

"Oh, Gleb!" I squeezed his hand, smiled at him. "Let's go and see your room!" To be alone—just for one moment to be alone with him! Then I thought of my trunks; they had to be taken off the ship as soon as possible.

"Seven trunks?" Gleb looked at me wide-eyed.

Natalia Ivanovna came to his rescue. Such a small matter, she'd take care of them. She began collecting the cups and glasses from the table.

Gleb's room was far out at the other end of the city in a low block of houses. The landlady, plump and jovial, greeted us at the door. "*Oy, oy,* what a day we've had! God be with you, Gleb Nikolayevich, is this your wife?"

Her pale flabby face gleamed with sweat and goodwill. Her upper lip was adorned with an astonishingly luxuriant black moustache. It was easy to smile and to assure her that I was very happy to be in Russia.

The room was at the back and could be reached only by going through the whole of the landlady's crowded and untidy apartment. At Svensksund we had closets bigger than that room. Yet the landlady obviously thought that while renting it she could quite properly also use it as an extra storeroom. One corner was piled high with her unsightly belongings. Only the table and the narrow bed looked as if they belonged to Gleb, for they were covered with his own blankets, the table with a fine green plaid one that Mother had given him. The view from the window was dreary, a dirty gray uninviting backyard.

"Lisa, let's not look at this—just look at me!"

And in a flash I regained my full equilibrium and with that all my courage. Now even the small inglorious room seemed a wonderful place, and all I wanted was to stay there.

"Yes, darling, stay if you wish and I'll go somewhere else." Gleb laughed. "Here there isn't even room enough for me to stretch out on the floor, much less in that bed. Feel how hard it is! Do you think you can sleep on it?"

He looked at me quizzically. The bed was hard, it had no spring, no mattress, just bare boards laid loosely on the frame. But if he had been able to sleep on it, so could I.

"But where will you go?" I was suddenly full of concern.

He told me that Trebinsky had arrived from Copenhagen not very long ago, and he was now Gleb's superior. He had a large comfortable room where Gleb, alas, would be far more comfortable than I would be here.

"But tomorrow, Lisochka, we'll find a place where we can stay together!" And that was all that really mattered.

It took me a long time to fall asleep after Gleb left. Thoughts came tumbling into my mind, thoughts of Mother and the family and the home in Sweden, of the long journey that now at last was only a memory. The change was complete. Now I had nobody but Gleb—this boyish man, so tender, so impractical, so gallant, this strange being whose quaint sensibilities were so different from mine, whose bewildering and irresistible charm would tie me to him forever. I had chosen to share his life with enthusiasm, and whatever this choice might bring, so be it.

Feeling the hard boards under my body, I caught a glimpse of the special character that enabled him to accept life without complaint, without opposition. The thought brought hot tears to my eyes. Sobbing into his rough pillow, sleep caught me unawares.

Archangel, strange city of northern Russia, must have looked quite different from its original aspect in these days of Allied occupation and civil war. The low contours of its buildings, the breadth of its streets and avenues, the widening river coursing between the steep eroded banks suggested limitless space. Now an air of disrepair and abandonment adhered to its public buildings and to the former residences of its rich lumbermen and merchants. Indifference and neglect defaced the ornate elegance that in other days had made Archangel an attractive and prosperous port city.

From the Troitsky Prospekt, the main street, the town spread fanwise to the north and east. Here along the broad streets nestled small frame houses surrounded by trees and picket fences, some painted yellow and some unpainted and shining silvery gray from the harsh treatment of weather and wind. This part of the town gave the impression of unabashed penury, quite acceptable to the people under the circumstances because it was, on the whole, a natural and largely unalterable consequence of climate and locality.

On my first day in Archangel Gleb got off duty early. Walking down the Troitsky Prospekt in search of a room, we met a motley crowd. Soldiers and officers in a variety of Allied uniforms pushed past us. A short French zouave, pinch-waisted and dashing, seemed curiously out of place in the pale northern sunlight. A pair of English Tommies in blue hospital denim with broad red ties, on a pleasure jaunt downtown, eyed a slightly overdressed Russian woman who responded by clicking her high heels disdainfully on the wooden planks of the sidewalk.

Out in the street fast-trotting horses pulling droshkyes moved freely under their arched *dugas,* only slightly checked by the reins held in the coachman's stiffly outstretched hands. On the other side of the tramline, where the snow still lingered, three reindeer pulled an open sleigh. Their driver, covered from head to toe by a hooded parka, rode comfortably in his nest of hay. He must have spent days traveling from the northeast over still frozen swamps to do his business here in the coastal town.

A detachment of soldiers marched by with a prisoner between them, his hands tied behind his back.

"Is that a Bolshevik?"

"An enemy, a spy up for questioning. Remember, Lisa, this is not an ordinary war. This is civil war—brother against brother. This man probably knows every nook and corner of Archangel. Freed, he'd instantly vanish from sight. Many hiding places would be opened to him, many friends and relatives would be eager to save him. Harsh treatment? Do you know what would happen to any of us if we were taken prisoner? Dead bodies of our comrades have been found with nails driven into their shoulders, one for every star on their epaulets. Atrocities—hatred breeds atrocities. If you've never before experienced life stark naked, here you're not likely to escape it. And it's a kind of agonizing triumph." Gleb smiled as if contemplating an inner vision, but I did not fathom his meaning at all.

What he had said, however, filled my mind with forebodings. Until now the risks Gleb had been running since his return to Russia from Horserød had become known to me only after he had escaped from them. From now on, anticipation would be my anguish.

"And I also want to tell you this, Lisa, so that you will understand. Here in Archangel we can never count on the loyalty of the civilians. All of them speak the same language, all are natives of the same land, all know every road and hidden trail. Politically they belong neither to the Reds nor to the Whites. A wife sneaks across the lines to see her husband, a son his mother. This traffic is impossible to check. Fear, the need for security, and very often greed sway their loyalties. Natural, perhaps. As a result, riots sometimes break out unexpectedly. One did not so long ago, and two British officers were killed."

Having known nothing but security all my life, I had difficulty grasping that such things could happen. Gleb's story shocked me into a better understanding of the situation. It was like walking on quicksand. Only one solid point remained—we were together.

"I asked you to come here, Lisa, because I truly believed this was the only place where you really wanted to be. Isn't it?" His question cut in upon my somber reflections almost apologetically. His eyes sought mine anxiously. "Besides," he added in a soft voice, "I need you." His face lit up with a lovely reassuring smile, confident and unafraid. He took my arm. "And now let's look for that house. Oh, there it is! Sadovaya fifteen! How do you like it from the outside?" Laughing, he threw a critical eye upon the house before he led me through the little gate in the white picket fence. The small yellow bungalow stood back from the street in a grove of tall trees that soon would be turning green.

The landlady, a middle-aged woman with a gentle look, came shuffling to the door in soft felt boots. She stood there with her hands folded under her apron.

"A room to rent?" she said slowly. "Most certainly, *baren.* If you please, this front room."

When I entered the room, I thought at first that it was a small conservatory. Tall palms and fig plants stood in large green-painted tubs on the floor in front of the windows. More green plants were enthroned upon homemade stands. The room was bright, for it was blessed with an extraordinary number of windows for its size.

Except for the plants, all but the barest necessities had been removed from the room. A narrow crippled bedstead leaned against one wall and a spindly sofa against the other. Neither one suggested comfortable repose, but everything was spotlessly clean.

These details I noticed only later. At the moment I was entranced with the brightness of the small room. "This place will be light enough on the white nights in the summer," Gleb remarked dryly. And indeed it was, for at that time of year one day just eased into the next through three nighttime hours of vague twilight.

"Do the two of you propose to stay here?" the landlady inquired.

"I've no other bed," she added defensively. Clearly she was not pleased by the military decree that forced her to have strangers in the house.

Gleb laid his hand on her shoulder, smiling. "Don't worry, *matushka,* it doesn't matter. We'll manage. Perhaps you could spare us a table and a small chair?"

Suddenly her eyes, meeting his, became almost friendly. "Huh!" she grunted. "I'll see." And she ambled out through the flimsy double doors.

While she was gone I mentally refurnished the room. "The table, when and if we get it, goes here, and the chair goes there. We can put one of the trunks against this wall and it can serve as a side-board." We laughed happily. Gleb caught me up in his arms and said with gay mockery in his eyes, "Though I'm not all you imagined, Lisinka, please don't speak badly of me about town!" He was to say that often, and this whimsical saying of his, sometimes breaking through the clouds of impossible situations, never ceased to delight us and light up the dark.

The possibility that he might have to leave me and go to the front entirely slipped my mind. We were too happy. This was, at last, our real honeymoon.

With great aplomb I stepped into my new role of housewife, arranging our garden room with the table and chair the landlady found for us, and with rugs, cushions, and good china. I took over the management of Gleb's clothes, sewing on buttons, darning socks, and laying them out for him. We decided against taking part in the family ritual of daily ablutions at the washstand in the corner of the kitchen. Instead, I bought at the marketplace a large earthenware mixing bowl, meant to be used for making sourdough, and at night placed it on one of the trunks to serve as our bath. The modesty of existence in our garden room gave to our life during those few precious days in the shadow of war and disaster a certain indescribable luster.

We both worked, Gleb at his motorized unit and I at the American Military Mission, where I had secured a good position as a translator. The requirements of translating military orders, news bulletins, and intercepted enemy reports from Russian into English far exceeded my mastery of both languages. But I struggled with them, sometimes almost in tears, if only to try to justify the Americans' patience, leniency, and generous wages.

At lunchtime Gleb and I met at the Russian Officers' Club. Here we encountered many of our old friends from Horserød, who, like Gleb, had flocked to join Miller's White Army in the north and thereby earn the right, they hoped, to a tolerable existence when the civil war was at an end. Gleb had also come across boyhood friends from Tsarskoe Selo, linked to him by family and school ties. By means and routes too sensitive to be mentioned, they too had been attracted to Archangel to give their support to the Allied intervention. Among them was Sergei Vasilyevich.

The quality of this man was like the hard spark struck at the break of an electric current. Tall, slim, and broad-shouldered, he was handsome enough. His eyes were nut-brown, flashing. A rich, well-trimmed black beard encircled his lips, and the supercilious smile that sometimes played around his mouth revealed a set of even white teeth. His right sleeve was empty and tucked into his pocket. Several ribbons decorated his tunic and a group of wound stripes adorned his sleeve. But his undisguised arrogance and the sarcasm of his utterances seemed to negate both bravery and good looks.

"Lisa, will you permit Sergei to have lunch with us? He used to live in Tsarskoe Selo too. He's a marvelous soldier, was decorated with the Cross of St. George for bravery on the battlefield. Many a female heart has lain palpitating at his feet."

Gleb laughed heartily at his characterization of his friend as Sergei Vasilyevich blandly acknowledged the introduction. Quite obviously, these two knew and understood each other well. With his left hand Sergei Vasilyevich struck a match, but before lighting his cigarette he let it go out deliberately. Gleb struck another one for him.

I had a sudden feeling that Sergei Vasilyevich did not approve of Gleb's marriage. The brown eyes regarded me with mocking appraisal.

"Luisa Oskarovna sounds German," he said slowly. "Are you German?"

I tried to subdue my rising irritation. With some heat I denied the accusation. Was it an accusation?

"No, I'm Swedish!"

Gleb and Sergei exchanged amused glances. The name of Poltava flashed before my mind. They began talking about Tsarskoe Selo and the war, and I felt myself being rudely pushed outside the circle of their friendship.

By the middle of May spring had not yet arrived. The streets of Archangel were still muddy with half-melted snow that froze during the night. But the sun broke through the clouds capriciously to shine with some warmth upon the polyglot crowd on the Troitsky Prospekt. The onion domes of the cathedral transformed the sunlight into golden suns of lesser magnitude, and the daylight noticeably increased.

Then, a week later, it was suddenly spring. As if to make up for lost time, the sun in a passion of heat melted all the snow in one day. Overnight the leaves sprouted and through the wet soil the grass sent up green shoots. On the weather map of the north the magic metamorphosis occurred exactly at the designated time. Soft southerly winds broke down the lingering opposition of the northerly flow of cold air and turned the frosty landscape into a spectacle of tender glistening verdure and blue flowers.

That glorious day Gleb and I met as usual at the Officers' Club. Spring's abrupt arrival had an intoxicating effect upon the spirit. We laughed, joked, and were very happy. Gleb leaned forward, and I expected another joke. But he covered my hand with his and his face suddenly turned very serious.

"Lisa, I'm going to the front the day after tomorrow."

I sat motionless, his words falling like a crushing weight.

A small sharp voice rang in my ears unrecognizable: "Are you ordered out?"

"No, I volunteered."

My voice grew shrill: "You *asked* to go?"

Gleb nodded. "Lisa, listen. I didn't come to Archangel to stay safely at headquarters. I came here to fight—to fight for Russia. You knew that. Do you want a coward for a husband? Sergei is going too—and with only one arm! We're going to the Pinega front. I've already stayed here too long in safety. Would you really approve of my staying behind when crippled men don't hesitate to volunteer?"

"So it's Sergei who talked you into this!" Choking with fury and despair, I rose blindly from the table and, without waiting for an answer, left him sitting there.

Gleb followed me to the office. He asked my chief to let me off for a day, until he had left for the front.

"Lisa, come home with me!"

There was something in his manner that did not brook opposition.

Then, in our sweet garden room where only a few hours before we had been so happy with the brilliant spring sunshine streaming in, we tore at each other in a frenzy of wounded feelings and conflicting viewpoints. With all the passion of his sensitive pride, Gleb was distraught at the mere idea of hiding from the dangers of the front behind the skirts of a woman. Once again Russia was claiming him with all the irresistable force with which she always enslaved those who loved her well and belonged to her. His duty was clear and indivisible. He must go.

Anger and fear blinded me. I could not fathom that this fearless dedication represented the virtue that had captured my love, that bound me to him, that had made me willing and eager to leave everything in order to share his life. My love was too inexperienced, too untried. And this confused every issue except the sudden intense hurt of being powerless to keep him close to me. The realization that Russia, this enigma, this abstract concept, had such power and influence over him, far stronger than mine, made me ache with impotent jealousy.

So, like two overgrown children, we fought over our conflicting rights until, finally, exhaustion with a conciliatory hand touched our wounded hearts. Gleb sat down on the bed beside me and put his arm around my shoulders.

"Lisa, please don't cry. We can't alter the situation. Please don't make it so hard for me. Help me! We have tomorrow. Just one day, Lisa, of our own! Let's go out into the country and enjoy the springtime. Let's look at the flowers and the green leaves and *breathe*. Just for tomorrow let's forget the war, let's forget I have to leave you. One day, let's live only for each other. Come on, Lisa, please!"

I had longed to spend this springtime with Gleb—one month was all I asked. His offer of only one day brought another flood of tears. In the end, exhausted, I could not resist his plea for the gift of tomorrow.

Our single day of spring we spent far out in the open country at the small homestead of a Russian peasant, the father of one of Gleb's soldiers. In its rural peacefulness and simplicity, it was a day full of sun and the fragrance of flowers and the warming brown earth. We went for a long walk, walking slowly toward the distant horizon amid the delicate blossoms of the subarctic prairie, magically lured forth overnight, a mat of colors. We sat down together on the already dry ground, speaking little, just being together with a fierce intensity. When dinnertime came, we walked slowly hand in hand back to the house, where our hosts invited us to share their delicious meal of *pirogi,* cottage cheese, and sour cream. And it was good to be in their tranquil laconic company under the ancient icon.

Our one day, meant to exclude everything except the fleeting present, became a day that left us spent by its intensity.

The next day, in the dry heat of the noonday sun, I stood on the quay, watching Gleb and Sergei embark for the front. I could not speak; the hurt in my heart made me dumb. I had no words for either Sergei or Gleb. I could not lift my arms to embrace him or bring myself to return his kiss, because my mind could feel nothing except the dread that this might be for the last time.

Before the boat put out from the dock, with Gleb standing at the railing, I turned and walked away without looking back.

CHAPTER 11

NATALIA IVANOVNA SPEAKS

THE queen of spades goes on the king of hearts. And then the black five on the red six. That ace goes up—and the deuce and the trey.

One card was laid upon another endlessly. My eyes were glued to them with a kind of trancelike fascination. The solitaire did not work out. I tried again and again. When my luck would not turn, I tried an easier one. And that one I won.

Feverishly my hand shuffled the cards, mixed them. A quick harsh snapping sound—perhaps this time!

Evening after evening I sat in the friendly garden room, a recluse by my own unforgiving frame of mind, my heart stubborn, rebellious, and hard, a victim of a never ending train of thoughts and bitter recriminations. I would not write to Gleb. How could I write of things I could not feel? How could I say what I didn't mean? In my heart there was nothing but resentment, jealousy, and frustration.

"He didn't want to stay with you and you were not strong enough to hold him. He left you—he left you." The words kept repeating themselves in my mind.

"Lisa, please write to me." I could still hear his pleading voice as he stood at the railing looking down at me. No, I would not write.

The queen of clubs on the king of diamonds. He left me—I could also leave him. Let him go warring to his heart's content! I could go back home to Sweden. Better still, I could go to Murmansk, enroll as a nurse, and work there. And there he could find me—if he wished.

The days stretched ahead endlessly. The summer was going, fall would come, and then the winter, and there I sat in Archangel alone. Alone with the whole purpose of my being here forfeited, working at that boring job of translating reports meaningless to me, completely senseless, a life empty of ideas and of purpose.

The jack of clubs goes on the queen of diamonds.

He had said, "There is no place for women at the front." What about nurses? Aren't they of any use? This time perhaps the luck of the solitaire would change and I would make it. The mere handling of the cards gave me a certain measure of relief.

My thoughts raced on, then struck a new and jarring note. How would I have felt if the country my husband insisted on fighting for had been Sweden, my native land, instead of Russia? Would I feel the same resentment? The thought was upsetting.

Weeks passed. Apart from going to work at the American Military Mission and to the Officers' Club for lunch, I went nowhere, spoke to no one, did nothing but play solitaire. I was caught in an impasse of circular unreason; like water caught in an eddy I swirled and flowed but made no progress.

Then another idea came. On that first night when I arrived in Archangel and Lieutenant Smith had taken me to the Kovalevskys', I had immediately felt an unwilling attraction to Natalia Ivanovna. I say unwilling, for I had sensed that her kind of honesty and purposefulness could become intensely demanding. In her large brown eyes and in the way she spoke, I had read an insistence on the critical fundamentals of life. One might call this substance, or simply character. But it had appealed to me because it induced confidence.

Gleb admired her greatly, this had been obvious at once. Perhaps she would understand my feelings—perhaps she would understand my problem and sympathize. With a quick hand I pushed together the cards, their edges soft from much handling.

The evening was lovely outside. The sun threw long slanting beams across the treetops, which filtered through the gathering shadows down onto the wooden sidewalk.

Natalia Ivanovna sat at the table in her untidy living room. She was alone in the house. Beside her the samovar sang softly. The last cup of clear tea stood cooling at her elbow.

"Sit down, Luisa Oskarovna," she said without rising, hardly looking up from the book she was reading. We sat in silence for several minutes.

"What are you reading, Natalia Ivanovna?"

"Tolstoi." She pushed the book away from her.

I said that Gleb loved Tolstoi, that he was his favorite author, especially *War and Peace,* and that I had read parts of it but found it a bit heavy to read in Russian.

"It's his best book. It's Russia!" Natalia Ivanovna's voice blossomed with tender affection as if she had spoken of a lover.

"Russia—Russia! Tell me, Natalia Ivanovna, what is Russia, the Russia you are speaking of like that? To me Russia is nothing. I don't know it, I hate it!" And then suddenly all the thoughts harbored in bitterness deep inside me poured forth: "Gleb should not have left me, Natalia Ivanovna. I almost hate him for leaving me!" At last I was able to express in words all the pain that had been plaguing me for so long.

"Sshh!"

The sound was like a period after a sentence. When Natalia Ivanovna spoke again, her voice was subdued and slightly vibrant:

"Russia is indescribable and unfathomable. Russia is all and nothing. Russia is as perplexing as an unsolved riddle, simple as a straight line. Russia is inexorable to her children and sublime to her lovers. Russia is here," she laid her hand on her breast, "here in the heart of every Russian, no matter how badly she may hurt us or how mercilessly she may crush our hopes or steal our lives, so that she may go on eternally. We who are born within her immense expanse are tied to her with indestructible bonds. We can never detach ourselves from her—never!"

"Russia is taking Gleb from me," Natalia Ivanovna."

"You should give Gleb to Russia."

"I can't—I won't!"

"This you cannot escape, Luisa Oskarovna. Russia needs her true sons now more than ever in her great crisis. How do you think we Russians feel about this intervention by foreigners? It is humiliating beyond words to be obliged to accept help from these strangers to fight our own domestic battles. It's an unenviable necessity, a bitter confession of our weakness. Every true Russian feels this sorely and suffers under it, Gleb too. Could he have stayed behind in the shelter of foreign flags now, when every Russian should fill the foremost position on our front, whether our cause is won or lost? Would you honor him for it?"

In the long silence that followed, every word she had said reechoed between us.

"But can't you understand, Natalia Ivanovna . . ." I pleaded desperately.

"Yes, I understand." She put warm emphasis into every word.

"To me Gleb is everything—Russia is nothing."

"To Gleb Russia is even more than you."

"Oh, such hard words, Natalia Ivanovna! Why do you say them? Why don't you help me instead? For weeks I've been trying to realize what happened that Gleb should have hurt me so. But I cannot understand. . . ."

"It doesn't matter."

"How can you say that? I shall lose Gleb! Can't you see? It's inevitable!"

"You may." Her voice was quite toneless. "It's natural." I did not understand what she meant, or, if I did, I didn't dare translate it into words.

Once again a prolonged silence fell between us. Natalia Ivanovna sat motionless, her hands passively folded in her lap. Only her large brown eyes seemed living and warm.

"I must go," I said at length, rising.

"Yes, you must go," she answered gently.

I left her. Back in my lonely room, I felt more desolate than ever. Natalia Ivanovna, the only person I had thought would understand and help me, had spoken in riddles. I went to bed and tried to sleep. Outside the white night filtered through the open windows and its soft transparent twilight would not allow forgetfulness.

The short riotous springtime of the far north had come and gone, and now the fierce subarctic summer, with a heat that withered the grass and flowers and bred clouds of flies and mosquitoes, painted the lowlands a sun-baked brown.

On a stifling hot day while I was having lunch at the Officers' Club, Lieutenant Smith came over to my table.

"Your husband—did you see him? Marching at the head of his company, leading the singing? He's one of the best singers we have around here."

I sat dumfounded. Gleb home? Without telling me? My heart beating in my throat, I hurried back to the office.

A moment later he stood before me, sun-tanned, fresh, and happy, caked mud on his uniform and high boots, just as he had come from the front.

"Lisa, I'm home!" His face shone.

But my heart was obstinate and I steeled myself against him.

"So I see," I murmured, and busied myself with the typewriter.

The expectant smile drained from his face.

"Let's go home, Lisa."

Silently I put my things away. We left and, walking single file along Sadovaya Street, we passed through the gate of the yellow house among the trees. Gleb opened the flimsy double doors to our sunny room and closed them behind us.

"Lisa, look at me! Don't turn away!" He put his hands on my shoulders. "I've come back to you for two short days. I've been in charge of a company putting through telegraph lines ninety-two versts through no man's land from Pinega to Mezen on the northeastern shore of the White Sea. We crossed swamps and tundra, often sinking up to our armpits in mud and water. Look at my clothes! Flies and mosquitoes by the millions. We slept in our wet uniforms; your picture here in my breastpocket got all wet. And, Lisa, I thought of you all the time. On the steamer from Mezen all the way to Archangel I thought only of the moment when I'd be seeing you again. I hoped you'd see me marching with my men down the Troitsky Prospekt and be proud of me. Oh, Lisa, all these days and nights I've longed for you—how much you'll never know."

As I listened, the passion and persuasion in his voice reached my heart and the hardness inside slowly dissolved. The bitter arguments evaporated; the massive grievance I had felt abated like dust in a summer's rain. In that undefended moment a strange feeling came over me that now, for better or for worse, I was entering the portals of Russia without return.

Two short days we had together in abandoned happiness, two days that also were marked by a change in plans. To be together, we agreed, was the most important. And as Gleb's place was at the

Pinega front, there also should I be. I enrolled in the Russian Red Cross and soon received my orders to report at the Pinega Military Hospital. I was to leave Archangel in about a week, depending on when transportation would be available. My superior at the American Military Mission received my resignation with a benign smile, and I left my good friends there with regret.

When Gleb's leave came to an end, a Russian nursing sister in her white veil and black apron with a large red cross on the breast saw him off. This time no tears dimmed my eyes as I watched him and his men boarding the river boat on their way back to the front. Very soon I too would be leaving Archangel for this unlikely place called Pinega. But all apprehension had disappeared with the pride of having been, at last, accepted as an authentic part of Gleb's life.

As I stood on the quay with the fresh wind from the river billowing my veil, the company filed past me one by one. Loaded with creaking accouterments and with their caps jauntily cocked over one ear, bearded men and smooth-faced youths saluted my red cross and respectfully murmured, *"Dosvidanye, sisteritsa."*

The wheels of the river boat began to turn, churning the clay-laden water, and the vessel slid away from the dock into the broad river. Led by Gleb's warm tenor, the soldiers started to sing. I stood there waving until the sound of their voices died away across the water.

CHAPTER 12

JOURNEY TO THE FRONT

THE steamer was crowded with people. Peasants returning from a trip to the city squatted on their bundles, shrinking into the corners in their effort to occupy as small a space as possible. Their long hair was trimmed in an even bob around their leathery necks and from their low seats they sent furtive glances at their fellow passengers. There were also many soldiers in Russian and Allied uniforms, and the expressions on their faces suggested relief at returning to the restraining influence of military discipline after a few days of tumultuous leave. Some smartly turned-out British officers held themselves aloof, their short sticks tucked under their arms, while harassed canteen officials hurried to and fro, worried about late deliveries and unexpected shortages.

It was difficult to find a place to sit. I finally discovered a narrow corner to squeeze into and deposited my roll of blankets there.

It was long past midnight when we finally arrived at Ust' Pinega. In peacetime only an insignificant village, this was now a divisional point at the confluence of the Dvina and Pinega rivers, an important depot of reserve troops and supplies, serving both the main front in the south and the northeastern front of Pinega.

Upon disembarking I wandered in the unfamiliar clearing near the dock in search of the Military Control Post. The slopes toward the river were dotted with military tents gleaming white in the light of the full moon. At last I spotted the tent I was looking for. I raised the flap and found two British soldiers reclining on their sleeping bags, hardly distinguishable in the hazy obscurity of cigarette smoke and a dimly burning oil lamp.

I gave the sergeant my identification papers and asked when the boat for Pinega was expected to leave.

"Oh, sometime tomorrow—or the day after," he answered.

And could they suggest a place to stay?

The sergeant shrugged. "Don't know, lady, I'm sure. Perhaps in the village—if you can find your way there." The village, he said, was beyond the encampment some distance from the river. Meanwhile I was granted permission to leave most of my baggage in their tent, where I figured it would be comparatively safe.

The trail along the river, which I hoped would lead me to the village, was sandy and soft underfoot, and the moon illuminated my path. As I walked I heard voices, educated English voices. Relying on the respect commanded by my Red Cross uniform, I accosted the late wanderers. Did they know by any chance where I could stay until the boat for Pinega was due to leave?

The two stopped in their tracks and eyed me quizzically. One was in the uniform of a naval officer; the other was in pajamas, which somewhat dismayed me, with a trench coat flung loosely over his shoulders. Perhaps, as the day had been very hot, he had been taking a moonlight dip in the river.

The naval officer smiled at me. "Of course, madam, please consider my cabin yours for the rest of the night. Our hospital ship is moored not far from here." Had I felt the slightest hesitation about accepting the offer, it vanished completely at the mention of the hospital ship.

The ship, which proved to be the *Mesopotamia,* looked like a large clumsy shadow upon the moonlit water as it rode at anchor offshore. A long gangplank extended across pontoons from the riverbank to the ship. We crossed a covered deck that accommodated about a dozen men sleeping on high cots to a cabin at its far end. The mahogany wainscoting of the cabin and the wide berth across the wall opposite the door gave me an impression of comfort and space, almost elegance.

It was late, nearly 2:00 A.M. I stood for a moment, waiting for my newfound benefactors to leave. But they lingered.

"Sit down and make yourself at home." The first mate's voice was distinctly impatient. "Here!" and he produced from his pocket a bottle of whisky and set it down heavily on the spindly table. "Have a drink."

I declined. The two men mixed themselves stiff drinks in toothbrush glasses. The time passed interminably while they drank, and the conversation lagged. I watched the whisky bottle getting emptier and emptier. At last the naval officer, flushed and a bit unsteady, left the cabin, leaving me alone with the man in pajamas.

He sat down beside me on the bed. A brief awkward silence followed. Suddenly he leaned toward me, his flushed face close to mine.

"I love you," he whispered hoarsely, and the smell of whisky came full in my face.

Only then the meaning of the whole thing struck me—the offer of the cabin, the whisky, the departure of one of the men.

Slowly I drew back. His bloodshot eyes met mine, and I saw his expression change. He sat bolt upright on the edge of the bed.

"I—beg—your—par-don!" The words came slowly, with emphasis on each syllable. Then he rose, stood briefly at attention, and was gone.

The tension suddenly relieved, I still felt doubtful. Should I stay? Could I find another bed? I was so tired! I locked the cabin door, took off my dress, and lay down on top of the bed.

The rattling of the door awakened me. I stumbled out of bed, still half asleep, and grabbed the handle of the shaking door. Outside a voice roared:

"Who the hell'sh in my cabin? Open up, you damned fool!"

The door shook and creaked. Wide awake now, I held on to the shaking door with one hand while with the other I struggled into my dress. I flung open the door in the face of the cursing first mate. The beam of his flashlight struck my eyes. Enraged, I slapped it out of his hand and it flew clattering along the deck. Outside, I pushed the man back into the cabin and he fell on the disheveled bed, curses dribbling from his lips. I banged the door shut on the ugly sight.

The noise of the fracas awakened the sleeping men and one of them raised himself on his elbow. A burst of loud laughter followed me as I strode across the deck toward the gangplank.

The rest of the night I spent in the woods under the open sky. On a bushy bough above my head my white veil hung suspended as a warning of inviolable occupation. The voices of soldiers in the distance occasionally disturbed my rest, but no one discovered my place of refuge. Soon neither fear for my safety nor the discomfort of my bed could keep me from sleep.

The next morning I went in search of the captain of the *Mesopotamia.* I discovered him striding up and down the bridge with the grace of a great cat. A red beard encircled his ruddy face. As he listened to my story, a smile began to play in his piercing blue eyes and spread to his wide mouth.

"And what would you propose I do with this man?"

I felt my temper reddening my cheeks.

"Madam, it's for you to say."

"No, Captain, it's for you to act!" And with these words I turned and walked off his bridge.

The small river boat for Pinega departed the next afternoon, earlier than expected. Laboriously it made its way out into the broad Dvina, pulling at the end of two taut hawsers a pair of barges, majestically broad-beamed and inert, loaded to their gunwales with artillery, men, and mules. We rounded the point and then headed into the narrower Pinega.

In a quandary about where to put down my bedroll, I was glad when two Englishmen came to my assistance—one a British naval officer known as Cheerio, the other a lieutenant in charge of canteens. They ordered a cot set up for me in a secluded corner of the canvas-covered afterdeck. Chairs and tables were brought up, and during the two-day voyage this became a place of pleasant sociability, where passengers and ship's officers gathered.

I became absorbed watching the northern Russian landscape pass slowly in review. The somber virgin forest pushing right down to the steep riverbanks hung over the edges like scalloped green draperies. In some places erosion had created tall cliffs, some of red sandstone, others gleaming white, and their images were mirrored upside down in the black oily-smooth water. Here and there less spectacular vistas opened in the forest where collections of small gray houses snuggled in sheltered bends of the river. The farther inland our convoy penetrated, the greater the distances between these peopled nests.

The front between the Red and White lines was fluid and stretched along the river slightly beyond the town of Pinega. Each village on either side was protected by fortifications and garrisoned by an occupying detachment of Russian or Allied troops. Between the villages large areas, sometimes for distances of thirty to forty miles, were no man's land. And here Reds and Whites struggled for dominance, each conducting daring patrols with small mobile detachments of picked men far into each other's territory. Shielded from reconnaissance planes by the dense forest, these patrols crept upon each other along hidden trails and in the quagmires of spongy swamps fought their desperate battles.

Sometimes Red patrols, penetrating to the river, staged surprise attacks upon the villages. On such occasions convoys plying the waterway were often ambushed and forced to run the gauntlet of enemy machine-gun fire pouring from the riverbanks. The transport preceding ours had been attacked in this way.

Another danger to navigation was the constantly shifting sandbars. The man in the bow with his long sounding rod called out the changing depth of the river in a singsong voice. On one occasion the ship actually ran aground.

"What a convenient opportunity for the enemy!" Cheerio remarked dryly as with a rolling sailor's gait he betook himself to the bridge. Every man was hastily ordered overboard and, thus lightened, the ship soon cleared the bar and was on its way.

On the evening of the second day the winding river brought us within sight of Pinega. High on top of the white cliff the low weather-beaten houses of the town surrounded like gnomes the golden-crowned cathedral. A sunset of rare beauty illuminated the scene, painting the high clouds in vivid hues of gold and orange, imperceptibly shading into carmines and ochers. And at the foot of the cliffs the river, divided, encompassed like two arms of molten gold a dark-green island.

Gleb and Sergei stood waiting for me at the dock. To celebrate my arrival, Sergei played the host. And that night a new and strangely charming Sergei revealed himself. Gone was the mocking insolence, and spontaneously the two men included me in their friendship with a warmth of welcome and affection I had never dreamed possible. The world seemed to me bright and beautiful as the dangers of the war and the risks we now shared appeared unreal and remote.

"This time," Gleb boasted, "I've found a room for you to live in, Lisa! And good news, I've just been named liaison officer to the

British command. This means the possibility of a day's leave tomorrow. So when you go to report at the hospital I'll go with you, and perhaps we can both get the day off before you start to work. Another day to ourselves! Would it please you, Lisa?" He took my hand in both of his and kissed it.

I was rapidly learning to discover the modest flowers blooming by the wayside and to pluck them, one by one.

CHAPTER 13

PINEGA

On the outskirts of the town Gleb had found quarters for us. The house was modest in size, unpainted, smooth and gray from the effects of wind and sun. But its porch and cornices and window frames were richly carved in elaborate peasant designs.

At the back, stables and barns circled a roomy yard. Here also was the *banya,* the bathhouse, without which no Russian peasant's home is complete, a low building of solid logs, divided into two compartments.

Gleb gave me a vivid description of the procedure: "These wooden buckets are filled with hot water, and first they scrub themselves clean. See, with these hard brushes. Then they wash their clothes. The peasant never takes his clothes off between baths, from one week to the next. He goes into the steam bath—it's suffocatingly hot there. White clouds of steam from the water thrown on those red-hot stones in the corner over there hang under the ceiling. He stays there till sweat pours from him, and he emerges as clean as a new-born babe. Somebody throws a bucket of cold water over him, or he runs out and rolls in the snow." He threw back his head and laughed heartily. "Who dares insinuate the Russian peasant isn't clean? What do you say, Lisa? Shall we ask them to heat it for us?"

We were given two rooms, a small apartment, and to me it seemed the height of luxury. One room, small and dark, had a narrow bed in it, a mere skeleton compared to anything I was used to thinking of as a bed.

Gleb noticed my hesitancy.

"Don't you think our apartment looks cozy?" he asked.

"Of course I do, and we can make it beautiful!" The view from the window was a striking panorama of land and water. "But the bed in there—let's make a bed on the floor in here instead."

"Why? Isn't the bed in there all right?"

I told him I had had enough of hard narrow beds. So I was going to create one with hay, wide and soft. Just wait and see!

The peasant sitting by the window in the kitchen gave Gleb permission to take from the barn all the hay we wanted. He and his wife came to the door to watch our preparations, standing there silently side by side.

Soon I had a large bulky mattress fashioned out of two blankets held together with safety pins and stuffed with fragrant hay. White sheets on top and then blankets covered the bed; two pillowcases were filled with soft clothing. The result was magnificent. Gleb led our hosts gently away from the door, wished them good night, and closed the door softly behind them.

In the middle of the night I awoke with a start. "Gleb, something is crawling on me and biting me!"

"Shush, Lisa, go to sleep."

"But I can't!"

A candle stood on the floor by the bed. I lit it and watched veritable armies of flat brown bedbugs crawling over the white sheets.

"Gleb—bedbugs! Hundreds of them!"

He sat up and looked at me disapprovingly.

"The wife of a soldier who wants to be with him at the front does not bother about such trifles!" With this he turned over and was soon breathing evenly again.

I dared not complain any more, but I could not bring myself to ignore the unpleasant invaders. In a tin can half filled with water I began drowning the bedbugs, one by one. As the sun rose, my flickering candle spluttered and went out, and I fell asleep too tired even to wonder if any of the crawling creatures had escaped my avenging hand.

When Sergei heard about my dreadful experience, he shouted with laughter.

"Didn't you know, Luisa Oskarovna, that bedbugs love the smell of fresh hay?" he teased.

I couldn't help laughing too. Although my long acquaintance with bedbugs had only just begun, I never again complained. From that day on, with a never lacking supply of insect powder, I waged battle silently and desperately. In the more doubtful quarters we later came to occupy I always pulled the bed well out from the wall and placed its four legs in large tin cans filled with water.

We left the ornate house the next day and found lodgings in a small white-painted frame house perched high on the cliff above the river. Gleb was able to procure two army cots, a few boards knocked together and resting on two trestles. With them came mattresses and pillows made of rough burlap and filled with fresh straw. It did not take me long to become reconciled to their lack of downy softness, mainly because, being new, they had not yet been discovered by any bloodthirsty bugs.

The base hospital was quartered in a building adjacent to the cathedral. Never having been intended for a hospital, it lacked the traditional connecting corridors. The wards, the emergency room, and the operating room opened directly upon one another. In spite of the rows of low hospital cots filling every available space, the large and lofty wards looked half empty. The front was quiet and there were no patients, and the fresh clean smell of astringents lingered upon the air.

Most of the nurses were fugitives from behind the Red lines, who concealed their destitution under ill-fitting surgical gowns tied around their waists with lengths of gauze bandages. Sadness and resignation imprinted upon his bony face, the chief surgeon wore his draped quaintly over his gaunt and stooped figure. But let an emergency occur, and he and his motley staff of nurses sprang into action, a highly coordinated body of efficiency and courage. My appointment as nurse in charge of the British wards conveniently solved the hospital's linguistic problems.

A week after I began work at the hospital, Gleb was ordered to a small village called Vonga, on the other side of the river. There he was to join a party of British officers to assist in the training and instruction of the Russian troops.

Isolated within a maze of wild lonesome forests, marshlands, and tundra, an uninterrupted battle line could not be held and defended.

With the ever present menace of mutiny among troops of wavering allegiance and with the river the only link with the rear, the situation at the Pinega front was at best precarious. Under these conditions the prospect of another parting swept away my happiness over our reunion, and fears for Gleb's safety assailed me anew. Premonitions beset me and the purpose of my being in Pinega was lost. All I asked was to remain close to Gleb, for as long as we were together, shared dangers held no terror.

"Gleb, let me come with you!"

"But your work, your hospital, your patients! Without your work you have no legitimate reason for being here, Lisa."

"I know. And I've no intention of giving up my work. But Gleb, Vonga is just across the river. Let's keep this room, and you'll have a room over there also. And it'll be very simple for me to go over there whenever I'm off duty."

Gleb wouldn't hear of it. "Four versts across the island and two rivers to cross! How do you suppose you'll get to the hospital in time in the morning? Besides, it's dangerous for women to be so close to the front. A riot in the village next to Vonga a month ago took several lives. Lisa, it's impossible!"

The mention of the riot lost him the battle. I persuaded him to let us try the scheme with a solemn promise that should I not be able to make it to the hospital on time in the morning, I would stay in Pinega without demur. And with that I began packing some things together, ignoring the glint in his eyes, half pleased, half resigned, which he tried hard to hide.

Once again we were to inhabit a Russian peasant's home. It stood in a row of similar houses on the brow of the bank high above the eastern arm of the river. From the eight small windows of our room we looked out upon the two rivers encircling the island, Pinega in the distance, all against the backdrop of the strongly etched black line of the somber northern forest. It was like living in a watch-tower overlooking this land of witchery and kaleidoscopic color changes.

The room itself, on the top floor, reached by a creaking stairway at the side of the house, was charming in its simplicity and hominess. Chairs, bed, wall-fast bench beneath the windows, and the table in front of it were painted blood-red. The backs of the chairs and the ends of the bed were decorated with carved hearts. In one corner, close up under the ceiling, an ancient icon shed faint glints of old gold from its madonna face.

The hearth, the mainstay of every rural Russian household, stood out from the north wall almost to the middle of the room. A monster of white-limed stone and mortar, it was a versatile utility without equal. Large log fires lit in the cavernous low oven transmitted to the massive stonework heat that lasted for hours. And after the dying embers and ashes had been removed, all the food could be prepared there and kept warm, huge bowls of borsch, delicious thick meat pies. In winter a specially constructed place on top of the hearth provided warm sleeping quarters for all the members of the family.

Although there was no need for heat now in the summer and all our cooking was done outside over campfires, the hearth played an important role in our lives. Every day, on Gleb's insistence, we practiced emergency drills and used it as a barricade. He figured that if a riot broke out, we would take cover behind its enormous solid bulk and thus be able to defend ourselves until help arrived or our ammunition ran out.

The back of the room opened on a hayloft, which was simply a layer of planks placed across the beams of the stable below where cows, horses, grunting pigs, and chickens lived. Empty until harvest-time, the loft ended abruptly a few feet from the wall, leaving an opening through which fodder was thrown down to the cattle. Here too the indoor lavoratory was located, a slit cut in the planks that emptied into a convenient corner of the stable.

The peasant, his wife, and their well-mannered and industrious children lived in the summer in the room below ours. We saw little of them. They worked from the early dawn through the late evening, brown-baked and antlike, wrestling from the soil the hard-earned supplies that were to last them and their animals through the long winter. They ignored the war; whether their land was occupied by Red or White troops was of little concern to them.

At five each morning, the wife, smiling a cheery good morning, brought in a singing samovar trailing a light stream of vapor and smoke. I had little time to spare. I brewed tea and put the teapot on top of the samovar, dropped a couple of eggs into the boiling water, and breakfast was soon ready. At seven it was time for me to leave.

"Can you manage, Lisa?" Gleb inquired anxiously when he saw from the window that the ferryman had not arrived at the dock yet.

I assured him I would be all right, that I was getting quite good at maneuvering the single oar in the stern of the rowboat. Halfway down the cliff I turned and saw Gleb at the window, watching me. I blew him a kiss and ran down to the landing. Poling the boat out into the stream, I began to push the oar furiously back and forth. But the current was fast, and in spite of all my maneuvering it carried me almost a quarter of a mile past the opposite landing. I left the boat where it was for somebody else to retrieve. At this hour the countryside was deserted and I had the road and the soft sands and the morning breezes all to myself.

On the return trip in the late afternoon the traffic was lively, winding columns of troops, clanking artillery, and trains of mule teams moving across to the forward positions. I got a ride on a rattling mule wagon, but this was of little advantage because much time was lost when the balky animals held up the ferry at the crossing below Vonga.

When at last I ran up the creaky stairs to our room, Gleb was already home waiting for me. Eagerly he told me his impressions of the day's events while I prepared supper. He liked to work with the British officers. He admired their nonchalant courage, their military competence, but most of all their sportsmanship. To Gleb the matter of trust was paramount, and he got on well with them.

For supper that evening we had porridge cooked over the fires the Russian soldiers had built in long trenches. It was one of those magic evenings when another brilliant sunset drenched the whole sky and the land in vivid golds and saffrons, and the thin bluish ringlets of smoke from the fires drifted into the color-burnished air.

After supper we wandered along the dusty village road skirting the high cliff above the river. Just a few houses beyond ours was the Russian officers' mess.

The captain in command of the company rose from the table where half a dozen officers sat with their glasses of clear tea and charmingly welcomed us.

"*Milosti prosim!*" There was a moment's confusion while they got us seated in the most comfortable chairs.

Gradually, inevitably, the conversation turned from workaday matters and the latest news from the White fronts of Denikin and Kolchak to prewar Russia, the Russia of beautiful women and wild parties, the Russia of the Cossacks and the Tatars and the patient muzhiks and the fantastic revolutionaries. Presently the men began to sing, the wistful stirring tunes never far from Russian lips, songs of wild exuberance and hopeless nostalgia. Why should these Russian songs, the deepest, most eloquent expressions of the Russian heart, always be so filled with sadness? Why should they carry such a penetrating sense of gloom, darkening all gaiety, all passion, all love and happiness?

"Child, do not reach for the roses in the spring, but hasten, hasten to gather the violets! When summer comes the violets are gone."

"Coachman, don't urge your horses on! My beloved has left me, and I've nowhere to go."

Gleb took up the well-known stanzas of a student drinking song, and with eyes flashing and young voices laughing defiance at an evil destiny the others join in the rousing chorus:

"Pour out the wine, comrade, God only knows what will happen to us in the future!"

As the shadows began to lengthen, Gleb and I said good night to our friendly hosts and went out into the deepening twilight. Silently we walked home on the high road. In the west the sun was about to disappear like a glowing ball that sent a blushing shimmer to touch each fleecy cloud above the horizon.

The refrain of the drinking song kept ringing in my ears, repeating itself again and again, and made my heart ache with sudden apprehension. Nearer to home a bugle sounded taps. And then through the evening stillness came a chorus of men's voices, strangely muted and mellow. It was the Russian soldiers chanting their evening prayers, the notes melting together like droplets in a mist.

"Our Father, which art in heaven . . ."

Beautiful! We stood there listening until the chanting ceased. I pressed Gleb's arm closer to me. Then we climbed the creaking stairs to our room and gently closed the door behind us.

The summer wore on toward September. Rumors began to circulate that the Allies were preparing to leave the northern fronts. The news took us by surprise. We could not believe it. Yet apparently it was true. The renowned British Field Marshal Henry Rawlinson had already arrived in Archangel to carry out the evacuation.

How could this have come about? It seemed incomprehensible. Just a few months ago Gleb and I had stood in the window on the Troitsky Prospekt and watched the debarkation of reinforcements for the British Expeditionary Forces. They had come marching up from the quay through the town with flashes of white stars on blue diamonds on their shoulders, bagpipes skirling and drumsticks forcefully whirling. The white stars had seemed emblematic of crusaders come to the deliverance of Russia, and the success of the counter-revolutionary forces had seemed very close at hand, almost certain. But now, with their task far from accomplished, the Allies were departing, leaving the White Russian forces to their own devices.

"The British Labour party has demanded the immediate withdrawal of British troops from Russia," Gleb told me, shrugging his shoulders.

"Then far better if they'd never come at all!"

Characteristically, momentous events like these always found Gleb with a reserve of strength. He simply redeployed his defenses.

"And the others, the Americans and the French?"

"One leaves, they all go. Probably a few foreign volunteers may remain."

This politics was incomprehensible. So long as it had not kept us apart, I had not thought of it much. But suddenly it posed a threat to us. And those undefinable premonitions? Was this the beginning of an end?

"From the military point of view, we've got three alternatives," Gleb said. "Either we abandon the northern fronts and transfer our men and equipment to other fronts, or we give up Archangel and concentrate our forces on the Murman front, or we continue to be supplied and supported from overseas and fight to the bitter end. The decision rests with General Miller and his staff."

"What would you do?"

Gleb smiled. "Our opinion is seldom asked. We only obey orders." He paused for a moment. "It seems to me we're far too weak to hold these extended fronts through the wilderness and at the same time make any significant gains. Our troops are so unreliable." He sighed. It was a shameful confession. It was a bitter truth. Suppose there were a mutiny at Pinega, on the Kotlas front, at Onega, a breakthrough on any front! There was only the Arctic Ocean at our backs.

"I'm thinking, Lisa, that the wisest thing would be to give up Archangel and establish a strong front along the Murman railroad. Sergei is of the same opinion. But that also involves great risks—a tight corner with far-extended supply lines."

What about Kolchak? What about the need for the Pinega front to penetrate eastward for the linkup with the Siberian White armies? Gleb thought it more important, indeed more feasible, to take Petrograd from the north than from Estonia in the south.

"But I'm partial. I'm thinking of Marie and Tsarskoe Selo, and how I'd like to be there when it falls into our hands, our capital. You understand what it would mean to our cause to recapture Petrograd?" He hadn't needed to say it—his feelings were eloquently reflected in his eyes and in the clutching of his hands.

"The decision will be known very soon, and whatever it is, I'll stay with our army. That one thing is inevitable, you understand that, Lisa?" He looked at me searchingly. "But you can leave with the Allies. You're absolutely free to go. Never, never forget that! It might perhaps be better for both of us if you left. Lisa, do you wish to go?"

Had it not been for an almost imperceptible inflection in his voice, I might have had greater difficulty separating the kernel from the chaff when making this momentous decision. As it was, I recognized immediately not only Gleb's innermost wish, but the imminent division of the road ahead. And, as once before, I did not feel the slightest doubt about which choice to make.

"I've only one wish, to stay with you. You know that—you know that." My voice was high and shrill in my eagerness to convince him I had never uttered a greater truth.

Gleb sighed. In his eyes a smile dawned and spread like a sunrise across his whole face.

"Yes, Lisa, I know."

One evening a few days later I returned to Vonga slightly delayed after a heavy day at the hospital. Gleb was not at home. This was unusual. Ordinarily he was resting on the bed when I arrived home. The wound in his hip sometimes bothered him, it swelled and ached from too much exertion. I wandered about the room for a while, feeling a bit uneasy. Then my eyes fell upon a note lying on the table.

"Darling," it read, "go back to Pinega and stay there until I return. Keep in close contact with Sergei, he'll look after you, and don't ask any questions. Please don't worry. Gleb."

Now what had happened? Don't worry, he said. How could I help worrying? Where was he? My head swam. Preparations for an attack? A patrol behind the lines? That was it! He had often spoken of these daring patrols far behind the enemy lines, reconnaissance, feeling out enemy positions. I could never share the thrill of excitement that made Gleb's eyes shine when he spoke of them. What if something happened to him? Would they bring him back? Oh, God, let him be wounded and not dead!

The next morning I got up tired from sleeplessness and stumbled down the cliff to the river. This time I did not look back, for there was no one standing at the window waving, watching me with loving concern. The beauty of the rivers, the tang of the crisp morning air as I walked across the island were wasted on me. At the hospital I performed my duties mechanically, absentmindedly.

After supper I went in search of Sergei. Blithely disregarding Gleb's admonitions not to ask any questions, I begged him to tell me where Gleb was. Sergei was attached to the Russian headquarters, so he should know. But he shook his head.

"Come for a walk, Luisa Oskarovna. Let's walk along the cliffs and look out over the rivers." He took my arm. "Now look at it! It's beautiful, isn't it? Especially like this in the evening, with all the colors of the sunset. I often come here."

With my heart heavy and troubled, I walked along with him a bit unwillingly, seeing nothing.

"Where is he, Sergei? Tell me! If I knew, I wouldn't worry."

"I cannot tell you." His voice was soft and very sincere.

"But Sergei, that's cruel!"

"War is cruel, Luisa Oskarovna."

Sergei's soft sympathetic voice momentarily soothed the pain of my uncertainty. Had he urged me to be courageous, I would have screamed and run away from him.

"Is it decided yet what they are going to do when the Allies leave?" This was a safe question. What did it really matter? What did anything matter except Gleb's safety?

"We're staying in Archangel." There was no need for him to say he disapproved; the tone of his voice, the expression on his face told me only too plainly, but for some reason I persisted:

"You don't approve?"

Sergei shrugged. Perhaps, then, he had already reached his own decision. But at the moment my anxiety about Gleb crowded out all thought of the significance of military maneuvers.

The days passed. Had Gleb only hinted at the kind of mission he was being sent on, I could have borne the uncertainty better. Military secrecy meant nothing to me. The necessity of it entirely escaped me, or, perhaps more truthfully, I refused to acknowledge it. It appeared to me an exasperating means of tormenting people who, after all, had a right to know what was happening to their loved ones.

I walked past the British headquarters, then suddenly turned about and went in.

"Captain White, my husband has been gone four days and I know nothing. Please tell me where he is."

"Kirilin is safe. Don't worry about him."

Was he with Major Collins and Captain McLeod? I asked. If I knew this, I would have a better idea of what was involved. Captain White rose from his chair and took my hand. His smile was warm and understanding. "I want you to take my word, Kirilin is well. And if anything should happen to him, I promise, we'll let you know at once."

So Gleb was working in close contact with the British—whatever consolation that was! But it did give me some relief, some confidence. I had the highest opinion of their officers' skill and courage. And they were dependable. They would never abandon a comrade. Come to think of it, the three men Gleb had worked with at Vonga had disappeared at the same time as he.

After that, I gradually succeeded in training my thoughts away from my gnawing anxiety, at least while I was at the hospital, although the hours on duty dragged, for there was so little to do. Most of the patients were ambulatory. Still, the few that required full care gave me back some of the undiluted joys of nursing, of competence and skill, of the ability to cope with emergencies. This at last helped to release the grip of abnormal self-absorption into which I had fallen.

Sergei came to see me almost every evening after supper. He sat down by the table where I was occupied with my eternal solitaire. He looked at me quizzically. Then, abruptly, he pushed all the cards together.

"No more cards for tonight, and that's an order. Come on, we're going to have a cup of tea at the club. And let's talk about things! Tell me, Luisa Oskarovna, what's your opinion on free love?"

He burst out laughing. I had an opinion, of course, but he had taken me by surprise. In vain I searched for the right words to express my thoughts in Russian. Again we laughed at his joking challenge and my confusion. His efforts to cheer me up were irresistible.

Great crises often foreshorten time and distill experience. And during this difficult period I gained a startling insight into an unusually versatile, uncommonly warm, and nobly self-confident character. Sergei was incomparable. He would juggle before me all kinds of farfetched topics until I was carried away by his sparkling wit. Or I would sit listening fascinated while he spoke of his cherished subjects, Russian literature, the arts, the history of Russia, learning about this land that he so aptly and vividly represented. A man of complete loyalty, like Gleb, he was modeled upon the best and the purest of the Russian character, in love with the beautiful, the gay, and the simplicities of heart, mellowed even in his most reckless and sarcastic moods by the inevitable Slavic melancholy.

When Gleb had been gone two weeks, it became evident that things were moving toward a decisive battle at the front. And one morning when the airplanes began zooming overhead at daybreak, we realized that the battle was joined. The objective, it was rumored, was to occupy a certain important point farther up the river. Then the big guns began to speak, distant booming noises, now louder, now dying away, and sometimes in the lulls the angry sputterings of machine guns. This went on all day and the suspense became a dull ache.

At the hospital we were all at our posts, waiting for the wounded to be brought in. I peered into the faces of the other nurses as we moved about silently; faces full of anxiety for the safety of loved ones, tense and expectant.

Toward evening the wounded began coming in, and for a while we became very busy. But the stream ended quickly, so quickly that we became uneasy. Had the great advance, the significant break-through petered out prematurely?

"Have you seen Lieutenant Kirilin?" I whispered to everyone who I thought might know. But the answer was always the same: "No, sisteritsa, I haven't seen him."

I went looking for Sergei, but I could not find him. The hospital was the only place where I could bear to be, where my hands were kept busy while I waited. I stayed at the hospital until late that night.

The next few days crept by. All seemed to have returned to normal at the front, and still no word about Gleb.

"Where is he, Sergei?" I asked in desperation when he came in the evening. "Why didn't he come back with the others? The battle's over, what has happened?"

But Sergei would not or could not tell me. The cards flew through my hands down upon the table. My anxiety was so absorbing that I could not even listen to Sergei. And when he left I was relieved.

The time was approaching for the evacuation of the British forces from the Pinega front, and still Gleb had not come home. Would he ever come back? I made up my mind that I would wait here in Pinega until I found out what had happened to him. And with that decision my anxiety slowly drained from me, and I waited passively, moving my hands with hardly a thought, dressing wounds, changing pillows, making beds.

The gray light of the northern dawn came through the windows and outlined them mistily. A sound intruded upon my dream. I woke with a start from a fitful sleep. I heard the click of the gate. I sat up in bed. Footsteps crunched upon the graveled path. I rushed to the window.

"Gleb! Gleb!"

In an instant I was outside. He came toward me, dragging his feet in his big boots, grasping his rifle by the muzzle and dragging it along the pathway. His face was gray and drawn under a week-old beard; his eyes were red-rimmed. His uniform hung upon him stiff with caked mud.

"You're back!"

"I'm back, Lisa, exhausted." His voice was dry, harsh with fatigue. In that moment all my anxieties of the past weeks were forgotten, all the burning questions, even the incredible joy of his safe return. For the love that had grown with the agonies of suspense craved only to prove itself in tender service.

CHAPTER 14

IN NO MAN'S LAND

GLEB required several days to recover from his deep exhaustion. His patrol had traversed dense forests, waded through bogs. They had slept in wet clothes through the chilly nights of the burned-out summer. They had ambushed enemy patrols and their tightly knit group had successfully penetrated some fifty miles behind enemy lines. Gleb had required all his tenacity and determination to keep up with his hardier companions. The long years spent in the German prison camps had drained from his system the resilience needed for prolonged exertion. But the lives of all of them had depended upon the stamina and the grit of each, and this alone had prevented him from reaching the breaking point.

We returned to Vonga, this time for less than a week. The British were leaving and Gleb's duties as liaison officer were ending. On the last evening the British officers invited us to their mess in the next village for a farewell supper.

The night was dull and a fine drizzle fell as we walked across the stubbled fields separating the two villages. Darkness came earlier now, and with it a warning of the impending fall. The brief northern summer with its magic white nights and its accelerated growth of leaf, flower, and seed had passed by all too quickly and a presentiment of dissolution, a disquietude about future events filtered into our mood.

In the bright warmth of the mess hall a chorus of gay voices greeted us. The joyous prospect of the departure for home, mixed with good drinks, put everybody in high spirits. Gleb's friends started to ply him with questions about his plans, half seriously, half jokingly trying to persuade him to leave Russia with them.

The colonel, a pleasant man named Hargraves, turned to me smilingly. "I hope you and Kirilin have given serious consideration to the opportunity you have of leaving with us. Your husband should not hesitate. He doesn't need to worry about the future, his place among us is assured."

What a wonderful prospect—security and Gleb's military proficiency recognized! "But," I told him, "General Miller has decided to stay in Archangel, and under these circumstances Gleb will not leave."

The colonel gave me a long thoughtful look. "It's unsafe to remain here," he said quietly.

Supper was announced. A festive table had been laid. Three lighted candles reflected the subdued highlights of coarse army cutlery and chipped chinaware. Gleb leaned forward and blew out one of the candles, and then stood rigid, his cheeks flushed, contrite apology in his eyes.

"Three candles are lighted only around a coffin," he said softly. The gay murmur of voices hushed. Someone removed the extinct candle and a draft of chilly air ran through the warm room.

McFee's gay voice broke the awkward silence. "Aye, you superstitious Russian!" he exclaimed, swatting Gleb on the shoulder. "Three on a match, three candles, eh, Kirilin?"

Gleb smiled. "And yet," he mused, "perhaps . . ."

But the laughter and the din of voices drowned out his words. He shrugged, grasped the mug by his plate, raised it high, and started to sing a refrain of the student drinking song:

"Pour out the wine, comrade, God only knows what will happen to us in the future!"

His young voice rang warm and fearless and the others joined in the refrain. No one knew the words, but the roar of their chorus filled the room.

The next day a letter arrived from Zinaida Andreyevna. "At last we also have come to Archangel," she wrote. "My husband is on General Miller's staff and I am going to organize a hospital of my own here. I wish you were here to help me. I am so anxious to see you. I have so many greetings to you from your mother and all your friends. I hope we shall see each other very soon."

How I longed to see her and hear all the news about Mother and Tante Jessy! I could hardly wait to get home to tell Gleb. Minutes later I perched on the arm of his chair. A thought flashed through my mind. Did he think we could possibly get two weeks' leave and go to Archangel? We had both been working hard these last months and he in particular needed a rest. Afterward, full of restored energy, we would return here for the winter.

I hoped silently, fervently that if we could go, something would happen to prevent us from coming back to Pinega. The prospect of the cold weather, the deep snow, the hardships of winter warfare in this godforsaken relentless wilderness disturbed me. Yet even so, Pinega's terrible isolation and odd beauty held a mysterious fascination, and this was also part of the reason for Gleb's wish to stay here. This was Russia! I knew it to be true.

Gleb sat silent. If we could get leave, perhaps the British would allow us to travel with them when they pulled out. Why not try? We would soon be back here again, rested and fresh.

I waited for him to speak, hoping that his lingering fatigue might weigh in favor of my proposal. For many minutes he sat silent. I thought he had not heard what I said.

But at length he spoke: "Perhaps you're right, but I hate to ask for it." He looked at me as if begging indulgence. There was another prolonged pause before he said slowly, "But—I think we'll ask for leave!"

Without difficulty the Russian command granted us two weeks' leave. But the British ruling—no women aboard troopships—threatened to dash our hopes of going with them. On the basis of my service in care of their sick and wounded, we appealed the ruling. Nobody could tell when the next opportunity might come. It was now or never.

The morning dawned when the British were to leave. Gleb, who by this time was as keen to get away as I was, told me to wait at the hospital while he took our baggage to the dock. He could not believe that Collins, McLeod, and McFee would desert him at the last moment. The British were to leave at eleven. The clock struck ten, and still there was no word from Gleb. Too late, too late! The words kept ringing in my ears, and with each minute that ticked away, hope faded.

"You're wanted at the entrance!"

I rushed out. A British orderly handed me a note. It read: "In recognition of your services to the British Army, General Langford herewith grants permission for Sister Louise Kirilina to travel with the British Headquarters to the village of Ludovaya."

As we stood on the dock waiting for orders to embark, my feelings of relief mingled strangely with regret. Would we return to this crisply chaste land where Gleb and I had experienced some of our most enchanting days of deepening intimacy? Indelibly imprinted on my memory was the room in Vonga with its red hearts, the sunsets over the twin rivers seen from its windows, a fantastic landscape of shifting colors. Unforgettable the soldiers' mellow chanting in the evenings, the changing emotions tearing at the heart, the luster of blossoming friendships in a life almost too stark and demanding. Would we come back?

Sergei was there at the dock, and he smiled as he held my hand in his warm left-handed grasp. "So you made it, Luisa Oskarovna!" There was no trace of censure in his voice, but I knew what he meant.

"Perhaps we'll be back." But Sergei knew better and he shook his head.

We went aboard and the boat cast off. With its railings crowded with Tommies singing, whistling, shouting, it drifted slowly on the current into the river. The engines started up. The last we saw of Pinega was Sergei, the bearded Muscovite, standing erect and strong, with the upside-down reflection of Pinega's white cliffs and its white cathedral, fatalistic and aloof in its brooding isolation, at his feet.

By nightfall the transport made fast at Ludovaya, where we were to disembark. The possibility of a surprise Bolshevik attack required every move to be hushed and hurried. Along the protracted spy-infested front line the departure of the British could scarcely have remained a secret.

Gleb was traveling in the capacity of a courier. The night was moonless and he was set on continuing down the line under the cover of darkness. We hurried into the village in search of the elder. We found him asleep and Gleb mercilessly aroused him. The old gentleman's annoyance at being thus rudely disturbed became awed subservience when he realized Gleb's authority.

"A horse and a cart at once, please!" Gleb demanded curtly.

"Where do I find them, your honor?" His watery eyes peering abjectly from under bushy brows.

"Find them, little dove, at once!"

"Yes, your honor, at once. But it will be hard to persuade anyone to drive so far in the dark, very difficult, your honor."

"How far is it to the next village?"

"More than twenty versts. Very dangerous to travel at night," the old man insisted.

"Quick, be off with you, Grandad, I'm in a hurry!"

The old man shuffled to the door.

"I said hurry up!" Gleb shouted after him.

A short while later wheels crunched on the gravel outside. The old man appeared at the door.

"A muzhik and a telega at your service!" He bowed. A relieved look came into his eyes as Gleb pressed a few coins into his wrinkled hand.

We got into the basket-like vehicle. Made of slabs joined together by pliant roots, it was filled with fragrant hay and rested without springs upon the low axles. We covered up with blankets, for the night was chilly. The muzhik, his jovial round face fringed with a shaggy beard, rode sideways upon his lean pony, his sheepskin coat falling like a mantle over its rump.

"Get going!" Gleb urged him impatiently. Kicking the horse into an unwilling trot, the rider bounced upon his rough-gaited steed and our carriage rattled down the village lane. Heavy rains had fallen and promise of more rain hung in the air. The roads were soft and muddy, full of water-filled ruts. Heedless of the rider's kicks, the horse soon slowed to a walk.

Beyond the village the forest took over and tall trees edged the narrow road. Here darkness closed in upon us, impenetrable, tangible like the vaulted walls of a cave. For fear of attracting the attention of the enemy we dared show no light. The coachman trusted the horse's instinct to find the road.

Gleb trusted neither the darkness nor the peasant. I could feel him fumbling for his revolver. He drew it from the holster. Our eyes ached from the intense effort to see in the darkness. The cart jolted in the ruts, the horse clopped through the mud, and the water in the puddles splashed high up on the animal's legs and belly, cold and wet.

Suddenly the horse stopped. "A bridge, your honor!" shouted the peasant over his shoulder. "Maybe it's down!"

"Shut up!" Gleb admonished him sternly, and in a whisper: "Get off and find out."

I felt Gleb's muscles tighten. What if the man had driven us into an ambush? For several minutes he was gone in the darkness. At last we heard the muted sound of footsteps, and then his shadowy form disengaged itself from the obscurity.

"It's not down," he hissed, and his small eyes twinkled like distant stars in his hirsute face.

"All right," Gleb whispered back. "Let's get going, quickly! Lead the horse across the bridge. How far still to go?"

"Ten versts, your honor."

We jolted across the battered bridge and then down on the road again, lurching, and there seemed no end to the journey. Blissfully I fell asleep against Gleb's shoulder. Gleb kept patient and vigilant watch.

Day was just about to break when we arrived at the next village. Here we had a short rest. Luck was with us, and we chanced upon people who received us with hearty hospitality. The suspicious eyes of self-appointed spies and opportunists could not penetrate past their tight family circle, and our hosts were full of friendliness and warm sympathy for the traveling White Army officer and his wife.

The buxom housewife, spotless in her ample dress covered with an abundance of gay embroidery and with ribbons floating from her tiny cap, pressed good food upon us, warm soup, deliciously crusted meat pie, cottage cheese, and sour cream. The bearded husband, hungry for political news, drew Gleb aside and plied him with questions. How long would the present situation last? What were the prospects? And we found it to be true, that wherever in these villages strewn along the valley of the Pinega River we came upon some traces of old-time affluence and stability in the midst of the prevailing mistrust and uncertainties, there loyal people lived with whom we were secure.

For a week we traveled by day and by night, changing horses and coachmen at each village. We depended directly for our food and safety on the inhabitants, a pure Russian breed. Although their political leanings often emerged, a certain political balance was evident. It derived less from any active political interest than from the temperament of a people living precariously by the grace of God, clinging to their land where hardships and the pressures of self-preservation continually shaped and reshaped their hearts and their destiny; and their behavior was natural and self-explanatory.

When we arrived at the last village before reaching Ust' Pinega, Gleb had a severe attack of asthma. Having had no previous experience with this frightening shortness of breath, I did not know how to deal with it. Heat? Should I apply heat? But the condition did not improve. Hour after agonizing hour he lay there, panting and wheezing. All I could do was sit beside him and hold his hand, watching his painfully heaving chest.

We might have hoped for some sympathy from our hosts in this extremity, but they were afraid. They withdrew silently casting dark glances in our direction. I did not know whether their fear concerned the illness or guilt at harboring a White Army officer. After a day and a half the attack finally subsided and we were able once again to be on our way.

At noon on a bright and sunny day we arrived at Ust' Pinega and the comparative security of the military encampment. The Military Control informed us that a passenger ship had left for Archangel less than an hour earlier.

We went outside, undecided about what to do. A large vessel was coming down the river at full speed, obviously with no intention of stopping. To our surprise, the sergeant of the Military Control came rushing out and signaled the ship. Would he be able to stop it? We saw it slow down, and then very carefully it sidled in toward the small dock. Then I recognized it. It was the *Mesopotamia*, the hospital ship of late unpleasant memory. On the bridge stood my sarcastic antagonist of yore, the redheaded skipper, critically observing the delicate docking maneuver.

The sergeant's request that he take us aboard for Archangel met with courteous agreement. As we met again, the captain expressed his sincere regret over the unfortunate incident involving one of his men and apologized to Gleb. The man had been duly disciplined, he said. During the trip down the river, which lasted until late evening, the captain showered us with special attentions and courtesies. The first mate remained conspicuously invisible.

CHAPTER 15

ARCHANGEL ONCE AGAIN

On our arrival at Archangel we found the town outwardly unchanged. Crowds thronged the sidewalks of the Troitsky Prospekt, to all appearances ignoring the international political byplays that had unexpectedly forced the government of northern Russia into the role of a hapless pawn. Except for the inordinately large number of ships riding at anchor on the river, a casual glance could detect nothing that might suggest any significant movement of troops prior to the imminent evacuation of the Allies.

Yet nervous tension was in the air. Without warning a guilty gleam in the eye of an Allied friend might suggest: "It isn't our fault, for Christ's sake don't blame us!" Or the sudden explosion of a Russian's loud cynical laughter: "It's happened before, hasn't it, but what the hell do we care?" Across the levity there was the ghost of panic. "Didn't you hear . . . all very hush-hush? The Allies are dumping weapons and ammunition into the river. Didn't they tell you? Boxes and boxes of supplies are being destroyed. What for? Why?" All this was fine kindling for suspicion and fear—questions to which there were no answers. And then billboards appeared, bearing offers of safe evacuation at no expense to anyone wishing to leave with the Allies.

The morning of September 27, 1919, presented a change as striking as it was momentous. Overnight all evidence of foreign intervention in support of the great counterrevolutionary adventure in the north of Russia vanished. Nowhere was the uniform of an Allied soldier to be seen, nowhere did a foreign flag float upon the breeze over buildings that had been flying them for months. In one short night the Allies had evaporated, as if ashamed of a retreat so closely resembling a flight. And on this significant morning Archangel awoke outwardly calm, almost indifferent, showing not even a sign of surprise at its desertion.

Thus the White Russians of the north were left alone with their own land. Their choice had been voluntary. They had elected to remain, to accept victory or defeat. Was this choice forced upon them by a hopeless lack of vision on the part of their leaders? Or was it one of sublime courage and sacrifice? I thought of Natalia Ivanovna's words:

"We'd rather fight our own battles and perish than have others fight them for us."

Below the massive cathedral square the Dvina flowed quiet and peaceful. We stood there high above the river, looking out across the vast land now wholly our own, free at last from foreign intervention. Gleb straightened his shoulders and filled his lungs with a liberating breath of pure fresh air.

That evening we had dinner with the Kliuevs. Zinaida Andreyevna plied us with questions about Pinega. She hoped we would decide to stay in Archangel, because she was so keen on having me there to help her with the projected hospital. I hoped so too, and Gleb did not seem fit to go back to the front yet. But his insistence on returning to Pinega appeared like an insurmountable obstacle to any such plans.

"I've heard they want Gleb Nikolayevich as an instructor at the machine-gun school," she said in a deep contralto. "Don't forget, we need loyal and capable officers here too."

I sensed a minor intrigue being set afoot to keep Gleb in Archangel, and a wisp of hope came alive that something might actually come of it. But I had learned to take nothing for granted.

With the Allies gone, good accommodations were plentiful, so we decided to move to an apartment in the home of a rich merchant who had fled the insecurity of the north with his family. It consisted of two large, airy, comfortably furnished rooms and a breakfast corner. The taste of the merchant family ran overly much to painted statuettes and sculptured vases, but by the time we had got ourselves installed, the less appreciated objects were out of sight and the rest were arranged according to our own taste.

I was thrilled with our first real home. The bedroom windows looked out upon the tree-lined Troitsky Prospekt and the living room faced a walled-in garden, now at the beginning stages of autumnal decline. A goodly part of the space was taken up by an enormous heater of green tiles, fired with wood, which kept the whole apartment at an even temperature. From this heating system a tiny fireplace opened into the living room and made it into a warm and cozy place during the chilly evenings.

The house had been left in the care of a servant, Dunya, a homely, colorless woman with a hard thin-lipped mouth and flinty pale eyes. Her hair, combed into a knot on top of her head, was drawn so tightly back that the wrinkles on her forehead disappeared.

Sour and exceptionally lazy, Dunya regarded our presence as a distinct nuisance foisted upon her and the master's premises under the duress of a political edict. All my efforts to make friends with her foundered miserably. Her unwillingness to cooperate bore striking resemblance to that of a mule, and she demanded payment for the smallest service. Whenever I dared set foot in the kitchen, she let me know that she regarded us as insufferable interlopers.

We had still ten days left of our leave. Happily I went about keeping house, pushing far from me all thought of a return to Pinega, nourishing the hope that something would happen to prevent it. In the mornings I went to market down by the river. There shaggy men and noisy, gesticulating women swathed in layers of shawls haggled over the price of milk and butter and sour cream. Here I also bought salmon caught in the Pechora and Dvina rivers, lightly smoked and marinated and recognized widely as a special delicacy. I served the fish raw, lightly seasoned with salt and pepper, and the pink flesh was so tender it melted in one's mouth.

At my insistence Gleb agreed to submit to a physical examination and I heaved a sigh of relief. But I had not expected that his rigid sense of duty would prevent him from staying at home.

"No, Lisa," he said with determination, "I'm not staying at home. If I need medical treatment I'll go to the military hospital. We're not here to play together. I'm a soldier first and last."

I was shocked and aghast. As a nurse and his wife, didn't I have the right to take care of him?

"I'm not going to stay at home like a baby." He looked at me sternly. "Ridiculous. I must submit to military discipline the same as everybody else, and that requires hospitalization for a complete physical."

His tone offended me. Such obstinancy seemed inconceivable, and all this for what I regarded as an exaggerated principle. Surely he could walk across the street for his tests and X rays.

While he packed a few things I stood there, refusing to help. "Won't you come and visit me, Lisa?" he pleaded wistfully, his voice very soft and loving. He got no answer. "Please come!" I'll be so lonesome without you."

My ears were deaf and stubbornly I refused to return the kiss he pressed on my cheek as he left. For the passion of love is perversely self-centered, and even in its most ennobling forms fundamentally powered by the natural all-pervading impulse of self-protection and self-preservation.

The following two days passed by miserably. I was still too painfully hurt to accept the situation. Finally I could keep it up no longer. At the hospital the strong odor of disinfectants irritated me and I noticed with disgust the soiled gowns of the orderlies. I asked for Gleb and found him among several officers in a large bare ward. He lay there smiling and patient on the dismal hospital cot, with none of the comforts I yearned to lavish upon him at home. The sight of him caused resentment to surge up within me anew. Inwardly and in self-defense, I cursed the patient resignation with which he mastered every situation. Against my will I envied him his incorruptible spirit.

I could hardly bear the look of unconcealed happiness that came into his eyes at the sight of me.

"You came at last," he whispered with no trace of reproach. "I've waited so long!"

He turned toward me, moving closer in a vain attempt to conjure a sense of privacy, and pressed my hand to his lips. Full of conflicting feelings, I could not speak.

He told me that he was coming home soon, that they had given him extended leave, that nothing was wrong with his lungs, and that he had to have another X ray.

"Is it nice at home—warm and cozy?" He had been dreaming of the comforts of home. I sat there until the end of the visiting time, speaking little, but gradually regaining my composure and peace of mind.

A few days later Gleb came home from the hospital. Meanwhile, he had received the proposal that he become an instructor at the machine-gun school, but he said very little about it.

One evening he complained of a bad headache. His face was flushed. I felt his pulse; it was racing. He told me that he had had chills during the afternoon while I had been away at the market.

The doctor came, the same one who had looked after him at the hospital. He was a tall, slightly bowed man with a serious, deeply furrowed face. With slow measured movements he gave Gleb a thorough examination. Then he stood there, pensively stroking his Vandyke beard. "Typhoid, I'm afraid. But we'll know in a couple of days."

Filled with anxiety, I asked if my husband would have to be taken to the hospital. Couldn't I look after him here?

The doctor gave me a penetrating look that lasted half a minute. "Sisteritsa," he said finally, "you shall nurse him here—by my orders."

I was unspeakably relieved. Later I understood that this arrangement also solved the doctor's problem of quarantine in the most practical way.

When I returned after seeing the doctor to the door, Gleb had fallen into a fitful sleep punctuated by jerking movements and incoherent mutterings. For a long while I stood watching him, and I realized from experience that a hard battle for his life lay ahead.

Confirmation of the doctor's diagnosis came the next day. After the precipitate climb on the first day, characteristic of a severe case of typhoid fever, Gleb's temperature remained typically high. With all the anxiety of one whose love is mercilessly drawn into the battle of life and death, I nursed him with detached skill and resolute tenderness.

The dim room was oppressively quiet, the hours trailed, the days passed, and there was no change. For hours he would sink into an unmoving torpor. His heavy quietude might easily have been mistaken for restoring sleep had it not been for the deep unnatural flush upon his cheeks. And then, feeling my hand on his, he might awaken and smile up at me feebly. He would make an effort to speak, but his words would trail off into delirious mutterings, sometimes turning into excited shouts. I whispered soothing words to ease his restlessness. Unheeding, he would fight me until exhaustion at last forced him back against his crumpled pillow.

Dunya watched the regular comings and goings of the doctor and my elaborate precautions against the spread of contagion with hostile and suspicious eyes. All the used linen, everything we touched in the sickroom I plunged into a large tub. And when, after the appropriate period of soaking in disinfectant, I called to her to come and pick up the linen to get it washed, I could see the unspoken protest forming on her bloodless lips: This is an outrage! In the pesthouse this man should be, not here infecting my master's house! But she dared utter no word against the doctor's authority. Or perhaps I failed to hear her mutterings, wrapped as I was in a defensive silence, absorbed in the fight for Gleb's life.

Days dragged into weeks. Gradually I could no longer visualize the possibility of a recovery from so virulent and protracted an onslaught. My hopes that he would pull through dwindled.

I sat there beside him, tense, watching his breathing, and the suspense of waiting for an unknown outcome banished weariness. The lamp shed its shaded light upon the green cloth of the night table and the book in front of me. Except for Gleb's breathing, the room was deathly still. Was there in that hard, slightly staccato rhythm a dreaded stertorous sound? Rooted to the spot, I stared at his heaving chest in a paroxysm of fear.

Many minutes passed. Gleb stirred, flung his arm over his head. "Lisa?"

I bent over him, my knees trembling.

"What are you reading?" His words came in a whisper. What strange lucidity!

"*Anna Karenina.*" I had difficulty getting the words past the lump in my throat.

"Tolstoi." He sighed happily. "I love Tolstoi. Read 'loud—for me." He closed his eyes.

I began to read aloud haltingly, with an effort. Was this a new phase of the illness leading toward the end? Was it possible his life was slipping away before my eyes? I dared not look for fear of seeing the signs of death gathering upon his face. He lay so strangely still. My heart beat suffocatingly, drummed in my ears. I could not control my voice, but I kept on reading. He doesn't hear me any more, I thought. The words stuck. . . .

"Why did you stop? Go on, Lisa." He looked up as I bent over him and smiled.

"How do you feel?" I touched his hand and it was cool.

"Fine. Just tired. I'd like to listen some more—then sleep."

I went on reading, and gradually my anxiety disappeared. The fever obviously had left him. A peaceful calm fell over the dim room. All was quiet and I read on, and the relief that came from these thoughts was so great that weariness sank over me like a pall. My head came to rest on the open pages of the book. When I looked up again, Gleb was sleeping quietly.

His convalescence stretched into many weeks. Regaining the strength the high fever had drained from him became a long uphill struggle. On many occasions jagged peaks of high temperature appeared on his chart, filling me with fears of a relapse. Long before he was able to hold the book in his own hands we had reached the end of *Anna Karenina.*

The day came at last when he was able to sit up on the sofa in front of the fire. With the return of his strength a great urge came over him to set thoughts into form and images into words. An impulse to create in whatever form, music or drawing or writing, drove him. For the first time in his life circumstances provided the necessary leisure and tranquillity to formulate and to carry out the great projects of his dreams.

Gleb began writing a novel. Plans for this story about life in Russia before the Revolution had occupied his mind during the tedious pain-ridden years of enforced idleness at the prison camp in Germany and later at Horserød. Parts of it had already taken form during the time we spent at Vonga. Now he worked on it throughout the days and evenings. He read parts of it to me while we sat before the fire. In his absorption he almost forgot his mission as a soldier.

These were memorable evenings when, through Gleb's sensitive interpretation on the pages of his growing manuscript, he imparted to me his own native understanding of Russia. More significantly he rendered Russia, now no longer wrapped in obscurity, acceptable to me as a reality unalterable in substance, evolved naturally from the constitution of the land, the people, their culture and history.

When this happy intermission far too soon came to an end and we were once again swept into the mainstream of events, Gleb's novel was well advanced.

The question of our return to Pinega was no longer discussed.

Gleb gave up the idea, not without regret. The advance on the Pinega front initiated at the time of his exhausting patrol behind the lines continued. It spread like wildfire and included a major advance on all fronts from Pinega to the Murman Railway. Hard-pressed on the Kotlas front in the south, which threatened the way to Moscow, and to prevent a breakthrough there, the Bolsheviks withdrew part of their forces from the Pinega front, and the decreased Red resistance allowed our troops to make significant advances across vast empty territories in the direction of the Urals and Siberia. Simultaneously Admiral Kolchak succeeded in reaching the Urals. In the south General Wrangel, who had taken over the command of the White armies there, was advancing upon Moscow, and in the west Yudenich stood at the gates of Tsarskoe Selo. Under the concerted pressure of these encircling White armies, the Reds were being pushed back gradually and relentlessly.

Had the departure of the Allies in the north actually been of little military significance? So it would seem. And might it not also have acted as an incentive to secure our position and to unite the divided people? Had the political prospect of replacing the dictatorial autocracies of the old regime as well as of the Communists with a healthy and just democracy exercising lessened pressure and spilling less blood actually gained enough in appeal to rekindle morale?

Wishing with all his heart that he could take an active part in these exciting events, Gleb followed the march of the white pins on the map with shining eyes. His enthusiasm was contagious. Indeed, the whole of Archangel was caught in a mood of high spirits and expectancy. Everybody exultantly talked of victory. It was assured, it was inevitable. Brief notes came from Sergei in Pinega. And then, quite unexpectedly, he appeared in person. He had been posted to Murmansk and was on his way there. He remarked sarcastically on the general euphoria. In his opinion, it was premature. And the arguments raged long into the night for and against ultimate success.

But the advance continued. Now the lakes and the rivers lay hard frozen and secure underfoot and the forests stood deep in snow, facilitating the maneuvers of our well-supplied and well-fed troops. Starvation among the enemy was an ally on the side of the Whites, demoralizing the adversary and in some localities causing wholesale surrender. The condition of the prisoners was appalling. On wintry trails criss-crossing the wilderness, relief supplies were distributed. The hour of Russia's deliverance seemed imminent and inescapable.

Then, without warning, the advance on all fronts ground to a halt. The long curving front lines froze in complete inaction. The news shocked us. Why? What had happened? Had the victory been too easy? Had we pushed ahead too fast and too far?

Gleb came up with an explanation. Here in the north the vast, thinly populated areas recently conquered presented grave economic problems. The people were in a state of utter destitution. There were disease, despair, and death to be dealt with, and the reorganization of these enormous territories was obstructed by the rigors of deepening winter and the consequent difficulties of communication and transportation across the great distances. So, Gleb argued, our army had to entrench and regroup. Just wait, when spring comes the offensive can be resumed on all fronts! And his optimism allayed my apprehensions.

By this time Gleb was well enough to take up his duties as instructor at the machine-gun school, and the work interested him. Zinaida Andreyevna's Red Cross hospital was being organized, and she put me in charge of the officers' wards.

The hospital was located in a magnificent private home, recently evacuated by its owners, just across the street from our house. The job of turning these spacious rooms into wards for our sick and wounded was interesting and rewarding. Along the ornate and mirrored walls we placed the comfortable hospital beds left by the Allies, and upon the shiny parquet floors I rolled my rubber-wheeled stretchers and surgical dressing tables. Supplies were plentiful. It must have been heavenly for the patients, after the hardships of midwinter warfare, to be taken into these halls of luxurious comfort and warmth.

Zinaida Andreyevna moved among us in her simple brown cotton frock, the red crest emblazoned upon the black apron and the immaculate veil encircling her rosy, matronly face. The sick men adored her. They clung to her warm hands as she sat down beside them, listening to their troubles and in her deep husky voice speaking to them of the stresses and anxieties she too had suffered and bringing them consolation and renewed courage.

Christmas came. During the short hours of daylight the noondays dazzled with their crisp and frosty luminosity and the nights sparkled with stars. Sometimes, when the moon bathed the landscape in its cold luster or the aurora's resplendent colors spread across the wide heavens, the nights dared compete with the snowy sparkle of the sun-bright days. In the middle of January the Russian New Year was ushered in with peaceable celebrations. Snow was falling, and with every new fall the plowed streets of Archangel had the appearance of deep ditches between the rising walls of snow. The relaxation of tensions obscured the fact that we were actually living in the rear of a fighting army.

My duties at the hospital were generally light because few wounded were brought in. A man with a frozen foot might require treatment with baths, or a case of acute bronchitis or pneumonia might need careful attention. I learned to apply suction cups, a surprisingly effective treatment for chest conditions. A small cotton-tipped wooden stick was dipped in alcohol, set briefly afire, and then quickly swished inside the cup before it was pressed down on the bare skin. A vacuum was created that made the cup stick to the desired spot, drawing the blood to the seat of infection. Eight or ten cups might be applied for ten or fifteen minutes, leaving the area a mass of rich coloration. The days of antibiotics were at that time still far away.

We spent the evenings quietly with the firelight playing softly upon the shadows of the room, Gleb absorbed in his writing or reading aloud from the growing manuscript. Friends dropped by for a glass of tea. Among these was Musmann, one of Gleb's fellow instructors at the machine-gun school. He was a giant of a man with a full ruddy face, an ample brown moustache, and the clumsy movements of an enthusiastic puppy. He showed an appealing enjoyment and trust in Gleb's friendship. His need for companionship became his admission into our home every night of the week.

Occasionally a sharp reminder of the fleeting nature of our peace interrupted our everyday preoccupations. Muffled drums sounded in the distance, approaching, and the compelling dirge drew us to the window to watch the slow, hesitating march of soldiers with reversed rifles, an open coffin carried high on the shoulders of the bearers. The cold still face upon the white satin pillow belonged to one of Gleb's fellow officers.

In the night the report of a gun sounded close by our window and brought Gleb out of bed, tense and alert. But it was only a party of carousing soldiers. Gleb crept back to bed and tucked his revolver under the pillow.

To inspire confidence, our crack regiment, the First Archangel Reserves, was often ostentatiously shown off, marching up and down the Troitsky Prospekt. Their ankle-length greatcoats flapped against their high polished boots, their arms swung smartly in time with their full-toned singing. These troops looked good and their loyalty was unquestionable. Revolts and riots? With troops like these there was no reason for fear. When spring came—ah, then the final march upon Petrograd would take place! Anything less than success was unthinkable.

One day at the end of January, an unexpectedly large number of wounded was brought into the hospital. Curiously, nearly all of them were officers. Before evening my wards were filled to overflowing. They came in shocked silence, not a moan to be heard, not an anguished cry of pain. Their faces were drawn. One man with a bullet wound in the back of his neck needed no words to explain from where that shot had been fired. Another, a tall dark fellow with his arm torn to shreds, whispered apologetically, "A shot from behind . . ." as if to excuse himself for not having been quick enough to face it.

A third one, a powerful athletic man, came in with his jaw shattered. The self-inflicted wound from a weapon awkwardly aimed at a moment of appalling shock had felled him without killing him, and he was saved only to become the prey of a numbing hysteria that robbed him of the power or the will to speak when he regained consciousness. He lay there mute, lacking words to tell exactly what had happened to him; only his eyes expressed deeply and wildly the anguish he had endured.

At the end of that awful day we knew that the Third Fusiliers, stationed at the Kotlas front, had turned upon their officers in revolt.

I returned home exhausted. Gleb was not there. At last I heard his footsteps in the hall. He came in silently. I waited for him to speak. At length I could not stand his silence any longer.

"What is happening?"

A long minute passed before he answered, "This, Lisa, is the beginning of the end." He spoke quietly, as if a different course of events could never have been imagined.

The end? What did he mean? I have often wondered if at that very moment what actually was going to happen suddenly stood before him crystal clear, as a shadowy contour emerges sharply when a dark cloud slips off the face of the full moon.

"But everything was going so well!"

"What we took for strategic retreats on the other fronts turned out to be routs. Kolchak in the east and Wrangel in the south are withdrawing as fast as they can. Yudenich too, and we don't know the reason. But without their support, what chances have we here in the north to succeed? It is fate," he added.

The emergency demanded a solution. "What can we do?"

"Nothing." He sounded very tired. "We can do nothing but wait."

So we waited. Everybody around us remained unruffled, as if what had happened at the front did not concern us here at the rear. It was, they said, nothing but an isolated incident. But the seething beneath the surface? Did no one realize the tremors of the precarious foundation upon which rested the existence of the government of northern Russia and its White army, ruled by Miller and his old-fashioned generals? No one but the officers at the front knew, those who had seen it happen, who had encountered the opposition with their own flesh and blood; only they knew and understood the undercurrents of revolt and hatred, the stark irresistible power of the Revolution and its triumph.

And they did not talk. What could we do? Gleb and I carried on as usual, working at our posts during the day, returning home to spend the evenings before the fire. All was as it had been, except that the carefree insouciance that had blossomed in other days was gone now. The music was muted.

One day as we went for a walk after Sunday service in the cathedral, we noticed that all the icebreakers that regularly shuttled between Archangel and Murmansk had disappeared. Not a single one could be seen at the moorings along the river, nothing but the yacht *Yaroslav* and a destroyer. What was the reason for this? If Archangel should fall, these ships were our only means of escape. Was it possible that our military leaders were not at this critical moment planning for an orderly evacuation of their loyal officers and men? To us this was a shocking discovery, and we returned home filled with dire forebodings.

On my arrival at the hospital in the morning a few days later, somebody told me that Zinaida Andreyevna had left. I was aghast, I couldn't believe it. She the faithful, the shining example of loyalty and duty, deserting her hospital!

"She left by sleigh during the night to join her husband," someone whispered. That explained it. She had told me some time ago that the general had been sent on a diplomatic mission to Karelia. I had felt sorry for her, having to be separated from him. But my disappointment persisted.

I found the hospital in a state of total dissolution. Officials and staff officers came and went. They spoke to some of the men, then left. During the forenoon those of the wounded and the staff who wished to be evacuated were taken aboard the *Yaroslav*. By noon half the hospital was empty and I went home for dinner.

Gleb was walking restlessly around the apartment, waiting for me. He said calmly, "Lisa, you must leave with your Red Cross unit. The front has collapsed. The Reds will be here in Archangel in one or two days."

"And you?"

"I'm leaving tonight by sleigh with the machine-gun school and what's left of the garrison." He spoke casually, as if talking of an ordinary journey. "Our orders are to get to the Murman Railroad, to hold the front there."

"Then I'm leaving with you tonight!"

There was a pause. "Is that your decision?" he asked at length. His question implied simply his acceptance of a foregone conclusion, and I had no feeling of having made a significant decision. "I'll be back in the evening. Pack a few things, especially warm clothes. Make it light so we can carry it on our backs. Pack as if we were going on a picnic." He gave a single shout of laughter at his flippancy, but instantly had himself under control again.

Action at last. I felt elated and very confident.

Back at the hospital I found no need to stay at my post any longer. The wards were nearly empty. Only a few officers and a nurse remained. They had refused to leave.

At home I brought out the seven trunks and began packing the various trivia gathered during the happy time now at an end, all the little things that make a home warm and dear. I gazed a long time at the beautiful Royal Danish tea service before wrapping each piece carefully and putting it away. All my dresses and Gleb's clothes that we would have no need for on the "picnic" I also packed away.

In a light suitcase and a brown duffel bag I put together warm shirts, socks, blankets, a few toiletries, cans of food. On the writing table by the window was my father's large portfolio of finely worked leather, now Gleb's possession. It contained our love letters. Beside it were Gleb's notebooks, his manuscripts. I could not bring myself to destroy them, and they must not be left behind, so I emptied the duffel bag and put the portfolio and the notebooks at the bottom. Then I folded a few trinkets, two rings and a gold chain studded with baroque pearls, Tante Jessy's last gift, into a £100 note we had bought recently for an emergency. This I sewed tightly into the brown cover of a first-aid dressing and then I pinned the whole thing into the knot of my hair.

Dunya was in the kitchen, and then I saw her sneaking up close to my half-open door. There was an ugly sneer on her pale sallow face. Treacherous Red cat!

I closed the trunks, locked them, and pushed the suitcase and the duffel bag into the hall. Then I sat down by the fire and gazed at the empty room, waiting for Gleb. At last he came.

"You're to travel with the chief's wife, Nina Aleksandrovna," he told me. "Your sleigh will be here about nine. We'll be following. Just go on, don't stop! At the first village on the other side of the river we'll meet again."

It was curious that at this moment, when we were about to start out on our momentous flight from Archangel separately, I did not feel the slightest anxiety about Gleb's safety. There would be many hours before we would be together again. For a moment we held each other close. And then without another word he was gone.

Dunya stood leaning against the kitchen door. She had seen what had passed between us, heard what was said. I caught her derisory glance at the trunks, and my temper mounted. I realized that as soon as I was out of the door she would take covetous possession of them. Oh, no, I would rob her of the perverse pleasure of acquiring them by default! In a white rage I swept up the keys from the table, and there must have been plain hatred in my eyes as I glared at her. I threw the keys at her.

"Oh, no, Dunya, you're not going to take them! I'm giving them to you!" I shouted at her.

My vehemence startled her, but the fine point of my intended checkmate ricocheted disappointingly against her dour wits.

The sleigh was at the door. Without a backward glance I walked out of the house. The chief's pretty wife motioned me to the seat beside her. Nina Aleksandrovna's dainty person almost disappeared in an abundance of furs, and I caught the fleeting whiff of expensive perfume. Her dark eyes glinted with subdued excitement in her rosy face. The soldier coachman stuffed my baggage under the wolf-skin robe at our feet. Slowly and deliberately he headed the single horse out into the Troitsky Prospekt.

A fierce blizzard swept the snow around the corners of the houses and the wind stung our faces. The street was almost empty. Only one or two dark figures were hurrying along the sidewalk, huddled deep into the collars of their greatcoats. The fall of Archangel into the hands of the Bolsheviks still seemed a hallucination mocking reality.

The horse picked its way down the embankment step by step and out on the snow-covered river. Not another living soul was to be seen. We were alone on a crazy flight into the vast white emptiness. Our straining horse plodded through the trackless snow. Presently the whirling mass, swept high before the hissing gale, swallowed the last twinkling light of Archangel. And there was nothing.

CHAPTER 16

THE RETREAT

THE whistle of the gale, the dance of the snow, the sting of the icy crystals in our faces! Cold snow whirled into every crease and fold of our covering. Here and there it collected into small drifts until dispersed by a strong gust of wind. The movement of a cramped leg caused icy currents of air to filter through our warm clothing, leaving us shivering. The horse floundered knee-deep in the snow, its tail and mane tossed sideways by the wind. Ahead of us the trail lay trackless.

My aching eyes closed, and for a moment—a minute or an hour—I drifted into sleep until a cold shiver jerked me awake again. I could feel Nina Aleksandrovna cuddling up against me to keep warm.

"What's the time?" she whispered.

"I don't know."

"Is it three o'clock? Perhaps?"

"Perhaps."

She sat up. "Are we on the right road?" she asked. "Piotr, are we on the right road?"

She pulled the fur collar from her face so that he could hear better what she said. He was tramping in the snow beside the sleigh to ease the load. He put his bearded face up close to Nina Aleksandrovna's. "What did you say, *barenya*?"

"Are we on the right road?" she asked anxiously. "The others, the soldiers, where are they? Can you see them? Piotr, are we lost?"

"Don't worry, Barenya Nina Aleksandrovna, we're not lost. We'll meet them soon. Trust me! I know the road well."

He spoke as a father to a frightened child. He gripped the sleigh, his hand buried in a snowy mitt. The snow covered his bushy beard and small icicles surrounded his nose and mouth.

"Piotr, I'm cold! Let me get out and walk," I begged.

Piotr drew rein and the horse stopped willingly. Its steaming sides heaved. I stumbled out into the snow.

After cramped immobility, movement was a relief. The blood surged back into my stiff limbs. But the drag of the drifting snow soon tired me. My eagerness to exercise vanished and I stumbled on almost exhausted, hanging onto the sleigh with a cramplike grasp.

Nina Aleksandrovna too wanted to get out and walk. Unused to any greater exercise than dancing, she floundered valiantly for two or three minutes. Soon her pretty face became deeply flushed and the ringlets of her dark hair, escaping from under her cap, clung to her moist forehead. She almost fell, but Piotr, broad-chested and strong leaped to her rescue and lifted her back into the sleigh.

In the cutting wind we could no longer tuck ourselves in airtight under the robes. The snow clinging to our boots and skirts melted. We cuddled up close to keep warm, but our wet clothes stiffened and clung to our bodies like icy sheets.

Again we forced ourselves to get out of the sleigh. For a while we floundered in the snow to feel once more the blood coursing through our veins, then stumbled back into the sleigh again. Each effort drained from us a bit more energy and warmth until we were almost insensible with cold and fatigue. Gently Piotr urged us on. And the snow whirled around the sleigh, rose into a white cloud, and swept on beyond in wild turbulence.

We went on like this for hours, endless hours, and we ceased to think, to feel, to wonder, or to worry.

Piotr's frozen beard touching my cheek startled me.

"The soldiers!" he whispered hoarsely. "Look!"

Ghostlike figures were moving up alongside us, blurred silhouettes bent forward against the driving gale. The faint creaking of leather, the hushed swish of feet plodding in the snow mingled with the gusting wind. We stared fascinated at the bayonetted rifles weighing down the shoulders of the weary men. Their packs looked like humps on their backs. Behind them came sleighs like ours, drawn by lathered horses, their tails and manes blowing in the wind. Again Piotr leaned over and whispered into our ears:

"Aleksandr Dmitrievich is coming up behind us. We'll soon be in the village."

It was high noon when I awoke on the floor of a peasant's house, pressed against the wall with Gleb's warm body protecting mine. Many other people lay packed on the floor beside us, men of the machine-gun school, Nina Aleksandrovna and her husband. The large Russian hearth loomed beside us, sending out gorgeous heat laden with the humidity that evaporated from our breaths and our wet clothes. The frost flowers on the tiny windowpanes were melting, adding still more vapor to the air.

I turned, met Gleb's kiss, and then caught sight of my boots crowded around the hearth in a motley company of leather boots, fur boots, and large clumsy white canvas boots. I wondered how my boots got to be there. I could not remember either taking them off or putting them away. Under the blankets my legs felt as if swathed in warm wet compresses. My wet skirts clung to them and I dared not move for fear of letting in a chilly draft of air.

Presently the people began to move and I got up and sat by the hearth to dry out my skirts. Everybody was buoyed by the rest and in a cheerful mood. Some of the men took turns shaving in front of a tiny pocket mirror suspended from a nail by the window. Long exhausting marches, sleeping fully dressed on the floor or on the ground were commonplace experiences to these men, and they knew how to make the best of it.

A fair young man, one of Gleb's fellow instructors at the school, came up to talk to him. His name was Dmitri Grigorievich, and not even a march through a wild snowstorm or sleep on the floor could blur the freshness of his face or his dapper appearance. While the two of them were talking, his eyes fell on my wet skirts.

"Luisa Oskarovna, you should wear breeches and not skirts! Haven't you got any?" he inquired. And then he turned to Gleb: "Gleb Nikolayevich, I've got a spare pair. May I give them to your wife?"

Gleb nodded his hearty thanks. He held up a blanket to shield me from view while I made the change. Dry clothes, what luxury! The breeches fitted perfectly. What a relief to get rid of those wet clinging skirts!

In the other room food was on the table, opened soup cans, bully beef, big loaves of crusty bread, bowls of sour cream and cottage cheese. At one end a huge samovar stood singing softly, cups and glasses beside it. Nina Aleksandrovna and her husband were already there having their breakfast.

Aleksandr Dmitrievich was Nina Aleksandrovna's second husband. She had loved her first handsome husband with an almost frantic passion. When he was killed in action half a year ago, she had thrown herself screaming in a paroxysm of grief upon his open coffin. A month later she had married Aleksandr Dmitrievich. He was a heavily built man and his square clean-shaven chin gave to his pleasantly homely features a look of power and determination. His eyes were gray, penetrating, and honest, and he nurtured for his dainty doll-like wife an adoration implicit in every word and action. Gleb regarded his chief with unreserved esteem.

Outside the late February sun was past zenith but its slanting rays still touched upon the great mass of new-fallen snow and made it sparkle. The weathered houses stood well apart along the wide village street and cast blue shadows upon the white snowdrifts that half buried them. Fine scattered ice crystals floated through the crisp clear air like minuscule glittering diamonds. It was very cold.

At this moment the village was seething with life. Officers and orderlies hurried to and fro. Horses were being harnessed and sleighs mounted with machine guns and loaded with supplies and ammunition. A single light gun mounted on its carriage rolled rattling down the village street. The troops consisted of units that, after the collapse of the front, still remained loyal, and foremost among these was the First Archangel Reserves. Suddenly, relayed from house to house, the order came to form ranks, and company after company fell in line and began marching down the street. Sleigh after sleigh pulled out from the yards and followed the troops in a long line.

Shivering in the cold, small groups of villagers assembled at the corners of their houses, anxiously watching the activities of the troops. Some protested bitterly when their hay was requisitioned and their horses were taken from their stables to supply the needs of the military, but their protests were ignored. When the last sleigh pulled away it left the village impoverished and unprotected.

Aleksandr Dmitrievich had arranged for his wife to go up front with him. I was assigned to a sleigh driven by a clerk of the machine-gun school. When Gleb tucked me in, I asked why I could not go in his sleigh.

"No, Lisa, I'm in charge of a machine gun. Remember, darling, our safety depends on discipline. We're all under orders—no questions asked. A long road lies ahead." He pressed my hand to soften his stern warning.

My companion was a young man with round rosy cheeks and a formless body. His uniform was several sizes too large and hung from his shoulders awkwardly. Did he know, I wondered, how to fire the gun stuck into his sagging belt? To ride with strong solicitous Piotr, whose presence assured security and protection, was one thing. But this juvenile!

Late in the evening I was preparing our bed on the floor of a small dingy room when Gleb came in looking tired and annoyed.

"Look here, Lisa, your horse is still outside not unharnessed, not fed."

"But wasn't the clerk supposed to . . ."

Gleb took me out into the stable. It was full of horses and the steamy pungent odor of fresh manure. Beside each horse its harness was laid neatly in a pile ready for immediate use. The sound of the animals' rhythmic hungry chewing mingled pleasantly with the men's soft remarks as they worked around their charges.

"From now on, Lisa, I must hold you responsible for this horse," Gleb said. "No matter how tired you are, you must first look after the horse, see that it's unharnessed and fed. This is the way you undo the *duga*." And with a deft twist he loosened the wooden archlike device fitted over the shoulders of the horse.

Soon we had the tall black animal thoroughly rubbed down with straw and fed. Piotr was in the stable. "I'll water him for you after a while," he offered with a broad smile. Piotr never left the horses except to eat; he slept with them.

"Thank you, Piotr! Will you help the *barenya* to harness the horse in the morning? And don't forget, Lisa, always fill your sleigh with hay before starting out. This is important!"

When we got back to the house, many were gathered around the table eating with hungry energy. Others, to whom sleep was more important, had already occupied the choicest places on the floor, curled up in their blankets. In a far corner the clerk was snoring loudly.

Early the next morning I was out in the stable. Piotr showed me how to fasten the shafts to the ends of the springy *duga* with a kick of the foot to hold them out from the sides of the horse, thus allowing it to move within them freely. My early training with horses served me well, and it did not take me long to become an expert in harnessing horses in the Russian way. I was elated with the chance to fulfill my part, however small, in the general operation, to cease being a piece of baggage.

Slowly the long train of sleighs headed by the column of marching soldiers wound its way across the bleak white northern landscape like a huge black serpent. Its immediate destination was Onega, a lumbering town at the southern tip of the White Sea. Gleb had told me that, if we got past this critical point, our chances of reaching the Murman Railroad before that front collapsed would be good. And secretly I envisioned the security of the Finnish border, only twenty versts west of the railroad.

On roads tracked only in winter across bottom-frozen swamps our long cavalcade traveled past scattered scrubby spruces eking out a lean existence in the peaty soil of this harsh environment. Occasionally we passed through virgin coniferous forests where the clangor of the moving column and the creaking noises of the metal-shod runners reechoed under the vaults of the tall trees. Small villages lay scattered along the route. Furtive glances and stony silence greeted our appearance. The inhabitants knew only too well the depredations of the military that left hardship and woe in their wake. Red or White, the difference was nominal. The former took without paying, the latter paid with worthless paper money.

Meanwhile, on information gathered by the forward reconnaissance party, the need for haste became urgent and the daily marches were increased in length. The lassitude and boredom of the endless hours of cramped sitting in the sleighs dulled all sensation. The clerk beside me, with his incredible capacity for sleep, blissfully dozed away his weariness and tedium, and I envied him. Time and again I gathered the slackened reins from his inert hands until finally I refused to let him drive any more. He did not mind.

The stops for rest provided little more than a chance to ease cramped muscles while others were brought painfully into action in the care of the tired horse. Then on and on without rest until darkness long since had descended upon the landscape before we reached a village where at last we sought shelter and rest and something to eat. Never before had I known such torment—not of exhaustion, for that dulls sensation, but the simple tiredness of an aching body kept forcibly in action beyond its actual capacity. Up before daybreak, out into the stables to harness the horses, hitch them to the sleighs, and then the hard relentless order to move on.

A commotion at the front of the line momentarily lifted the lethargy of monotony. The long train of sleighs came to a hesitant halt. An emergency? But no orders came to man the rifles propped up in the front corners of the sleigh, no permission was given to get out to stretch stiff limbs. Three shots rang out unexpectedly, crisply staccato in the cold air. And then the sleigh in front moved ahead and our black horse followed without urging. Presently we came to a well-trampled place beside the road and a splash of red blood on the snow. Aghast I stared at the booted foot of a soldier sticking awkwardly up out of the snow.

The next day we passed a soldier sitting in the snow resting against his pack, wearily following the passing sleighs with a guilty look in his eyes. Nobody spoke to him, nobody picked him up. More and more often this happened. Soon deserters littered the roadsides. At every village men disappeared in the forlorn hope that their desertion would induce leniency from the Reds at the ultimate moment of surrender.

Four days out of Archangel and darkness had already fallen. Since daybreak we had traveled over forty versts. A broad river and twinkling lights emerged through the mists outlining the shadowy contours of factories and sawmills along the frozen banks and the streets beyond. We crossed a wide bridge and drove into the town.

Onega! The critical point! The advance party brought back the good news that all was peaceful. And now the tantalizing prospect of a good rest lay ahead. It had been a gamble, a calculated risk to try to reach this place before the Reds. So far we had been traveling in a southwesterly direction; the next part of the journey would take us slightly north of west. Would we be able to reach the railroad safely?

I tumbled out of the sleigh stiff and numb. To walk erect was exquisite relief. I began to unharness the horse, and suddenly, tired and irritable as I was, I found myself shaking with annoyance at the clerk's lack of assistance. He had disappeared.

Gleb found me in the stable. He took my arm, smoothed away my anger. We crossed the courtyard, leaning on each other. The house was bright, warm, clean, roomy. Its welcome chased away at least a part of our exhaustion. Incredible luxury, the married couples were given beds to sleep in. A generous supper was laid out on the table. Obviously the people who lived here were neither poor nor unsympathetic to the Whites. The warm food, the friendly atmosphere quickly erased the lines of fatigue furrowing many faces, and soothed frayed tempers. And gradually the conversation around the table became colored with renewed confidence. Tonight the possibility of reaching our goal safely seemed assured.

A shouted command: "To the sleighs!" The order reechoed from house to house until it died out in the distance.

Shocked silence and immobility. Then of one accord everybody sprang from the table. In frantic haste our half-unpacked belongings were collected and we rushed out to the stables. Curt orders flashed across the heavy moist air. The horses stamped as they were pulled from their half-eaten bundles of hay and reharnessed to the sleighs.

Gleb gripped my arm hard as he put me in the sleigh with the clerk.

"Down the street!" he commanded the boy holding the reins in trembling hands. I grasped his arm before he was gone. "Don't get lost!" I begged stupidly, clinging to him. He tore himself away.

Awkwardly the clerk whipped the tired horse into a lumbering trot. Sleighs dashed out of the yards ahead of us to fall into line. I looked back and saw Gleb jump into the sleigh with the mounted machine gun. Thank God, he was only two sleighs behind us.

Down the street! I gazed at our two loaded rifles and wondered how soon we would have to use them. Would I know how to use mine, how to cock it, how to aim it?

At the end of the street a group of officers stood at attention, letting the sleighs pass in review before them. Suddenly a burst of machine-gun fire came in angry spurts from the river below. The crackle of fire continued, but the officers remained motionless, as if they had heard nothing.

I wondered who of our men were down there on the river engaging the enemy. Later I was told that Musmann had been one of them, and neither he nor any of the men who had been with him returned to fill the places in the column they had left empty.

The lighted outskirts of the town gradually blended into the darkened countryside. Expecting momentarily another burst of machine-gun fire, we crouched deep down in the sleigh. Around my heart suspense tightened like an iron band. The tall forest closed in around us and the evergreens, heavily weighted with large pads of snow, looked like hooded ghosts keeping eerie vigil alongside the road. How many hostile eyes followed us concealed in the deep recesses? A blank moon, approaching the last quarter, slid from one sharply silhouetted treetop to the other.

A gunshot cracked jarringly on our taut nerves. A shout sent us grasping for our rifles. Tense, ready at the next command to fire into the shadows at the enemy we could not see, we waited. There followed only a heavy silence, irregularly broken by the creaking of the runners and the soft sound of reins slapping loosely against the horses' flanks. An irrational fear of the recoil of the rifle should I have to fire it suddenly flooded my consciousness. But the continued silence, aching, throbbing, almost unendurable in its persistence, gradually drowned out this fear.

There were no further interruptions and the journey resumed its monotonous pace. My companion fell heavily across the butt of his rifle, fast asleep. His even breathing kept pace with the soft creaking sound of the horse's harness. I put the safety catch on my rifle and, resting the barrel on the front end of the sleigh, took the reins from the boy's hands.

Interminably the night wore on. The effort to stay awake became agonizing. Imperceptibly sleep crept upon me and within minutes it was invariably followed by a painful start back into consciousness. As I hovered between sleep and wakefulness, my head began to swim. Rocks by the wayside, trees and shadows took on strange shapes; they vanished, then abruptly loomed up again in another place. Eventually, with that useless inert form beside me, I found myself sobbing from loneliness. Why could he not keep awake? I wanted to shake him, to shout at him, hit him, claw at him until he sat up to share with me that awful vigil in the night. But finally derision at his weakness, pity, a wave of nausea left me indifferent.

Up front a horse fell in its tracks. It lay there in the deep snow. The sight of its glassy eyes and stiffening legs shocked my thoughts into lucidity. Somebody lost his horse! What if I should lose mine? And, as if to emphasize its weariness, my horse stumbled. It stumbled again. And now, clearly awake, I gathered the reins and, applying the best of my driving skill, I strove to support the poor beast's faltering gait. We passed another horse lying dead in the snow.

It must have been between three and four o'clock in the morning. I noticed a flickering light playing on the horse's ears and the snow became tinted with a bright reddish glow. Where did it come from? I looked back and saw a sea of fire coloring the entire southeastern horizon like a brilliant sunrise. Flames leaped high into the somber sky, like avid tongues. Onega was on fire, the whole town was burning!

Slowly the meaning of the fire penetrated my dulled wits. Those good people, the clean spacious house where we had been so well received and where we were to have spent the night, the generously laid-out supper. . . . Who was responsible for this deed against the peaceful, friendly town? Was it an act of retribution by the Reds, to avenge the escape of the White fugitives? Or was it our side, the Whites, carrying out a scorched-earth policy? Either way, the fire of Onega burned itself deep into my memory of this retreat. Inexperience is the cradle of unreasoning optimism. Now events were forcing me to look upon this military maneuver in another light. Where, when would the ultimate encounter with the enemy take place? Under what circumstances? The hope of reaching safety across the border into Finland suddenly appeared unreasonable. Had Gleb ever thought that this retreat would end successfully? The look in his eyes when we separated just before leaving Archangel on this momentous journey had told me differently, but at the time I had been too eager for action to pay any attention. He had said then, "This, Lisa, is the beginning of the end."

Dawn broke when at last we reached the next village. The glow from Onega still illuminated the sky.

The retreat of what was left of the once-proud northern White army now became a headlong scramble to escape the hot pursuit of the Red forces. Hard on our heels, they poured like spilled water from one village to the other. On the narrow trampled road our column pressed forward, allowing men and horses only a few hours to eat and to rest at long intervals. The once smart Archangel Reserves, the example of loyalty and discipline, finally reached its total dissolution. Nobody marched on foot any longer. What was left of the rank and file rode in the sleighs with the officers. Hardship erased all differences of rank. Horses fell and were dragged to the side of the road. In the villages bitter threats and protests made the requisitioning of horses and supplies difficult. The people knew the Whites were defeated, and to cater to them either by force or out of commiseration was a risk no one could take. The black horse was hardly able to stand any longer and Gleb succeeded in exchanging it for another.

For three more days we forged ahead; the trail behind us was littered with the frozen carcasses of fallen horses. Our men tore down all the wires from the telegraph posts and they, too, lay trailing in the snow. To do away with superfluous baggage, rifles and ammunition were silently dropped through holes chopped in the ice to the bottom of the swamps and creeks. Occasionally the lone figure of an exhausted man sat huddled by the wayside, unable to move. And the fate he was destined to meet after the last sleigh passed him defied speculation.

On the fourth day we met an occasional small group of soldiers still wearing British uniforms with White Army insignia, going home.

"Where are the Reds?"

"Ahead."

"Where?"

"At the railroad."

At last we knew where the meeting with the Reds was to take place. Fighting weariness, the column moved on. With tempers on edge and patience worn to shreds, hope still persisted. Perhaps there was still a chance we might reach the railroad before the Reds were able to amass a sufficient force to stop us. The men braced themselves for the last battle.

All that night the column pushed onward. No longer was I aware of the boy in the sleigh beside me. No longer did I care whether he was awake or asleep. I was entirely alone, the horse and I forming a single link in a long chain of slowly, eternally advancing sleighs. My one sharp sensation was Gleb's presence behind me, though I could not see him. But he was there, and we must not become separated, lost to each other. That alone must never happen. Nothing else mattered.

The next day and the following night the column pressed on without stop, without rest or sleep. At dawn we reached Sumskiy Posad, the last village before the railroad. Somehow I became aware that Gleb was no longer behind me. In a panic I tumbled out of the moving sleigh and began to walk against the flow of men and horses. The passing sleighs crowded me into the snow, but I was past caring, past exhaustion. Only one sensation motivated me, a frantic fear that he was lost somewhere far back. I must find him, dead or alive.

"Gleb! Gleb!" My cries were lost in the cold air as the impassive column moved by.

Innumerable sleighs passed me, but Gleb was in none of them. The last sleigh came by and he was not in that one either.

The road opened before me, empty. How far back before I found him? Oh, God, how far back? Then in the distance I saw a stumbling figure. I ran. It was Gleb, dragging himself toward me.

"My horse fell," he whispered hoarsely, his lips rough and dry. I brought his arm across my shoulders. "Lost my revolver in the snow. Couldn't find it. Found another." He could say no more.

Supporting each other, we walked slowly, stopping and resting often. Finally we arrived at a house. There they told us that the Red Army was in the next village. The long-expected meeting with the enemy was at hand.

"How long have they been there?"

"Two days."

Two days? Clearly this terrible retreat through the vast tracts around the south end of the White Sea had been doomed from the start. And we realized with appalling certainty that the premature fall of the Murman front had made our desperate effort to reach it in time a strategic impossibility. The agonies of the retreat had been suffered in vain.

CHAPTER 17

THE ISSUE OF SURRENDER

GRAY daylight filtered weakly through the windows. But the house was warm and filled with the smell of wood smoke mixed with fresh lumber and tar. It had just been built and had no furniture in it. The owners were absent; the territory had recently been occupied by the Reds and no one knew what had happened to them.

In the crowded room there was no thought of sleep. Worry, anxiety, fear filled our minds. The final decision must be reached on what action to take now, how best to extricate these exhausted men from the claws of a notoriously relentless enemy, from the trap set by defeat. It was a momentous and a brutal decision that involved the lives of all of us.

Nina Aleksandrovna and I sat on our beds on the floor, watching the men. Restlessly they paced to and fro, finding no peace of mind. Occasionally some of them gathered into small groups, discussing the possibilities of a last-ditch breakthrough, assessing the chances of success. No one thought of giving up. When life hangs in the balance, hope, however preposterously illogical, is the power that sustains, the finger that indicates the loophole to success where none exists. Surely there was a way! Finland, the land of safety and freedom, beckoned on the far side of the barrier thrown up by the conquering Red Army. And hope and fear and stubborn determination sometimes do contrive the impossible.

Was it suspicion? Was it a creeping sense of distrust in their senior officers that rendered the waiting intolerable? One by one the men left the house. I watched Gleb walking across the village street, nervous and tense, dragging his left leg slightly, as he always did when excited or upset and his old wound bothered him.

Nina Aleksandrovna and I remained where we were in silence, each of us in paralyzing suspense. Time went by—an hour—much more than an hour.

At last through the window we saw the men returning. They were walking slowly, wearily. Gleb and Aleksandr Dmitrievich entered the room together. No one spoke. Hopelessness, dejection, utter discouragement were written on their faces. Their lips were pressed together in rigid lines. The silence became almost intolerable. At last I heard Gleb's voice:

"It is decided." And then with grim emphasis: "Surrender." The silence closed upon his words like a lid.

Gleb threw himself on the bed. I lay down beside him, wondering uneasily if I were the only one who felt a cowardly relief at the prospect of escaping a deadly engagement. For surrender temporarily removed the sense of impending disaster. It promised at least a postponement of the threatening fatality. At what price was entirely beyond my sphere of experience.

Gleb stirred. He put his arm around my shoulder, and we became wrapped in our own inviolate privacy, detached from the presence of all the others.

"This is an impossible situation!" he whispered in my ear. It was as if for the first time in his life he had faced the notion of giving himself up, and it revolted him. "Everything was decided before we got there," he said bitterly. "They didn't even ask us our opinion. We pleaded with them, reasoned, begged them to change their minds. We begged them to let us fight, whatever the risks."

His words were those of one who had reached the depth of disillusionment, whose faith in those he had believed responsible had been destroyed. Capable, brave men had been ignominiously betrayed and their enthusiasm was being turned to ashes.

"They made that decision without us," he repeated, as if this had been their greatest sin. "The Reds are at Kem, armored trains, machine guns. I suppose it would have been impossible, unless we had been on skis. Few of us would be left to continue on the other side. But this—is this better?"

It relieved him to speak. "The terms of capitulation are reassuring enough, on paper. Those wishing to swear allegiance to the Soviets are promised immediate freedom upon arrival at Moscow. An alternative is not mentioned." He spoke passionately. "How could they let themselves be so duped? A Bolshevik promise! Have they forgotten the Cheka, the firing squads, the terror?" He spoke as if I were not there to hear him. "And yet—I wonder. Was the counterrevolution ever the right way to save Russia? I wonder. . . ."

This was the first time I had heard Gleb express doubt about the wisdom and the merit of anti-Bolshevik politics. Once before in Copenhagen he had hinted, but I thought then that anxiety for Marie's safety had influenced him.

After a long silence he spoke again: "Lisa, I can't do it! I can't! We must try to get away on skis somehow. Wait here!"

He got up hurriedly. The door closed behind him and the sound of his footsteps outside died away.

For a long time I waited. Surrender meant no immediate exposure to danger and death. Surrendering, we would still be together, or so I hoped, and his life would be spared. Courage, what is courage? What is the price of courage? To flee, the two of us alone, what would that mean? A rash plan but worth the risk to be together to the end. I tried to imagine running on skis over unknown trails, hiding, darkness, interception, fighting with the enemy. Would we know how to find our way, how to avoid detection, how to survive?

Gleb's return interrupted my thoughts. "It's no use. Without a compass or maps we can't do it. Oh, Lisa . . ." He hid his face in his hands. I realized that had I not been with him, he would have gone to his death.

"Perhaps later, Gleb." Later! What a dubious notion! But at that moment I wished so desperately for that "later" that I believed my own words.

"Do the Bolsheviks actually mean what they say with their offer of freedom? Is this fate pushing us? It must be—but now I am so tired. . . ." And almost before he had uttered the last word he fell fast asleep.

I awoke with a start to find Aleksandr Dmitrievich standing over us.

"It's time to go, Gleb Nikolayevich."

Gleb sat up. "I'm ready," he said quietly.

Stiff and unrested, we packed together our belongings, rolled up our blankets. We took with us every can of food we could find; where we were going, food was scarce. I adjusted the little package of money and jewelry hidden in the knot in my hair; it represented all our wealth.

"It doesn't show, does it?" I asked Nina Aleksandrovna anxiously, turning around for her inspection.

"No, no, it's all right." She spoke nervously, her hands fidgeting. "They search everything for valuables, even sanitary towels." There was suppressed panic in her voice and for a moment it transmitted itself to me.

The men began to leave the house. Gleb and Aleksandr Dmitrievich went out to harness the horse. The four of us decided to go in the same sleigh. We had not far to go—about fourteen miles.

They had filled the sleigh with fresh hay. The day was cloudy and dull but not cold. Outside the village a soldier in the uniform of the White Army was gathering together our rifles, abandoned by the roadside. By performing this unnecessary service, was he trying to insinuate himself into the favor of the Reds?

Our sleigh moved on slowly. There was no longer any hurry. We talked little. Gleb moved beside me. Suddenly he drew his revolver from the holster. He gazed at it, lips compressed, eyes blazing. Then he threw it as far out as he could into the snow. It fell with a muffled thud. No one uttered a word.

Several of the sleighs in front stopped, and then moved on again. Aleksandr Dmitrievich said softly, "Remember, any fuss is undignified."

We approached the checkpoint. A soldier in Red Army uniform, the first I had ever seen, came toward us. His greenish ankle-length greatcoat flapped loudly against his knee-high boots. A round good-natured Russian face with high cheekbones, expressing neither hate nor pity, looked at us under the peaked felt helmet. The oversized red star in front, sewn on with unmatching thread, suddenly made me think of boys in homemade uniforms playing soldiers in the back-yard. His right hand never let go of his rifle with its fixed bayonet.

"Any arms?" His tone of voice was abrupt but not uncivil.

"Please search," Gleb said quietly.

We got out of the sleigh and gave up our remaining revolvers. The soldier gave Gleb a questioning glance, surprised he had none, but said nothing. He searched the hay under the seat and found five or six cartridges, which he collected and passed to his comrade without a word.

A row developed at one of the sleighs. Voices harsh and strident with pent-up animosity cut into the air, and for the first time in direct conversation I heard the word *tovarishch*—comrade. The faces of Gleb and Aleksandr Dmitrievich expressed nothing but bored indifference.

"All right, move on, follow the others!"

We drove into the town of Kem. At long last we arrived at the Murman Railroad, but in what a vastly different way from that in which we had striven so desperately to reach it! A few people in the streets stood looking at us with strange expressions of fear and pity in their faces; others peered with curiosity from behind the corners of their houses. This was the place, the goal set before our flying column of officers and men by a decamping high command. The cost to get here had been exorbitant in casualties, honor, and freedom. To me the loss of freedom still seemed only a dream, unreal and unimaginable.

They lodged us in unheated barracks at the outskirts of the town. There was a small room at the end of the long dormitory. Four men who had taken possession of it before we arrived immediately offered it to our husbands, and they gratefully accepted this doorless haven of pseudoprivacy. The room was icily cold and there was nothing to sleep on but the bare floor. We were soon busily carrying in the precious hay from the sleigh and spreading it thickly on the floor. Bedding down under the blankets, we huddled close together to generate warmth and comfort. In a few minutes we were asleep, merciful exhaustion obliterating all sensations of cold and the bitter defeat that had turned us into prisoners of the Bolsheviks. . . .

Slowly and reluctantly consciousness returned. And with it came, piecemeal, the full realization of what had actually happened to us, how we came to be here in this dirty barracks, evil-smelling from a multitude of previous uses. Now no longer were we able to feel a hard revolver under the pillow, to find a rifle leaning against the wall to give a sense of armed security. No longer were there horses to harness, endless distances to travel in cramped positions to reach a goal long since disintegrated.

The thoughts mingled with dreams. What strange rot had attacked the White forces to cause all resistance on the whole front from Pinega to Murmansk to deteriorate so quickly? How could that fateful error have been committed that sent the last loyal regiment on a fool's errand to support the already tottering Murman front?

The trend of thoughts persisted. What mysterious ideas had motivated the high command in the first place to carry on the fight on the northern front against wiser counsel after the Allies left? And when the breakthrough came, why did it turn a deaf ear to repeated warnings about what was actually happening? The menace of a serious revolt was temporary and quite manageable, they said. It would pass. And so did the last chance of a safe withdrawal.

The idea would not leave me. And after the final collapse, by what reasoning were arrangements for an orderly evacuation totally neglected and two precious weeks allowed to slip by in idle waiting? Why were the icebreakers permitted to leave Archangel empty, never to return, destroying the last chance of escape? Incredible! And to crown it all, then to send the remainder of the loyal troops, the cadre of the White Army officers, all with a price on their heads, on this fatal wild-goose chase, too late—indeed, at the very moment when the high command itself abandoned ship in the only boat left, the *Yaroslav!*

Gleb stirred, awakening at last from many hours of exhausted sleep.

"Gleb, we were miserably betrayed!"

"Hush, Lisa," he whispered in my ear. "Don't think. Let's just face it together."

Together . . . I desired nothing else out of life but that. Whatever hardships were in store for us, nothing mattered provided we were together. Only this! And I said to him, "Should you be lost to me, and I would not know where to find you, or what had happened to you . . ."

Gleb did not speak. But had I been able to read his thoughts at that moment, I would have known that he had already measured the full implication of these events and had in sober thought accepted the consequences.

There was no rancor against fate when he smiled at me, only love and serenity. "Lisa, I'm hungry! Shall we have something to eat?"

We emerged reluctantly from under the warm blankets into the chill of the dismal barracks. A thin slanting sunbeam penetrated with difficulty the dirty windowpane, announcing that the day was well advanced. Aleksandr Dmitrievich got some water from the guards' enclave. We used half of it to wash ourselves with our handkerchiefs and brewed tepid tea out of the rest. Thus refreshed and sitting cross-legged on our beds of hay, we watched through the doorless opening of our cubicle the figures of our fellow prisoners lounging and moving around among the dirty double-decked bunks in a haze of cold tobacco smoke. Their voices, hushed and dejected, mingled with the sound of their heavy boots tramping on the rotten floor.

For the first time we had unlimited empty hours at our disposal, strangely free from pressure to plan what to do the next hour or the next day. The condition was still too novel to have become irksome. The long idle hours ahead were welcome. And to save energy and enjoy more rest, we crept willingly back under the blankets to sleep, temporarily oblivious of the uncertainties of the future.

A few days later, in the early morning, the prisoners were ordered to line up outside with their belongings. In captivity, where one is bereft of the elemental right to move freely, to plan the next activity in a more or less predictable environment, the dread of change becomes paralyzing. To the prisoner who with enormous effort, ingenuity, and self-constraint has finally adjusted to the situation, any change seems a drastic and frightful threat.

Anxiously I walked close beside Gleb, carrying my bundle, I a minor member of the long column of prisoners shuffling their feet in the snow. I glanced at Gleb's face and a wave of pride and confidence surged within me. There he walked beside me, young and tall, carrying his bundle lightly upon his shoulder. A look of complete tranquillity illuminated his features, as if the surroundings and his defenseless future were matters that could not touch him. On a few other occasions and in the hospital at Archangel I had seen this same expression when conditions through which he must pass became irredeemable. Where, I wondered, did he get that inner strength of detachment and unshaken dignity that no situation, not even the foulest fate, could demean?

The day was bright with the sun shining on the white snow. The trampling of many feet soon destroyed its whiteness. Finally the long column was drawn up alongside the railway tracks and a long train of boxcars. Their sliding doors opened upon grimy interiors built to hold eight horses or forty men. Now they were fitted with wide wooden shelves, one above the other, and a small wood-burning stove stood in the middle of the floor.

Subdued conversations among the prisoners filled the protracted interval.

"Where are they taking us?"

"Petrozavodsk, they say."

"What then?"

"Somebody said an investigation of some kind. Then to Moscow."

"Investigation? What does that mean?"

A shrug, then silence and more waiting.

"Stand up for roll call!"

We stood up with our bundles at our feet. The droning voice of a Bolshevik officer began calling out names, names that from that moment were entered upon the Soviet lists of prisoners, unlikely to become erased except by a successful escape or sudden death.

"Kirilin, Gleb Nikolayevich?"

"Here!"

"Gleb, why didn't they call me?" He gave no answer, only moved a little closer.

The sun dipped westward in the cloudless sky. We sat on our bundles, waiting, talking, and getting hungrier as the day passed. Time was the one commodity in Soviet Russia of which there was never an insufficiency.

"Line up for rations!"

The mere mention of food made our mouths water. Our supplies had dwindled to a few cans of soup and bully beef and a small bag of tea mixed with sugar.

"What are they giving us?"

"Flour, five pounds. Lisa, for heaven's sake, what shall I take it in? They're giving it out loose!"

"Here, take this pillowcase!" someone offered.

Gleb got his flour. "And for my wife?"

"Red Army rations, women don't count!" A leer accompanied the words.

When Gleb came back, Nina Aleksandrovna gave him a sweet smile. "Never mind, Gleb Nikolayevich, with a few cans of soup and ten pounds of flour between us we'll manage until the next time."

Gleb smiled but said nothing. His previous experiences of Soviet

Russia did not permit him to be too hopeful as to the next time.

Late in the afternoon they finally ordered us into the boxcars. There was a furious scramble as everybody tried to get the best place for himself on the shelves. Yet the men did not ignore the presence of us two women. Protecting us from the crush, they immediately gave us the choice places on one of the upper shelves next to the ventilator. With our husbands acting as bulwarks, we were afforded not only a certain measure of privacy, but also the comfort of being near the source of light and fresh air.

We were like sardines packed in a tin. One of us always had to get up to allow the others enough elbow room to turn around. Some of the men had even to forgo the luxury of a small space on the shelves and were forced to huddle on the dirty drafty floor, to await the opportunity of a charitable brief spell on a shelf.

As darkness fell, the guard slipped out and pulled the doors closed. There was a sound of rattling chains and the iron bolt being slipped into its socket. For the first time I experienced the uneasy feeling of being forcibly locked up and robbed of my personal freedom. In the darkness nobody spoke. Somebody moved, trying to relieve cramped muscles; someone else scratched an itchy spot. Drowsiness overtook us until in the middle of the night the doors clanged open to readmit the guard. Soon, jolting noisily, the train began to move.

The distance between Kem and Petrozavodsk was about 220 miles. Months of protracted warfare had scrambled communications and in many places damaged the roadbed, leaving an emergency passage to be negotiated not without considerable risk. This caused many delays and added days to the journey, giving us plenty of time to become accustomed to the cramped and hungry life as prisoners of war.

The mechanism of adjustment in human beings is extraordinarily efficient in making terrible conditions quickly seem not only tolerable but livable! Nights spent fully dressed in no more than a scant foot of space by no means prevented me from awakening in the morning quite refreshed. And a small can filled with melted snow served quite well for washing face and hands. Heavy beards soon accentuated the hollow-eyed look of our companions, although some of them tried desperately to maintain a civilized appearance by shaving crouched over a small mirror in a dim corner. It became a daily ritual for the men to sit stripped to the waist and with concentrated interest pick lice from the seams of their clothing, and the fact that

Gleb and I had so far escaped an invasion of these typhus-carrying parasites was nothing short of a miracle.

The relations between the guards and the prisoners were distinguished by distant civility. No one suffered any reprisals, and any feelings of hostility and fear were fastidiously kept within bounds. The Red officer in charge wore a perpetually worried look on his sallow face, and we regarded our own guard in his oversized tunic as an inoffensive youth, not overly endowed with brains and given to giggles and practical jokes.

Without sanitary facilities of any kind, the scene at the frequent stops was shocking and tragicomic. With a wild look on their faces the prisoners charged out of the doors in a scramble no guard could withstand to secure half a minute's use of the open-air latrines, nothing more than overflowing holes in the ground. With our husbands standing guard, Nina Aleksandrovna and I discreetly retired under the cars, always with grave risk that the train might start up without warning.

The decrease of the pain as we became more or less accustomed to hunger was a surprise and afforded a certain relief. We found also that abstention from unnecessary exertion and longer intervals between the scanty meals likewise reduced discomfort. With our limited store of soup and bully beef almost gone, we had to think of some way to make use of the flour in the pillowcase. Most of the men simply ate the stuff raw. What else could they do? And this probably accounted for the chronically upset stomachs. Without utensils and other ingredients, not even salt, it was a puzzle.

Suddenly, an idea! A frying pan could be fashioned out of an empty can, with a stick for a handle. Soon I was experimenting with a bland batter of flour and melted snow, baking it in the firebox as in an oven. The bannock that eventually resulted stubbornly stuck to the ungreased can, but when pried out at last proved eatable though rather tough. To improve our diet, Gleb and I allowed ourselves possibly the most extravagant luxury of our lives. At one of the stops, in exchange for one of our blankets, we acquired from a peasant woman a small bag of sugar. She walked away hugging the blanket, and no doubt came out the winner of that transaction.

Emergencies often arose to delay progress. Snow sometimes accumulated in huge drifts in front of the train, and the supply of fuel was depleted. Peremptory orders drove the prisoners out to man the shovels or to cut wood from the surrounding forest to stoke the wood-burning engine. These would have been welcome diversions had it not been for the weakening effects of the prolonged fasting. Frequently our train, which was of secondary priority, was hurriedly shunted onto a siding to let by freights with mobs of free-loading passengers clinging like swarms of bees to the ladders and platforms. Or we were pushed aside to make way for northbound troop trains, from which poured the triumphant notes of the "Internationale," the German song of the radicals turned into a Russian hymn. The song sounded strangely foreign when sung by the Russian soldiers with the red stars emblazoned on their helmets, who filled to overflowing the swaying coaches. Constant hairbreadth escapes from threatening accidents and head-on collisions seemed the normal conditions of the Soviet transportation system at this time. We had, in this respect, the kind of unexplainable luck that sometimes favors the persistent gambler.

As the journey progressed, whispered rumors began to circulate among the prisoners. Significant events were due to occur soon and speculations stirred hope. Hints were passed around about the staging of a mass escape now while the transport was still running close to the Finnish border. Help would be forthcoming; secret Allied missions were just across the border, waiting for the right moment to act. There would be a sign.

Freedom! To be abandoned this way in the clutches of an enemy whose hands were notoriously bloody seemed to the prisoners a betrayal unworthy of great nations like the United States, Great Britain, and France. The intervention in northern Russia had been the fond idea of the Allies, Churchill's especially, and it had been directed at the encirclement of the Bolsheviks. It had lured Russian refugees to flock to Murmansk and Archangel. They had been assured the strong backing of the Allied forces, and they had fought together. Then in the dead of the night the Allies had left. The debacle foreseen by many had followed within months. At this time what actually took place must have been well known abroad. Surely there must be a strong feeling of obligation on the part of the Allies to come to the rescue of their former comrades in arms, to snatch them now from the jaws of a relentless enemy. Any other outcome, the prisoners felt, was unthinkable. But Gleb and Aleksandr Dmitrievich shook their heads.

In the middle of the afternoon a loud report suddenly rent the air, followed by a fusillade of explosions. The train jerked to a stop. The engine and the two cars attached to it became detached from the rest of the train, which began rolling backward downhill, gathering momentum. In the rear someone worked frantically at the brakes as the runaway section approached a curve at high speed. Just in the nick of time the brakeman succeeded in bringing the wildly clattering cars to a jolting halt.

The barrage continued, the loud thunder of exploding shells mingled with the angry reports of small-arms fire. We were all on our feet, listening tensely. Was this the sign? The men pushed aside the guard, who was as shocked and curious as they, and jumped down onto the tracks. They began running alongside the cars, trying to see what was happening.

Then the truth dawned on them. The two cars next to the engine, loaded with captured ammunition, had caught fire from sparks from the engine. And as they stood there listening, watching, the look on their faces changed from high elation to bewilderment to despair.

That moment might indeed have been the one single auspicious opportunity for a break for freedom: the guards were distracted, and we were in an isolated wilderness not far from the Finnish border. But no daring leader emerged, and so the moment passed.

The guard locked the doors of the car and the men lay down to sleep, still waiting for the sign. Then a flash, an explosion, and yet another, and the closed car filled with fire and fumes. Everybody sat up.

"What in the name of God?"

The young guard sat by the door with his rifle between his legs, his eyes gleaming in the dim light of the lantern above his head. A mischievous smile played upon his lips. Giggling, he leaned forward and poked the pieces of two spent cartridges from the top of the stove. And the men, no longer believing in the miracle of an Allied rescue mission, turned around and went back to sleep.

At midnight on the seventh day our train rolled noisily onto a siding at Petrozavodsk. The prisoners were allowed to sleep until morning. Anxious thoughts had troubled me during the night and prevented sleep—the terrible dread of the coming change, the menace of the unknown, and the pangs of hunger, for the flour had come to an end twenty-four hours ago.

CHAPTER 18

IN A SOVIET PRISON

THE prisoners poured out of the cars. Seen in the brilliant early March sunshine, the change wrought by seven days of short rations was astonishing. Some of the young and the fit still wore their caps at a flippant angle, still believed in the future, but with sobriety imposed upon their youthful zest. Others, like Gleb, clearly preserved in dress and mien a look of dignity and proud resignation.

Those who wore the stigma of imprisonment most conspicuously were the former commanding officers. Deep lines furrowed their faces, thick stubble on cheeks and chins dulled their features. Gone was the elegance that once had distinguished them, their swagger and arrogance, the air of authority, they who had once commanded the destiny of men whose welfare and lives had depended on their decisions. Now weariness and hunger and remorse had destroyed their confidence and left them haggard and dispirited.

The men lined up four abreast with their bundles at their feet. Gleb found a small abandoned sled by the tracks and we piled our baggage upon it. No one knew how far it was to the concentration camp, and the effects of the starvation diet could no longer be ignored.

Flanked by the helmeted guards, rifles slung upon sagging shoulders, the long line of prisoners began to move ahead, feet shuffling in the snow. Gleb pulled the sled while I pushed from behind. We were a bedraggled pair. Gleb still preserved a soldierly air; an onlooker would have had a hard time telling whether his companion was a man or a woman. A long leather coat reached below my knees and hid my borrowed breeches. The shoulder strap from Gleb's Sam Browne served me as a belt, and on my feet were oversized Shackleton boots of dirty white canvas with thick corded soles. People in the streets stopped to watch us trudging by. Mingled with their covert curiosity was a look of fear. Yet compassion flickered across some of these faces and set them apart.

The sides of my stomach felt as if stuck together from sheer emptiness. But my attention was soon diverted to the new surroundings. Even in these times Petrozavodsk was an attractive town. On its wide streets, among many trees and open spaces, small houses mingled with larger ones, with enough room between them to provide fine views of Lake Onezhskoye. The municipal buildings had obviously been designed by skilled architects. The golden domes of a multitude of churches gleamed richly in the sun. Passing them, the prisoners reverently crossed themselves.

How far could it be to the concentration camp? Surely, there at last we would eat!

The long lines of prisoners were finally brought to a halt outside the tall ornate iron gates of a large building situated on a height with a panoramic view over the town and the lake. We sank down on our bundles with sighs of relief. The concentration camp at last. Before the Revolution it had been a seminary. An immense Greek Orthodox cross with its slanted crossbar still shed its golden blessing over the Gothic portals. But behind the tall iron fence another brotherhood now crowded the spacious grounds, a brotherhood of suffering, of physical and mental captivity. These men thronged against the fence, clasping the bars with bony hands, to stare at the new arrivals. The expressions on their gaunt, unshaven faces were frightening and pitiful, some crafty, some depraved, all bitterly hostile. Was the stamp of imprisonment already so plainly written on our faces?

The concentration camp soon refused to admit any more prisoners. The last ones to enter the gates were Nina Aleksandrovna and her husband. We were ordered to march on. Wearily we picked up our bundles. Where to now? Someone whispered, "To the prison of Petrozavodsk." In my ignorance I hoped that the prison would prove to be a less depressing place than the concentration camp.

The forbidding gates of the prison were swung open and banged closed behind us. Prison guards surrounded us on all sides, a dirty-looking crew with high cheekbones and untrimmed whiskers. One was clad in blue breeches, another in khaki ones, one wore a military tunic, the next one a belted Russian blouse, one high boots, another clumsy straw shoes. Only one item was worn by all: a black leather belt with a revolver in a trim holster. Apparently this place too was overcrowded. Again we sat down on our bundles and waited.

The warden appeared. He came into the yard with his hands deeply buried in the slanting pockets of his black leather jacket. The jacket looked new, and so did his khaki breeches. His high boots were polished to a gloss. He was a square, short, powerfully built man, but the shape of his legs suggested a serious bout with rickets in his infancy. His wide-set eyes, high cheekbones, and large mouth contradicted the weakness of his receding chin. Still his face was not unpleasant. Its roughness was relieved by an unexpected glint of humor.

"Hmm, women!" he muttered.

Then I discovered to my surprise that there were other women in our group of prisoners, and I wondered where they had come from. One was a tiny, timid-looking mother with two girls about ten and twelve years old. They huddled close to their father, seeking the protection he was unable to give them.

The prisoners clamored for food. The warden grinned and raised his hand reassuringly. "You'll have dinner in a moment, you're just in time. Now quiet, please!"

Presently the warden separated about twenty of us from the others, including three couples, the two children, and a single woman. The latter was a handsome middle-aged person, her face framed with gray hair. She was wearing lipstick. She looked like an actress, and later I found out that she was one. Actresses in Soviet Russia were a privileged class of people. How she fell in with our disreputable company, I never discovered.

"Gleb, they're not going to separate us, I was so afraid they would!"

"No, darling, just keep calm. *Tout vient à point . . .*" He never finished the saying.

Smells are far more than indicators of what may be pleasant or unpleasant. They are also characteristics of lands, people, places, dwellings, and situations, and when encountered they can recall often with wonderful subtlety, sometimes with great insistence, certain situations and events of the past. The smells of Russia were mainly of the good earth, the tangy scents of forest and open steppe mixed with the refreshing essences of water and frost, and the delicate odors of burning charcoal around the ever present samovars. The Revolution added the smells of greased boots and *makhorka,* a cheap pungent tobacco that impregnated hair, clothing, trains, buildings, the very outside air with its heavy musty odor.

When the door clanged open upon the inside prison passage, the prison stench hit me full in the face. It filled every breath, hesitantly drawn, to sicken the stomach. The walk down that foul passage was an almost intolerable ordeal.

Then dimly, through the haze and the stench, I saw the barred iron doors and behind them crowds of pale-faced disheveled men staring at us with expressions that shocked me beyond words. Surely such faces belonged only to fiction, to antirevolutionary propaganda! These grotesque masks, eyes burning like coals in sunken sockets, possessed something of medieval horror. Brutish yet pitiful, they aroused the most profound compassion. The men began shouting words I could not understand. Gleb's expression hardened as he looked stonily ahead, and his hand in mine shook slightly.

One of the guards touched the gun at his side. "Shut up, you dogs!" His command met with loud mirthless laughter.

Near the end of the passage a key scraped in a lock. An iron door opened, and we filed into a rather large room. The door closed upon us, the key rattled in the lock. Some time later the guards brought an enormous bowl of soup, a pitcher of steaming water, and five loaves of bread. We sat down at a long table. With gluttonous eagerness that not even the stench could dampen, we pounced upon the food. We did not notice the dishwater consistency of the soup, in which an odd small fish floated whole amid strands of green weeds, its glassy eye staring blankly. Neither did the tea seem too weak, brewed as it was from a few tea leaves found in somebody's pocket. With relish we sank our teeth into the coarse black sour-dough bread. An Epicurean repast could not have been more satisfying or have tasted better than this first prison meal. For the first time in a week we ate well.

Having finished, we sat back in relaxed contentment and our spirits rose. We even found courage to joke about our predicament. Whatever other drawbacks affected Soviet prison life, we observed, we could at least count on being fed.

In other days this room obviously had been the prison library. We could count the nail holes and marks on the walls where the bookshelves had been. The room was about fifteen by twenty feet, large enough for all twenty of us without being too crowded. The sun shone brightly through the large barred window looking out over the snow-covered roofs of the town to the lake and the horizon beyond. The naked walls had in the course of time become the keeper of records, dealing with personal data, thoughts, and events concerning the occupants. Awkward tracings gave grim evidence of human courage and crushed hopes. Names had been painstakingly inscribed at odd angles together with relevant dates and a cross of finality. A multitude of comet-like strokes drawn with blood where a bedbug had been crushed to death crisscrossed many of these records.

With their usual consideration the men arranged for the mother and her two daughters a good place to sleep off the floor on two benches pushed together. The rest of us camped on the floor. The space under the table was at a premium, as it provided some protection from the bedbugs that dropped from the ceiling. Gleb and I found a corner of comparative privacy up against the wall, but there was no escape from the bedbugs.

I needed to go to the bathroom.

"Gleb, what will I do?"

"Ask one of the women to go with you, call the guard!"

He called the guard himself. The key rattled in the door and the actress and I walked down the corridor. At the lavatory a sudden terror seized me. I dashed back to our door and shook it.

"Gleb, I daren't. There's a hole in the door!"

A guard came up hurriedly. Quietly Gleb explained what was the matter. The guard smiled indulgently and permitted Gleb to accompany us to stand outside the door.

The sewage system of the prison must have been out of order for a very long time. The bowls, mounted on a dais level with the peephole in the door, looked like thrones. A stinking overflow poured in rivulets down from the dais along the walls under the door out into the passage, revealing the source of the unspeakable stench. Sick with disgust, we picked our way between the streams and returned to our room.

In vain we waited for supper. At last we realized that the one midday meal we had devoured was the ration for the whole day. Tomorrow we would know better than to eat so greedily.

When twilight came, lanterns were lit and shone dimly in the corridor, but the cells remained dark. A rumbling noise was heard, doors opened and banged closed. An evil-smelling wooden tub sodden with urine was pushed inside our door. The men surrounded it defensively.

"Not here with women. Get it out!"

"Call the warden!"

Shrugging, the guard muttered something about the damned bourgeois. The warden appeared and in a quiet authoritative manner reassured the men. It was not necessary to use the tub, of course. Anyone wishing to leave the cell during the night could just knock on the door. The guard would let him out. Obviously political prisoners were treated differently from criminals, and the Petrozavodsk warden observed the rule. Many of us took this as a promising sign.

The contrast between this practical and efficient man and the deplorable state of his prison was incongruous. Clearly, poor administration was not the reason for either the breakdown of the sanitary system or the starvation rations. The economic chaos that followed the Revolution, the incompetence of a government bent on establishing drastic changes in mores, philosophy, and social order overnight, the political brutalities inevitable with such a course, these and a host of unfavorable consequences made impossible the normal functioning and organization of any part of life, prison management included. Everything had ground to a standstill, repairs, maintenance, the production and transportation of food supplies. The warden worked with existing means under the heavy pressure of extreme overcrowding, filth, and corruption, and under the circumstances his performance was commendable. And with his surprising display of discretion he proved, all evil tales to the contrary, that humane prison wardens did exist in revolutionary Russia.

Appeased, we went to sleep. The faintly snapping sound of vermin dropping from the ceiling, the monotony of the guards' footsteps walking up and down outside the door, the sudden scream of a nightmare-ridden inmate in another cell occasionally broke in upon my sleep.

Two days later, just after we had returned from exercise in the prison yard, a guard ordered the women to pack their things.

"To the warden's office, you and your husbands!"

The sudden possibility of separation terrified me.

"Ask them—beg them for special permission for me to stay with you!"

Gleb's voice was very soft. "Darling, don't you see, we'll still be in the same prison, and they'll let me visit you after a while," he reassured me.

"I can't bear it!"

"This may also mean that they'll put us both in better quarters." Gleb put his hands on my shoulders. "Imagine my Lisa in a Bolshevik prison! What will the aunts and cousins say when they hear of it?" He smiled. But he quickly changed his tactics: "Seriously, Lisa, don't you see that without me you are innocent? Don't you see what that means? They'll have to set you free. While you are in prison you can do nothing—free, you will at least have the chance to work for my release. Your freedom is important for both of us."

Tears dropped wet and warm on my hands as I put my things together.

"Take everything, Lisa. All I need is a blanket and perhaps a small pillow."

Another tear dropped, and the act of putting away into a corner these pitiful items for him, all he would need when I was gone, released a flood of them. And with humility in my heart I realized at last that all my fierce insistence on sharing his hardships could not match in quality the love drawn from his decency and remarkable calm.

In the office the warden sat at his desk, his red-starred helmet on his head. The place was surprisingly neat and clean, the air heavy with tobacco smoke.

"Please, open your bags for inspection." His voice was firm and polite.

So it was not enough for him to separate us? Search, you devils, search! Outraged, I seized the canvas bag, tipped it upside down, and shook out its contents on the floor. Aghast, I watched my father's precious portfolio with all our love letters and Gleb's manuscripts tumble out on top of boots, sweaters, and shirts. Before I could think of a way to hide them from view, the warden pounced on them. Everybody stood rigid in deep silence.

The warden glanced through the manuscripts and then threw them one by one back upon the pile of clothes. I sighed with relief. Then he picked up the portfolio and with curiosity examined its blazing coat of arms. At length he opened it and slowly turned over the letters.

"With your permission, citizeness, I'll keep these."

I pleaded in French: "They're only our love letters—only our love letters! I swear! Gleb, tell him!" But Gleb stood silent.

"When we have inspected these papers, we'll return them to you." The warden's manners were faultless, but I knew then that they were lost forever.

"Our love letters, Gleb . . ." I could not finish the sentence. His stony face confronted me. Gradually I realized Gleb's hurt and the possible consequences of my rash act. I could not think clearly. But to Gleb with his intimate knowledge of Soviet Russia the meaning of the event presented no mysteries. And yet when he held me close as we took leave of each other, the hard look had vanished from his face.

"Just keep calm, darling! The advantage is all on their side, the disadvantage all on yours. Don't let go of your one good weapon—a level head."

CHAPTER 19

THE ESSENCE OF LIBERTY

"WELCOME, comrades in misery!"

These words, uttered with studied dramatic effect, came from a large formless woman in striped prison garb, standing in the bare cheerless kitchen of the annex where the women prisoners were held. A hardened harlot might well have possessed that face of coarse features, flushed blotchy red. Upon her ample heaving bosom a rosette of red ribbon was prominently displayed. She stood there and with obvious relish and considerable dignity performed her self-assigned role of welcoming committee of one.

Following so close upon the ordeal at the office, the comedy of the scene caught us unprepared and we burst out laughing. For an instant the woman looked perplexed. Then, resuming her role, she advanced one step, her face wreathed in the smile of the charming hostess. But the words she was about to utter died on her lips as the matron intervened impatiently:

"What are you doing here, Manya? Back to your cell, quick!"

Thus abruptly stripped of her role, the woman scuttled sheepishly down the corridor to the right.

The women's section of the prison was housed in a low, broad-beamed bungalow built of sturdy logs, stained brown inside and out. Before the Revolution it had been the prison hospital. The passage to the right led to a row of cells, some of which faced south, with the sun streaming through regular-sized windows. To the left was a small apartment, formerly used for the isolation of patients. A short passage led to two rooms. At the end of the passage was a cramped lavatory, the cleanest we had encountered so far. A stout door closed off this part from the rest of the house.

The matron ushered us into these rooms with the fussiness of an annoyed hen mustering around her a flock of wayward chicks. In the stark prison environment this tiny round matron seemed a quaint figure. Framed by a somber silky kerchief, its ends wound around the neck, her gray steady eyes looked out from a wrinkled unemotional face. A black shawl was crisscrossed over her breasts.

The eleven women taken into the apartment to the left were either wives or relatives of counterrevolutionary Whites or simply former residents of the conquered territories, all detained for political reasons. We soon discovered that the matron carefully discriminated between the common lawbreakers in the cells and the victims of political vicissitudes. We enjoyed free use of the whole apartment, and the door leading to the other part of the house was not locked in the daytime. Tacitly the matron put us on trust, and we were careful not to take undue advantage of her confidence. Only at night, after she had removed the last samovar, we heard the key turn in the lock and the heavy sense of imprisonment descended upon us.

The rations given us were also of a different class. At breakfast each of us received a pound of heavy black bread brought in on a wooden tray scrubbed white. By dividing it into three equal parts, we checked any temptation to gobble up the day's ration at once, although it took some self-control not to filch from the portions set aside. Dinner at noon provided the single variation of the menu: a green fish soup, served day after day. A simmering samovar accompanied each meal. Prisoners were supposed to provide their own tea. Having no friends or relatives in this strange town who might bring some welcome variation to the frugal diet, we soon used up every scrap of tea we possessed, and nothing remained for us to do but to let our imaginations create tea out of the hot water.

One day I was called upon to bandage the finger of an inmate in the other part, who had cut herself. She was a thin dark creature by the name of Anyuta. Two enormous brown eyes glowing from hollow sockets illuminated her pale emaciated face. She shared a small cell with Manya, the woman who had greeted us on our arrival. At the sight of me Manya went into a dramatic emotional display.

The cut in Anyuta's finger was trifling. A little blood trickled from it upon the dirty floor. But Manya and Anyuta made the most of it. Turning reproachful eyes heavenward before one who might listen, they called upon God with loud cries, thus relieving themselves of their accumulated burden of suffering and humiliation.

"She cut herself," wailed Manya, wringing her hands. "Look—the blood! My God!" And she heaved another sigh that shook her whole gelatinous body.

"Shut up!" came the matron's crisp command. "Let the lady attend Anyuta! Step aside!"

Manya heaved another deep sigh and reluctantly retired into a corner. I began bandaging Anyuta's finger. She oh'd and ah'd and her large velvet eyes eloquently expressed her woe. I told her that the cut was not serious and would soon heal. Like a stray whose injured paw is being tended, she abandoned herself to the small portion of sympathy that was hers at long last.

While we were thus occupied, the inmate on kitchen duty pushed a bowl of soup and two mugs with hot water inside the door. The matron left to supervise the serving of the food. I glanced at the soup. It was black. Manya emerged from her corner.

"Look, this is the soup they give us!" she hissed, seizing the bowl with her two hands and carrying it over for my closer inspection. "It's black, cooked blood. Blood," she repeated, and her voice became loud and strident. "This is what they give us to eat—soup of blood! Taste it, smell it!" She held the bowl up under my nose. "My God, what times! Starvation! Soup of blood!" The red rosette on Manya's bosom shook as she delivered herself of this impassioned speech with all the skill of an accomplished tragedienne.

"But you get bread also, don't you?" I said in an effort to lead the conversation away from the nauseous soup. "And tea?"

"Warm water, tea never. Three-quarters of a pound of bread. And those of us who have no one in the whole world to help—oh, my God, take pity upon us, for we are starving!" Anyuta's big eyes bore mute witness to the truth of Manya's pronouncement.

The return of the matron put an abrupt end to our conversation, and I left Manya and Anyuta to live out their sentences of miserable starved prison life.

The days dragged by almost tracelessly. A pack of cards tucked away in the top of my stocking, having passed through the search at the office undetected, proved a merciful diversion. Once again shuffling the cards and laying out another solitaire filled many a tedious hour. The actress became my interested watcher and adviser. At the sound of steps in the passage we quickly swept the cards under the blanket. The matron never spotted the strictly forbidden cards—or if she did, she gave no sign.

Had it not been for the gnawing hunger pains, our life in the prison might have been quite tolerable. But starvation upsets the emotional balance, nerves become abnormally sensitized, the mind becomes depressed. Hunger pains came in waves, never allowing forgetfulness. Sometimes, with almost masochistic enjoyment, we would indulge in animated conversations about fine foods and delicacies. The women who were blessed with phlegmatic dispositions bore it best, for they took things quietly, exerting themselves as little as possible. But those whose temperaments were high-strung suffered from fits of sobbing that alternated with hysterical gaiety. Occasionally I caught myself standing by the window, tears running down my cheeks. At other times I would fly into a rage directed at no one and nothing in particular other than our predicament.

About this time, I believe it was, feelings of bitter hatred began to pervade my thoughts. At first it took the form of impatient disgust with a people who allowed themselves to be pressed into accepting without protest the destruction of ordinary civilities in the name of the proletariat. These feelings of repugnance were not concerned with the general political situation, with the hostility of a despoiled upper class set against the triumphant masses, or with simple resistance against a ruthlessly aggressive revolution and the emergence of a new order. Mine was an entirely private and personal hatred that emanated directly from my own personal experiences and outrage.

It came to life during the nights when I heard the two little girls whimpering from hunger, and their timid mother—hungrier than they, for she had given them much of her own ration—trying to whisper soothing words to them while sighing softly over her own helplessness. It overwhelmed me as I lay thinking of Gleb, of his patient courage, of our enforced separation, and of the unthinkable dangers facing him. From these feelings it was a short step to seething rage at the mere sight of a red star, a red flag, the hammer and sickle, a black leather jacket. Hate is a disease that invades the body and the mind, causing acute physical malaise. It is like a poison spreading and embittering the thoughts, destroying all rationality, defying intelligence and judgment.

But these feelings were not yet fully crystallized or completely understood. Like a sickness that passes and then recurs again, they vanished for a time and then returned. Adjustment is a compulsive reaction that seeks to maintain balance in defiance of the pressure to yield and give up. And thus, almost without realizing it, I gradually learned to endure the confinement and the short rations. Having reached this stage, I found relief in the ability to laugh at various comic and absurd incidents, even at my bursts of anger.

Once my fellow prisoners and I overcame our objections at being forced to chop wood, we began to look forward to these half hours of exercise every day outside in the bright sunshine of the early spring. At the matron's command we would rush out and begin swinging our axes with an alacrity that was almost too strenuous for our starved bodies. The resurging appetite led us to commit acts that would never have entered our minds otherwise.

Thus, on my way through the kitchen after one such session of wood chopping, I spied a small pile of cooked potato peelings on the table beside the stove. Alone for a brief instant, I pounced on them and greedily devoured them before anyone discovered the theft. Another day the matron, frying pancakes with the gray prison cat sitting watching on the table by the stove, left just as the actress and I came walking through the kitchen. The fragrance from the pancake spluttering softly in the pan was too much. One look at each other was enough. The sizzling pancake was seized, torn in two, and swallowed before it had time to burn our fingers. At this instant the matron returned. We stood rigid. Had she seen?

"Who took it?" she demanded.

The actress pointed a slender finger at the cat, her face a study of innocence. "The cat," she whispered accusingly, as the animal blinked its green eyes and licked its chops.

But as we quickly withdrew to our own quarters, we heard the matron muttering, "Have to watch everything in this place or it disappears the moment your back is turned."

Every so often the matron ordered us out to carry water from the well just outside the wall of the main prison. This was fun. We swung along in single file, carrying between us on our shoulders a long pole from which a bucket danced on a rusty chain, with the matron bringing up the rear. A scaffold with a winch served to lower the bucket noisily into the well. Spring-clear water splashed from the returning bucket and it froze around the well head, making the ground slippery.

One day we met some of the men from Archangel on the same errand. Suddenly the idea struck me that the next time I might perhaps meet Gleb. And it did happen. Catching sight of him from a distance, I left everything and rushed to him. No one could have stopped me. The unbelievable joy at the mere touch of him drowned all planned questions.

"Are you well?" I repeated breathlessly, quite unable to think of anything else to say.

"Don't worry about me. Quick, now back to the others! We don't want any trouble," he whispered, smiling, as he tore himself away from me.

The men helped us to fill our buckets, but I had no eyes for anyone but Gleb. In a moment he stood beside me again.

"Arrange with your matron to send messages to me every night. She's doing it for some of the others. Send a pail of soup, slip a note with it. I'll return it." He fell back into line with the others.

"Come on, there!" With a jolt the command brought me down from the clouds. I joined the actress and we marched off, the bucket swinging between us and spilling much of the water.

That afternoon my playing cards remained idle under the pillow. I was too busy. I found a tin can and made a handle out of a piece of wire. I filled the little improvised pail with some of my fish soup, and one of the women who had a little flour left gave me half a teaspoonful with which to thicken the soup. A piece of paper served as a lid tied on with string. Under the string I slipped a small note written with indelible pencil in my tiniest hand.

In the evening, when the matron came in with the samovar, I followed her out into the passage with the pail in my hand.

"My husband—please, *milaya!*" I begged her in halting Russian.

She looked at me searchingly. Then she gave an almost invisible nod and took the pail.

"Thank you, oh, thank you!" I was so relieved I could hardly pronounce the words. She pushed me roughly aside, but I seemed to detect the glimmer of a smile in her gray eyes.

Nervous and excited, I brought out the cards. The actress edged over, the others gathered around. "You forgot the queen—see, over there!" Oh, yes. My hand shook slightly. What would happen to my note? Would she report our illicit attempt at communication to the warden? Nine on the ten. Would Gleb ever get the soup? Five and six up. Success! Everybody laughed. But the next play went wrong. Shuffle the cards thoroughly! The sound of steps in the passage, away with the cards!

The matron came in and handed me the pail without a word. When she had gone, I loosened the paper covering it and a tiny slip of paper folded over many times fell into my hand. The note ended: "I know how fond you are of sweets, so I am sending you two pieces of sugar. We sometimes get sugar with the Red Army rations. Chin up, dearest, *tout vient à point à qui sait attendre*." In the bottom of the pail, folded neatly in a piece of paper, were two cubes of white sugar.

Two pieces of sugar! Tears streamed down my cheeks as I held his priceless gift in my hand. Two pieces of sugar!

The next day I did business with the actress. We closed an important deal, my two cubes of sugar in exchange for four tablespoonfuls of rolled oats. With infinite care I cooked a mess of porridge that filled Gleb's pail almost to the top. With my note tucked into its hiding place, the matron carried it to Gleb. His note came back:

"Wherever did you get that good porridge? I do hope you did not deprive yourself of anything? That you must not do. It was the best porridge I have ever eaten. I ate and ate until my stomach was full. . . ."

About this time the men succeeded in persuading the warden to allow them two hours' visiting time with us once a week. They arrived Friday afternoon, accompanied by two guards. The meeting took place in the kitchen. Each family sat grouped by itself, but the emotional excitement of being together blotted from memory most of the things carefully planned for discussion during the preceding endless week of separation, and we sat there in silence, just holding hands.

Four weeks passed. With the approach of the vernal equinox, the sun shone strongly. The snow melted slowly and left small piles of sawdust and birch bark outside our windows were we had cut the wood, riding on mounds of unmelted snow. A rumor penetrated to us that the female political prisoners were soon going to be taken before the Petrozavodsk Cheka, the dreaded secret police. Gleb's notes came full of advice.

"Don't let on you speak Russian! When they find you are a foreigner, they will not bother to question you too much. I am sure you will soon be free. As for me, there will be no greater happiness than to know you are safely out of this prison."

The day finally came. In the late afternoon our group was ordered outside with our belongings. Surrounded by guards, we were marched along many streets. The two little girls kept fearfully close to their mother.

They took us into a bare stuffy waiting room in the Cheka building, impregnated with stale *makhorka.* One of the women, starved for a smoke, wheedled some tobacco from a guard. She picked a piece of newspaper from the floor, rolled her cigarette, licked the edges together, and began to puff nervously. A name was called. The timid mother quickly straightened out the crumpled dress of the elder girl before the trio went in through the double doors to face the commissar. When she came out again, her face was paler but she looked relieved. The actress was next. She returned with a small derogatory smile on her lips. Now it was my turn.

The square room was brown, tobacco brown. A few chairs stood scattered around the bare walls, and across one corner a large desk littered with papers spread itself. A regiment of rubber stamps on moist ink pads occupied an entire corner of the desk. Behind it sat the commissar under the benign surveillance of a large portrait of Lenin, draped in red.

The commissar's sharp features suggested keen intelligence. Almond-shaped eyes and pale olive skin betrayed his southern origin. The soft silky blouse he wore would have looked better on a dashing Cossack. A sly expression came into his eyes and my nervousness increased.

The secretary, a fair pleasant-looking young man, placed a sheaf of papers in front of the commissar. He leaned forward, arms resting on the desk.

"Your name, citizeness!"

Meeting his piercing glance, I shook my head. The commissar and the secretary exchanged puzzled glances, then looked at me sharply. I shook my head again.

"Nie ponyemayo," I said. "I don't understand."

"Sprechen Sie Deutsch?" asked the secretary. That didn't suit me at all, so I shook my head again. By this time I heartily disliked being left alone with these two, and I wished I could get the actress in to help me.

"Je parle français." With a series of gestures I got them to understand that out there in the other room was a woman who also spoke French and could act as interpreter. The commissar and the secretary debated the problem at some length. I followed their conversation with smug joy, almost forgetting my nervousness. Finally, with a wave of the hand, the commissar ordered the actress brought in.

She was given a chair beside me and the questioning began. My name? Where did I come from? Why had I gone to Archangel? To join my husband? Why was he there? I heard all the questions, and while the actress translated them to me in French there was time to think over the answers and quickly discuss them before she began translating them into Russian. When questions touched upon Gleb we knew almost nothing. As an interpreter the actress was perfect. With her ability to act she easily gave herself an air of being entirely trustworthy and plausible. We found our play-acting very entertaining.

Soon it was all over. We were dismissed and with smiles of relief withdrew from the presence of the Cheka. After the rest of the women had been interrogated, we were kept waiting for another hour before the secretary appeared.

"*Grazhdanki,* the commissar has found no cause for detaining you. You are all free to go.

Free to go! Warily, lest the reality vanish, we slowly crossed the threshold to liberty. Personal freedom now seemed to me a gift, a special privilege, its full meaning never before fully understood.

But no sooner had this freedom been bestowed upon us than it turned into a liability. What were we to do with it? How were we to benefit from it in this alien place? Dusk was falling, but for us there was no place to go. We stood bewildered.

"We're free to go out in the street without provisions or a place to sleep?" the actress said as though she could not quite comprehend what was happening.

The young secretary looked bewildered. Never before had prisoners just released quarreled with the gift of liberty.

"Let's go back to the prison," someone suggested. "The warden may let us back in."

"How will we find the way? It's getting dark," said someone else. The situation was absurd.

With a persuasive smile the actress turned upon the perplexed secretary. "Young man, you'll have to order the guards to take us back to the prison."

The secretary, relieved to find so simple a solution to the problem, smiled back at her. The unbending guard smiled. Everybody smiled.

"Convey these citizens back to prison," the secretary ordered the guard.

We trooped out of the grim building, surrounded by the relaxed guard. We chatted and laughed slightly hysterically. The sensation of personal mastery suddenly regained was like a heavy wine.

We crowded into the warden's office, taking him by surprise. Perhaps it was his humor that allowed him to waive any objections to our irregular request. Without much hesitation he accorded us the privilege of remaining in the prison as unpaying guests until we found other lodgings.

Once again we took possession of the rooms to the left in the women's part of the prison. The uninviting cells with their barred windows now seemed to us a haven of security and refuge. Again we spread our blankets on the rough boards with a feeling of comfort and lay down to sleep.

I felt strangely elated. What wonderful things I could now do for Gleb! The power of this freedom seemed to me unlimited. Wherever Gleb was taken, I would follow. I would buy his freedom at whatever price. I would never, never let him out of my sight. I would work to secure his lost freedom in all possible ways. Tenacity of purpose was mine, his the patience to endure. By sheer will-power I would force the fulfillment of these dreams.

That night we listened as for a familiar friendly knock for the sound of the matron's key turning in the lock of the door. But it never came.

CHAPTER 20

ON THE WAY TO MOSCOW

GLEB and I sat in the open door of the boxcar, dangling our legs over the edge. The train was moving slowly through the still leafless hardwood forests of central Russia. Our destination was Vologda, the large junction of the main railway lines running east-west and north-south about 225 miles north of Moscow. We had left Petrozavodsk and the prison with its stench and barred windows a few days ago.

Bidding our good matron good-bye, I had impulsively kissed her wrinkled face. "Thank you, *milaya,* for everything." And she had quickly turned away while her hand passed furtively across her eyes.

Most of the women had dispersed. The actress stayed in Petrozavodsk to look for work. The mother with her two daughters had sought permission to go to Petrograd, or Leningrad, as they called it now. There she had grown up and there she might have a better chance to adjust to the new way of life. With a heavy heart she had made the decision, for it meant leaving her husband, whom she might never see again, to save their children.

On the day after our release the rest of us had gone in search of a place to eat and had found a dining hall where the ration cards that had been given us were accepted. It was a dingy, dirty place full of people and the smells of greasy cooking and stale tobacco smoke. Here, unexpectedly, I ran into Nina Aleksandrovna. She told me that she and the other wives of their party had been set free a few days after their arrival at the concentration camp. Two other women were with her now, one of whom, to my surprise, addressed me in Swedish:

"Hello there! Heard of you long before we left Archangel, knew you were Swedish!" Her voice was loud and rasping. "How does this kind of life strike you? Dirt and smells! Heh! Nothing to eat! Ha-ha-ha!"

The words tumbled out of her mouth as if a response was of no particular significance to her. Her laughter was as strident as her speech, and the expression on her face suggested plainly that she considered her own situation a big joke.

Olga Stepanovna Kusnetskaya was tall and dark. Her movements, like her figure, were angular, yet with a certain bold and easy swing that disclaimed awkwardness. Her dark hair was smoothly brushed back from the white expanse of her forehead, allowing only a few frizzy curls to escape at the temples. Laughing, her brown eyes, like two peppercorns, darted around expectantly, seeking applause. Her air of mocking insolence discredited at the same time as it enhanced her personality. At close range a whiff of some kind of drug was noticeable. Ether? Yes, perhaps it was ether.

"This is Zinaida Vasilievna Smirnova," she said, introducing the third woman. "What's your name again? Oh, yes Kirilina. First names? Luisa Oskarovna! I'll call you Luisa. Well, you know the Smirnovs, of course, Archangel Reserves, the crack regiment, *tarra-ram, tarraram!* We're staying at the same place—won't you come too? Of course, we'll all be leaving with our men tomorrow."

Her questions came fast and breathlessly, giving me no time to utter a word. Besides, her last sentence left me stunned.

Seeing my look of consternation, she said, "Oh, didn't you hear? They're all being sent to Moscow by way of Vologda. We've already got permission to go with the transport. It's so easy—just smile, flirt, joke, and they do anything you ask. Ha-ha-ha!"

She went on: "Didn't you meet him, Ivan Zernov, the Cheka commissar? I'll take you over to him as soon as we've eaten." Her voice carried to the most remote corner of the dining room and by now people were beginning to look in our direction. Someone might understand Swedish and could be spying on us.

We finished the gritty buckwheat porridge that, with a slice of black bread, was the only course offered on the menu. Zinaida Vasilievna led the way out, her high heels clicking against the dirty floor. Her finely pointed face was lightly powdered and rouged, her lips carefully traced with scarlet lipstick. Upon her mound of blonde curls perched a small modish hat. I wondered what had prompted her to grab for that hat on the helter-skelter flight from Archangel. The heavy-faced proletarians looked up as her dainty figure passed between the tables and their jaws dropped. A long time had passed since they laid eyes upon such an apparition.

Brushing everybody aside, Olga Stepanovna burst in upon the commissar without ceremony, and I followed, worried and nervous. Nonchalantly she stationed herself on the corner of the great one's desk and forthwith went to the attack. Wheedling and demanding by turns, she was brazen, haughty, and coy. She flattered and she amused him. And with a half-self-conscious, half-patronizing smile, he finally succumbed to her persuasion. He reached out for a piece of paper, scribbled something on it, stamped it, and gave it to her. She grasped it and glanced through it carefully.

"Good! Luisa, there you are! Well, thank you." Her long slender hand brushed her forehead in a mock salute. "See you in Moscow!"

The next morning Olga Stepanovna had us bag and baggage down alongside the train of boxcars that stood waiting on a siding many hours ahead of the supposed departure time. Zinaida Vasilievna had demurred at the early hour, but Olga Stepanovna had insisted:

"These trains may leave at any hour and we don't want to miss this one, do we?"

She spoke from long and varied experience. More than a decade before, she had been a young barmaid in a Finnish café when a Russian general had fallen in love with her. Many years her senior, he had promptly married her and carried her off to live in Russia. At the time of the Revolution she was a widow with a school-aged son. When things became too difficult, she and the boy went to live with her mother in Sweden. There she met Boris Pavlovich Kusnetsky. After their marriage she went with him to Archangel, where she served as a nurse at the military hospital. Life had its points, she conceded. And that was true enough. But she was not one of those who just sat and waited for things to happen and then lamented when they went wrong. She had a strong predilection for the assisting action, the push, and a talent for organization.

In the short time available to us before we left Petrozavodsk, she managed to unearth from the caches and cellars of smugglers and speculators enough food supplies to last us for a few days. By means of secret and hard bargaining, she had acquired bully beef, cereal grains, and bread, which we divided between us. Afterward, along the way, we expected to pick up additional supplies from the people always to be found around the stations, looking for opportunities to barter foodstuffs for goods.

When the prisoners at last arrived, Olga Stepanovna's husband, unable to contain himself, rushed up to her, trying to catch her in his arms. But she evaded him and instead set upon the Red officer in charge of the convoy. She applied the same tactics that she had used on the commissar to extort from him the privileges she had in mind. Responding to her banter with hearty guffaws, he allowed our four husbands to ride with us. There was plenty of room, as only a score of Danish prisoners were assigned to share the boxcar with us. These men had served as volunteers on the Archangel front and after its collapse had been taken prisoners by the Reds at Onega.

Boris Pavlovich, tall and distinguished-looking, with an aquiline nose and fluid brown eyes, followed his wife's every move with an adoring gaze. Every so often he lunged at her to capture a kiss. But she only brushed past him, laughing, too busy arranging, organizing, unpacking their belongings in a carefully chosen corner of the upper shelf.

With Gleb's arms around me for the moment, the world was shut out. The train ran smoothly along the wide tracks, the sun shone warmly upon us. The ground was bare, only here and there in deeply shaded places a few patches remained of honeycombed crystallizing snow forming tiny droplets as it melted. Last year's grasses, flattened under the winter's heavy carpet of snow, were drying. Tender shoots of new green grass and the budding heads of spring flowers were pushing through into the light. The fragrances of rotting vegetation and promised blossoms reached us in elusive whiffs.

A wayward spark from the engine had set a small grass fire alight near the tracks. Blue smoke curled into the air, tiny flames licked at the dry grass and twigs, but the sun stole their shine away and they fizzled out in the melting snow water.

"Isn't she bewitching?" Gleb spoke dreamily, addressing himself rather than me, but I knew what he meant. Then thoughtfully he began to speak, pausing often between sentences. And this mono-

logue, together with the fragrances, the gentle motion of the slow-running train taking us into the heart of Russia, and the warmth of the sun, formed at this moment a strangely complete solitude.

"I've been thinking over things a great deal these weeks in prison," he began, "about my childhood, those wonderful days in Tsarskoe Selo, our family—affectionate, close, the happiest family—and our life so simple and unpretentious. Sunshine every day, it seems to me now." He smiled. "Then the years at Petrograd when my father was the head of the Military Academy and Volodya was in the Corps des Pages." He passed his hand across his eyes as if to recall more vividly these cherished memories. "Volodya was the one of us most like Mother, gentle, affectionate, sensitive, submissive. Boris and I were at school, Marie was just a baby.

"And then came the time for Boris and me to enroll in the Corps des Pages. Boris was handsome. And headstrong too. He did all right, but I wasn't much of a success." He chuckled softly. "I didn't like the swagger and arrogance of the seniors. The discipline seemed unnecessarily rigid. I would refuse to submit and got punished, of course, always in disgrace. I despised the professors for their favoritism and their fawning attitudes." He lost himself in thought.

"Yet, you know, I was very proud to belong to that famous exclusive college. And when I was chosen as *Kammerpage* to the Grand Duke Nikolai Nikolayevich, I was elated and flattered. My first assignment to the Winter Palace was at a gala dinner for the Persian shah. We pages looked so smart in our gold-braided tunics. We wore white pants that had to be drawn on wet so they'd fit skin-tight without a wrinkle. The patent-leather boots reached above the knee. Yes, we looked very smart. In every looking glass I passed, I remember, I admired my reflection." He chuckled softly. "Standing at attention behind the chair of my grand duchess was boring. So I amused myself with fantasies about anyone I thought looked strange or funny, and it helped the time pass. I dubbed the shah *le chat,* the cat. He looked like one." He laughed again.

"But then I began to think more seriously about all this . . . the pompous ceremonies, the people crowding in the anterooms of the tsar, the flattery, the glib talk. And the insincerity of it struck me. I didn't think the tsar should be kept so remote from the people behind this barrier of courtiers and selfish advisers. And the appalling extravagance! I felt it was wrong. It was false, the ideas at the bottom of the whole grand ritualism were distorted. Yet I couldn't define my objections. The contrast between the life of the aristocracy and the life of the common people had not yet occurred to me, simply because it was part of Russian life, always had been since the beginning of history. But I had a secret longing to find the truth about all this. It had really nothing to do with politics, but with the arts, the culture, the traditions, the land of the Russian people." For many minutes he sat looking at the passing landscape, a half-smile playing about his eyes as he gazed into the distance.

"Nothing thrilled me more at this time of my life than bravery . . . recklessness. I longed for the opportunity to do brave deeds. My father, grandfather, uncles, all were officers, and bravery was a part of the military traditions of our family. When the time came for me to join a regiment, I had set my heart on joining the Fourth Fusiliers, considered the smartest regiment of the Imperial Guards. Volodya belonged to it. But my father would not hear of it. I was furious.

"Then the war broke out. Suddenly things moved quickly. I found myself in a world of gallantry and courage. The old regimental traditions were put to the test." Gleb sat lost in the memories of those bloody days, Galicia, his comrades falling all around him, Volodya killed and he himself badly wounded on the same battlefield. And he learned what war was, this monstrous brutality mankind perpetuates upon itself, spurred by the most primitive of all passions—greed and hate.

"And they stood the test," he went on. "Then came the debacle, my family broken, destroyed. The Revolution shattered everything in my life—future, faith, the very foundation of our world uprooted and overthrown. I feel like a man who has fallen through the ice and is clutching desperately and in vain with his bare hands at the life-saving edge. All that my education and training commanded me to cherish and to fight for is subverted or wiped out. Now I am wondering—I am in doubt. Did the old traditions actually destroy themselves? Why should the whole structure of history—experience added upon experience—suddenly crumble? Why should the loyalties we grew up with and learned to honor be disparaged? And we ourselves be debased to useless encumbrances, doomed to total liquidation?" His voice was suddenly low and bitter. "Are these new standards actually any better, any more realistic, more adequate, or more viable than the old ones? I'm confused, Lisa! Which way leads out of the wilderness?" He fell into a brooding silence. It was some time before he spoke again:

"I know the change is inevitable. Why it is inevitable I don't know. But the old ways and the old style of living must change. There is no other way. Tolstoi recognized it long ago. The old system has lost its purpose and meaning, it has no longer any validity as the fundamental direction for Russia and our people to follow. Too narrow. The base must be broader, it must take in more people. Thinking, attitudes, and goals must change, and I want to work for it . . . for the creation of a new Russia. Kerensky saw that change must come. Autocracy was denounced and a new way of democratic rule devised. But the result was too vague, too superficial, too closely attached to the old. It could not, it did not arouse the necessary confidence. And so it was quickly smothered.

"Only exceptional men succeed in turning a vision into reality. Kerensky was not one of them. Perhaps he lacked the imaginative idealism and the iron-willed statesmanship. I don't know. Besides, history has shown that the initiation of drastic social change by an uprising against a long-established order too easily turns into a bloodbath."

Deeply immersed in thought, he sat silent until in the end a lovely smile illuminated his face.

"Spring," he mused softly, "springtime, the birth of new life!"

For a long blissful week we traveled across Russia; we saw it starved, ravaged, bleak, yet full of the special enchantments that belong to pristine nature and are indestructible. The warm weather, the soft sunshine, and our happiness at being together every minute of those unforgettable days took the sting out of the lice, the inadequacy of the rations, even the presence of the guards. In our car the social atmosphere was easy and congenial, like that of a large family bent on roughing it together with good cheer. Friendly even with the guards, we lost some of the sense of captivity.

We approached the end of the journey, but this time the prospect of impending separation did not seem so frightening as before. The fact that, instead of being dispatched to some peripheral region where in these days prisoners were often shot "by mistake," our men were being transferred to Moscow, the center, was a highly reassuring circumstance. We felt strong and in good spirits. Our capacity to deal with difficulties had improved considerably. Once the final investigations began, we hopefully believed, the end of our separation would surely not be too long delayed.

The train slowed down for a stop at a small station and across the flat landscape the low outline of Vologda was etched against the horizon. An old peasant woman stood by the tracks with a large round loaf of bread in her arms. As Gleb spotted her, he quickly took the green scarf I held out to him, jumped off before the train stopped, and raced to her. For a moment they were locked in argument. A minute later Gleb triumphantly reboarded the car with the freshly baked crusty loaf of bread held tightly in his hands.

What a prize! A large piece for Gleb to take with him and a smaller one for me would fill our greatest needs for the next few days. I got a knife to cut it.

"Wait, Lisa, let me!" Gleb grasped the knife, cut the loaf of bread in half, and before my unbelieving eyes offered the Danish lads one of the halves.

"But Gleb!"

He cut me short. "Here," he said to the Danes, "take this, divide it among yourselves." Then he turned to me. "Would it be right for us to keep all this bread to ourselves?" he asked simply. "These men are starving." And I had no answer.

As the train rumbled into the railway yard of Vologda, to avoid running into any inquisitive police, we four wives prepared to leave the train. One by one we slipped from the slowly moving car and the men pushed our baggage out after us. For a moment I stood looking after their car, jolting over the switch away from us. And then, stumbling across tracks and ties, we eventually made it safely into the town. There, somewhere, Nina Aleksandrovna had a friend who might be able to find us a place to stay.

Passion Week! In the midst of a pagan revolution, Vologda appeared strangely pious. The peel of numerous bells, large and small, made the warm air of the evening vibrate. And from the many churches, their golden domes glimmering in the rays of the setting sun, the notes of ancient hymns carried their Easter message across the town and out over the land beyond.

In the open door of a church we lingered for a while, listening to the chimes. From within wafted chilly air laden with incense.

Under the arches we could see the blue smoke issuing and diffusing from the swinging censers. In the background the golden iconostasis gleamed dimly through the haze and mitered priests in rich black and silvered robes moved solemnly around the altar. Here and there along the walls and around the pillars halo-crowned icons, once jewel-studded, shone with a tempered glow within their circles of flickering candles. Shadowy worshipers moved softly from one icon to the next to offer it a kiss and place a lit candle securely into an empty socket. Men and women stood or knelt on the ice-cold stone floor. Others, gripped with emotion, prostrated themselves several times, humbly touching the floor with their foreheads. There was hushed gentle movement, a constant coming and going in and out of the wide-open doors. The priests' monotonous chanting and the resonant voices of the hidden choir filled the holy room.

We found Nina Aleksandrovna's friend without difficulty. It so happened that she was a member of the House Committee, the inquisitive agency set up to handle the affairs of each house, whose members decided who should and who should not share the severely rationed living space in the building. Without undue publicity she was able to put us up in a small room, undoubtedly a hazardous gesture of hospitality on her part.

Our room boasted few more conveniences than the boxcar we had just left. Two twisted bedsteads represented all the furniture. They resisted every effort to straighten them out, so again we had to bed down on the bare floor. Nevertheless, the place was a refuge. It was clean and afforded us a measure of privacy. We succeeded in prying open one of the tightly nailed windows to let in the fresh air and the sweet smell of the budding linden trees along the avenue.

The next morning exacting tasks lay ahead of us, including finding out where our husbands were and securing permission to visit and to bring them food parcels. Since we had no ration cards, we had to search out illicit food outlets, an operation we were to find exceedingly risky.

In the process of social equalization the Soviet authorities had made a brilliant success of eliminating the bargaining power of money. According to graded scales in the order of their importance to the state, labor and political activities were now being rewarded by the direct provision of essential goods, including tobacco. At the same time, the calamitous scarcities caused by the prolonged war and by the drastic social changes of the Revolution effectively defeated all efforts to provide the people with the barest necessities. But the instincts of self-preservation demanding satisfaction at any price were uncontrollable. In secret and sometimes quite openly, speculation and the smuggling of food and other things flourished. The attempts of the government, though ruthless and often brutal, proved powerless to suppress the black market. At this epoch of Soviet history, the rulers, in possession of nothing but empty hands, in vain appealed for cooperation and true party spirit.

We divided ourselves into two parties of operation. Olga Stepanovna, bold and astute, together with Nina Aleksandrovna, who was not without her share of shrewdness, were detailed to find a jobber who dealt in valuables, so we could sell some of our trinkets. Among the four of us we did not own a kopek, and money, though incredibly inflated, was still useful in the black market. This mission obviously had to be carried out with utmost discretion. In addition, they were to approach the camp commander with a view to getting us into his good graces, not the easiest of tasks.

Meanwhile, Zinaida Vasilievna and I prepared to go to the black market. In these open-air bargaining centers, everything from bread and salt to Oriental rugs and exquisite antiques was sold for a price. So we collected shirts and sweaters suitable for barter, hid them under our coats, and set out.

In the former farmers' marketplace, Vologda's illegal commerce prospered. Evil-smelling throngs milled around a few ramshackle stands. Faces shone with sweat in the warm spring sun. Bearded peasants in belted sheepskin coats sat by their sacks filled with grain and flour, which had been brought out of hiding to provide them and their families with the supplementary supplies they so sorely needed. Broad-hipped *babushkas,* their wide skirts bulging over their clumsy felt boots, kerchiefs slipping off their foreheads in the heat of barter, loudly proclaimed the merits of their sour cream and cottage cheese. Behind them, dressed in tattered clothes to mask her gentle origin, a former lady timidly held out for sale in apologetic hands a golden chain of exquisite workmanship. A gang of Red soldiers, shamelessly bent on the same illicit errand as the rest of us, elbowed their way through the crowd jostling the lady. A streak of spittle landed in the dust at her feet. She merely turned her head away.

Keeping close together, hesitantly at first, Zinaida Vasilievna and

I mixed with the crowd. "We must not get separated," she whispered anxiously. She took out a sweater while I held out one of Gleb's shirts. Presently a peasant came up and thumbed my shirt with grimy hands. His small eyes gleamed under his bushy brows.

"How much?" he asked gruffly.

"What have you got?" I parried.

"Eggs."

A protracted argument ensued about the superiority of my shirt against the imperfections of his eggs, and vice versa. Tempers began to grow hot over the issue. Neither one wished to cede one inch. At length the peasant left in disgust. I wondered if I had been too insistent. But a few minutes later he was back again, edging up closer, trying to look nonchalant. Now the advantage was on my side. I set the price: thirty eggs for my shirt. Another vehement protest: "Are you crazy?" followed by a threat to leave. But the allure of the shirt was too powerful. With a musty oath the man produced the eggs, and Gleb's shirt disappeared behind the stiff folds of his old sheepskin coat.

That day luck was with us. Laden with bread, sour cream, eggs, butter, and cottage cheese, we had just reached the avenue bordering the marketplace on our way home when suddenly wild cries resounded from one end of the crowded place to the other.

"Oblava, ei, oblava!"

"A raid! The police!" cried Zinaida Vasilievna, her face pale. Shouts, shrieks, a storm of stomping feet, and a torrent of humanity poured madly toward the houses edging the square. Dropping a piece of clothing here, a loaf of bread there, men and women looked grotesquely funny as they ran, dodging, trying frantically to clutch, save, tuck away the damning evidence of their illicit operations. And on the crest of the peripheral shock wave of this tumultuous commotion, the two of us let ourselves be carried out of harm's way.

A glance back and the dust was settling on the empty marketplace again. A policeman walked across the vacant space. He picked up a flat loaf of black bread lost in the scramble. He broke off a good-sized piece, pushed it into his broad mouth, tucked the rest into the top of his boot, beside his spoon and knife, and sauntered on. In another hour the square would once again be bustling.

When we arrived home, Nina and Olga were already there, waiting. They had found a safe jobber with whom we could do business in the morning. They had also found the camp and met the commandant. And, amazingly, he had granted us permission to visit with our husbands in his office that afternoon, and every afternoon until further notice. Greatly encouraged, we chatted and laughed happily at Olga's vivid, always slightly smutty comments on their experiences, while we busily prepared a meal for ourselves and food parcels for our men.

The visiting hour passed in a happy mood. Gleb said that the prisoners were not confined to the barracks, so he spent most of the time outside sitting in the sun, dreaming of happier tomorrows. He spoke of visions of freedom and a life for us together, attuned to Russia's new aims and ideas. "The sooner we get to Moscow," he said, "the better."

A few days after Easter, word came that the prisoners were being sent to Moscow. Olga Stepanovna immediately tried to secure permission for us to travel with the transport, but the commandant categorically refused to consider her request, and all her cajoling and wiles were of no avail.

"I can do nothing for you, citizeness."

This sudden inflexible attitude worried me; it was not a good sign. Had the ruling anything to do with our getting closer to the center of Soviet Russia? Was the central soviet more to be feared than the local ones? Yet Moscow was the only place where, after all, there was any hope that the conditions of the surrender terms signed at Sumskiy Posad were eventually to be fulfilled. Upon those centered all our expectations, our faith in the future. For what other reasons had they taken the trouble to move this large number of prisoners across half of Russia? What would have been the sense?

The commandant went on, "But I will do this for you; I will arrange for you and your friends to travel to Moscow. That's all I can do."

This was actually a far greater concession than we could have expected from this man. To go to the station and to buy tickets and just take off was not possible. Travel was free, but for ordinary people to acquire a permit was a time-consuming and difficult process. This was especially true of people who had no legitimate jobs, partly because "essential" travelers, such as party members and officials, took precedence over all others, and partly because all transportation was in a general state of disorganization. Apart from this, it was of no advantage for this man to put himself out for two or three wives of political prisoners; rather the contrary. But there is to be found in the Russian character a certain spontaneous warmth of heart, an inclination toward compassion, often met when least expected.

When I told Gleb of our failure to get permission to travel with the transport, he said nothing but he looked disturbed. I hastened to reassure him. This arrangement was probably not bad, possibly even better, as we would arrive in Moscow ahead of them, and perhaps be at the station to meet them. On the trip nothing much could happen to us, traveling as we would be on Soviet passes. All three of us (Nina Aleksandrovna had decided to return to Archangel) had friends in Moscow.

"Be sure you go to see Nikolai Leonidovich," Gleb urged me. He was one of Gleb's best friends at Horserød and I, too, knew him well. I repeated the address: apartment 7, Myasnitskaya 18.

"Time is up, Lisa," Gleb whispered. He made the sign of the cross above my head. *"Que Dieu te bénisse!"* And as he embraced me a look of unexplained apprehension haunted his gray eyes.

If I had hitherto considered touring Russia in boxcars the most uncomfortable way of traveling, it was because I had not yet tried a fourth-class coach on a regular passenger run during postrevolutionary days. We boarded the train at noon. To say that it was crowded would be a gross understatement. Not only were all the seats occupied by more people than they were made for, but men, women, and children filled every passage and compartment, tightly pressed together, sweating, panting in the stifling atmosphere of *makhorka* mixed with the exudations of unwashed humanity. Hugging our bundles close to us, we could only abandon ourselves limply to the mauling of the crowd. Transported by the convulsive movements of the multitude, our immobilized bodies gradually gravitated toward the center of the car.

The pressure of the crowd reached its height at the stops. Cursing and screaming, people wanting to get off pushed toward the exits. Faces shone purple from exertion, excitement, and wrath. Only when the train stopped for several minutes was there the slightest chance for anybody to get off. Not infrequently many were carried, protesting and fighting, far past their destinations.

Between stations the passengers fell into a morose silence, broken only by an occasional outburst of cursing or a sudden frantic fight for a space to breathe. To get to the toilet was impossible.

Hunger and thirst assailed everybody, but none of us dared to open our food parcels lest we be robbed of the little we had. No one dared get off to fetch a pailful of water at the stations for fear of being left behind. Someone might occasionally voice a random call for water through an opened window, on the chance that some kind soul might respond by handing a pail full of water to the caller, and when someone did, it was seized upon with such alacrity that the water splashed over the loudly protesting fellow passengers.

Toward nightfall the pressure of the crowd eased somewhat and miraculously we found ourselves pushed into a compartment with two empty seats. Once we were seated, conditions seemed more endurable. We took turns lying down, somehow managing to wedge a body in behind the backs of the other two. Our spirits rose and Olga Stepanovna's jocularity returned. In French she treated us to rude jokes about our fellow passengers and their imperfections. With clumsy irony she praised the paradisiac conditions of the USSR until, weary and hungry as we were, Zinaida Vasilievna and I burst into hysterical laughter. Brown eyes darting highly gratified from face to face, Olga Stepanovna joined with her own hearty guffaws.

At a large junction halfway down the line a detail of railway police invaded our car, searching for "speculators," checking documents and baggage. They were looking for people who had gone into the country to buy up food from the farms with the intention of reselling it on the black market. A suspiciously bulky woman sat in a corner surrounded by her bundles. They pounced on her, seized all she had, and dragged her away, yelling, cursing, and kicking.

We sat in suspense, waiting for our turn to come. What if they discovered that some of our things were of foreign make?

The officer in charge reached our corner. He was a fair young fellow with blue eyes and smooth cheeks. His Russian-style blouse, khaki-colored like his trousers, was neatly gathered at the back under his black belt. He looked smart enough to have begun his military career in the old army of the tsar.

"Your papers, citizenesses!"

We gave him our passes.

"Personal belongings only?" he inquired. We said yes, and he went on to the next passenger. We sank back marveling at our incredibly good luck and at the magic power of the Soviet rubber stamp.

The night and the next day dragged on interminably. We were exhausted, uncomfortable, and hungry, and our tempers began to wear thin. We flared up at each other without cause. Even Olga Stepanovna's hilarity and free banter were silenced. She and Zinaida Vasilievna sat whispering together, and, feeling left out, I withdrew from them with rising ill humor.

All my fierce hatred of the Bolsheviks returned suddenly with full impact. The sufferings we were compelled to endure on this ghastly trip were their fault. They obliged people to live like pigs. They herded them like cattle and robbed them of every civilized right and amenity. No one, I raved in mute impotence, had any right to expose people to this sort of barbarous abuse. Never before had I found myself so closely surrounded and pressed and jostled by strangers, most of them unkempt and surly—as unkempt and surly as I was by this time.

Could this really be the people to whom Gleb belonged and whom he loved with all the passion of his Russian nature? Could these be the men and women for whom he was ready to lay down his life and whose destiny he had no greater desire than to share? No, these were merely the dregs stirred up by the agitations of the Revolution, risen like scum to the surface. These were . . . In this feeling of frenzied detestation, neither charity nor compassion nor good judgment had any part.

We reached Moscow toward the evening of the next day. Like sheep pouring from a fold, the released passengers tumbled out onto the platform of the Nikolayevsky Station.

The vast dimensions of the station at first impressed me. But then I perceived the degradation of the formerly luxurious building. Filling every inch of the platforms and the handsome waiting rooms, people sprawled, lolled, a motley crowd of peasants, riffraff, respectable citizens, northerners, southerners, all in dirty drab clothing; a huge congestion of would-be travelers assembled to wait hours and days for a chance to force their way onto a train. Here this mass of people camped, slept, ate, jostled each other with no sanitary facilities whatsoever. We had to make our way across these pulsating throngs of people, trying not to trample directly upon human flesh.

When we got outside at last, Olga Stepanovna urged me to come with them. But still feeling hurt, I told them to go on, I would be all right, I would find my own friends.

"But I don't like to leave you like this!" she insisted, and her tone was genuinely concerned. But I would not give in, and reluctantly they left me standing there. They found an *isvostchik,* a cab driver lording it over a scrawny hack. For several minutes they haggled over the fare before they piled their bundles and themselves into the sagging vehicle. I watched them drive off, mercilessly jounced on the rough cobblestones of the wide avenue.

So this was Moscow, the center of Russia! I looked around and found none of the bright golden domes so often shown in pictures of Moscow. Only a statue occupied the center of the circle in front of the station, covered by rough boards effectively concealing, I later found out, the likeness of one of Russia's mighty tsars. Beyond it monotonously rectangular buildings, some softly yellow, others drab gray, all sadly in need of repairs, lined spacious avenues and broad streets, fanning out endlessly in all directions. Wagons rattled over the cobblestones and the hoofs of the horses gave off hollow echoes. An occasional motor vehicle of ancient vintage chugged past with a leather-coated, red-star-helmeted driver at the wheel. A few gray-faced men and women in worn clothing, their eyes unfriendly, passed without offering the stranger a glance. And I myself, soured in mind, in my worn leather coat and dirty boots, in a hat and dress sewn together in the prison out of some brownish-gray material Mother had sent me, must have appeared as threadbare and hostile as any of these others.

Strapping together the bundle and the brown duffel bag for easier carrying, I slung them across my shoulders and went in search of Myasnitskaya 18.

CHAPTER 21

MOSCOW

IT relieved me greatly to find that one of the broad handsome streets fanning out from the open place in front of the station was indeed the Myasnitskaya. It could not be very far to number 18. With energetic steps I started off with my bundles on my back, not even glancing at the street numbers.

Tall office buildings lined both sides of the street; of course, nobody could be living there. This must have been an important business section before the Revolution. Now the gray stone of the walls was scarred by bullet holes, sad evidence of the bloody street battles that occurred here in 1917. The stores at street level, spacious and once probably well appointed, were nothing but hollow shells, their empty windows either boarded up or plastered with revolutionary posters: "Down with the bourgeoisie!" "Workers of the world, unite!" "Long live the Revolution of Workers and Peasants!"

But where was number 18? Aghast, I discovered that the next number was 1120. So the numbers must start at the other end. Where? At the center of Moscow? How far? The street led gently uphill. I walked on and on and my bundles became heavier until they seemed like lead. The evening was hot, with the kind of dry inland heat that sometimes strikes unexpectedly out of season. The sweat poured down my face, my knees shook from hunger and weariness, and I had to stop often to rest.

A terrible loneliness overwhelmed me. What if the prisoners were not being sent to Moscow after all, but to some other place far away? What if they had lied to us? How would I ever find Gleb again? I sank down on my bundles and sat there for a long while. What if I couldn't find Nikolai Leonidovich Grigoriev at Myasnitskaya 18? What would I do then? Where would I go? When Gleb was in Moscow two years ago on that near fatal trip, the Grigorievs were there. He had visited them. Much could have happened since then. My imagination refused to reach any further. How long was this street? How far to number 18?

Now the scenery began to change. There were churches and apartment houses with offices on the ground floor. Across the street I saw to my surprise the letters S. K. F. on a window. They were the initials of the famous Swedish ball-bearing company. The place did not look as if it were abandoned. Could there possibly be any of my countrymen still left in Moscow? Again I stopped to catch my breath and to rest. A red streetcar crowded beyond limit rumbled noisily down the street. Clusters of people clung around the entrances.

I sat down on one of my bundles to look around. A man stumbled over the other one. Enraged, he yelled at me, accusing me of tripping him. I was shocked into silence. The next number was 24. It could not be very far now. There was number 20 and there, just beyond it, number 18 blinked down at me from a small lantern-shaped entrance light. With a hollow sound my steps echoed under the vaulted passage into the yard. A man came toward me on his way out.

"Please, does Nikolai Leonidovich Grigoriev live here?" I asked timidly. He pointed at a back entrance across the courtyard, and I heaved a deep sigh of relief.

My heart pounded as I dragged myself and my bags up the narrow backstairs. Outside door number 7 I waited, nervous and excited. Finally I knocked.

Hurried footsteps sounded within and the next instant the door opened. A short woman in a light-gray dress confronted me. Her soft eyes looked tired. Her nearly white hair was brushed back, and little curls escaped to frame the upper part of her pale face. Her smooth skin lay in flaccid folds and her lips looked anemic. I asked for Nikolai Leonidovich.

"I'm his mother," she said. "He'll be home soon." She looked at me searchingly.

"I am Luisa Oskarovna Kirilina."

Her pale face suddenly lit up with motherly kindness. She must once have been very pretty.

"Come in, child," she said softly, and there was a warm welcome in her voice. "You are Gleb Nikolayevich's wife, aren't you? My son has often spoken of you. Your husband was here a few years ago. We heard nothing from him afterward and we have often worried about him, wondering what happened to him."

The room was dingy and overcrowded. A large oval table occupied most of the space and was set for supper. A cooking stove and a small sink were crowded into one corner; pails and boxes were ranged along the walls. Obviously the room was too full to be kept in order.

Anastasia Denisovna drew forth a chair. "Sit down," she said. "You look tired—you must be hungry. We will soon be having supper." She went about setting dishes on the table, attending to things at the stove.

What a haven of refuge! Without fuss, asking no questions, dirty, lousy, and half starved as I was, she simply accepted me, making me feel as if I belonged, as if I had come home.

Someone came leaping up the stairs outside. "Here is my son now!"

The door opened and there was Nikolai Leonidovich, looking exactly as I remembered him at Horserød. The same round-shouldered figure, the egg-shaped, almost bald head, the plain face with the thick horn-rimmed glasses behind which his eyes were hardly visible. One was vaguely aware that something was wrong with them. Oh, yes, now I remembered, the left one was a glass eye but the right one, acting for two, was doubly keen and alert. Nothing of all this was changed, only the color of his cheeks was of the same pallor as his mother's.

The sight of him brought Horserød back to my mind with overwhelming vividness, the green beech woods, my little room in the tar-scented barracks, those happy, happy days. How remote it all seemed to me now, far away in another world!

"Do you recognize her?" asked Anatasia Denisovna smilingly.

"Luisa Oskarovna!" he cried incredulously, and grasped my hands.

"Gleb's wife now," I said.

"Yes, yes, I knew that! Gleb Nikolayevich t-told me when he was here t-two years ago that he was going to marry you." He stuttered slightly, speaking in jerky sentences. How well I remembered that too! It was so good to see him, good to talk with him. His manner was quiet and his voice as warmly welcoming as his mother's.

The family was gathering for supper. Besides the mother and the son, there was Leonid Semyonovich, the father, a big-framed, stooped man with a sad look in his eyes, who seemed to have aged prematurely. With them was also Anna Petrovna, a tiny vivacious spinster. A certain frivolity was reflected in the sparse frizzy bangs falling over her high white forehead, instantly contradicted by her prudishly floor-length skirts and the prim blouse that was fastened under her chin with an old cameo brooch. She had lived with the Grigorievs since the Bolsheviks had come to power in order to occupy the surplus floor space of the modest apartment. As an old friend and delightful company, she was, of course, much to be preferred as a co-tenant to any stranger the House Committee might have foisted upon them.

The meal was of utmost simplicity, a watery soup made of dried vegetables, potatoes, black bread without butter, tea without sugar or milk. The supper seemed sumptuous to me, I had not eaten for so long, and my hosts' readiness to share the little they had with me touched me to the bottom of my heart.

They wanted to hear all about Gleb. I told them how he had been caught here in Moscow, how he had escaped into Finland and to me, about our marriage and the long journey to Archangel. I told them of our life there in the north on the other side, of the whole mad adventure, of the front collapsing like a flimsy card house, about our flight, how we were intercepted by the Reds, and about our surrender. They listened in silence.

When I had finished, Anastasia Denisovna said, "Poor Gleb Nikolayevich!"

"But," I said, "they are coming here tomorrow, and don't you think that shows they are not in any danger? Why else would the Bolsheviks bring them here? Doesn't that prove that they are intending to live up to the terms of the surrender?" In vain I scanned their faces for confirmation.

They sat silently around the table, sipping their amber tea, smoking their hand-rolled cigarettes. The samovar's simmering was slowly dying out. They had seen so many things happen during the perilous years since the outbreak of the Revolution. They had come through the first days of bloody revolts, the years of merciless reprisals and persecution. So far they had come through the awful suspense of the Red Terror, which had left few families unscathed. Though their son was a former officer, they had managed to survive, partly by sheer luck, partly by the force of their will, by adhering rigidly to a strictly nonpartisan course. It had not been easy, but they had succeeded in adjusting their lives to the demands and sacrifices the new socialistic society imposed upon them, suffering insecurity and privation in silence, but preserving their integrity, living without interruption in their work, and making their cultural contribution too.

"But don't you think—don't you think their being brought here means that they will be released?" I went on, anxiously trying to solicit their confirmation. "Don't you think they will fulfill the terms of the surrender? I am here now—I am Swedish and they still have respect for foreigners. I will find my way into the Kremlin, if I have to, to help Gleb!" In vain I looked into their expressionless faces for the smallest sign of reassurance.

At length Anastasia Denisovna said quietly, "Yes, it is better for Gleb Nikolayevich to be here in Moscow. Those who are sent out of Moscow are lost." She fell into a thoughtful silence, but only for a moment; then she smiled. "But now, of course, you are going to stay with us. Anna Petrovna will put you up on the couch in her room."

My most pressing problem was thereby solved, and my relief was as deep as my gratitude. "But what about the House Committee?"

"Don't worry, Luisa Oskarovna, my husband is on the committee and he will be able to arrange it."

Not until much later, when I had lived longer in Soviet Russia, did I fully appreciate the extent of the Grigorievs' spontaneous hospitality, the risk they ran of having their patiently and carefully achieved mode of living severely upset by taking me in.

That night for the first time in two long months I slept undressed between clean white sheets. I had never imagined that being able to use a clean toilet with running water could be so unparalleled a treat. But to get rid of the lice was another matter. Three weeks of washing, laundering, and shampooing elapsed before finally I was able to crush the last louse to death.

The next day Olga Stepanovna told me over the telephone that through her brother-in-law, who held a high position in the Commissariat of Communications, she had obtained official confirmation that the transport carrying the prisoners from Vologda would arrive that night at the Nikolayevsky Station. "And don't worry, I have found out plenty," she concluded enigmatically.

At dusk the three of us met at the station. I was amazed at the well-dressed appearance of my two companions, but said nothing. Far out by a siding we found the platform where Olga had been told the prisoners were to detrain. There, away from the crowds, we sat down to wait. In her rasping voice Olga Stepanovna proceeded to entertain us with a detailed description, liberally salted with witticisms, of her visit to the infamous Lubyanka 2, the headquarters of the feared and merciless Moscow Cheka. Zinaida Vasilievna, who had been with her, listened with a half-smile while she carefully applied the last touch of makeup to her pretty face.

"Well, Luisa, we did find out who is going to handle their case. Prosecutor Chidnov is the name, a redheaded Jew. Room Thirty-nine. Don't forget! They say he is one of the worst. He told us to come back tomorrow at eleven, he would then be able to tell us which concentration camp our husbands would be in. You had better come with us so you can get your visiting permit. Besides, it's good to know these devils personally and where to find them. Are they ever a sweet crowd! Ha-ha-ha!" She slapped her knee so that her satin slip rustled under her blue serge suit.

Against all expectations, we did not have to wait long for the arrival of the train. Soon the long row of boxcars rolled noisily in on the siding, and there was Gleb. He slipped down to the platform and came with long strides toward me, bareheaded and eager. The same detachment of soldiers that had guarded the prisoners on the way from Petrozavodsk to Vologda was still with them. They smiled at us and made no attempt to prevent us from approaching the prisoners.

Gleb's face was thinner but he had lost none of his serenity. We stood slightly aside from the others and spoke in whispers. We had only a short moment to be together, and there was so much to say, so much to plan. As the prisoners were being lined up on the platform, Gleb hastily ran to fetch his bundle and put it at his feet. He was delighted to know that I had found the Grigorievs and was staying with them. It was a great load off his mind. We talked of the chances of his ultimate release. It was then that I became aware of a peculiar change in him. Was it in his manner? Or in his voice or in the way he spoke? I could not tell, but it frightened me. Gleb's level eyes looked down upon me and he smiled, an expression of utter tranquillity and great tenderness on his face. Suddenly a violent, unreasoned anger consumed me—anger against fate, against Russia the archenemy, against the Bolsheviks, against all those that seemed to claw like vultures at the life of my Gleb.

"What cowards they were, all of them up there in Archangel!" I burst out in French. "Sneaking cowards, Miller and his staff! They knew well ahead of time their position was hopeless, just as well as you and I knew. They knew—yet they sent us on that insane errand to defend a front that was already collapsing while they made sure of their own escape. They left us to be caught like rats in a trap. We could have been saved on those icebreakers. Fools—cowards—goddamn fools!"

"Lisa!" I heard the catch in his voice. The anger evaporated as suddenly as it had overwhelmed me.

"But it's true, isn't it?" I said. An odd shine came into his eyes and he bit his lip to keep it from trembling. A storm of guilt swept over me. Defenseless, powerless, a prisoner, and I had hurt him! Holding his hand tightly I said, "Forgive me, darling!" But he was silent.

Nothing mattered but that he should be safe. Nothing! I tried breathlessly to reassure him, to encourage him: "I'll beg them—force them—persuade them to release you. There's no limit to what I will do to save you!"

Gleb swallowed hard. "Lisa, this you must never forget, and you must never try to change it. I shall never abandon my comrades. Their fate will be mine." Then he added, "I am a soldier, Lisa."

Once again Gleb had pronounced sentence upon himself. He had burned all his bridges, while I stood helpless and impotent. My heart filled with bitterness. Yet I realized that his supreme loyalty to Russia and to his comrades was the vital substance that allowed him to preserve his equanimity.

The prisoners were falling in line and we were permitted to walk through the streets beside our husbands. Gleb held my hand tightly in his. A guard with his bayonetted rifle slung over his shoulder marched next to us. There was no sound except the soft monotonous thuds of marching feet. We were held in a silence more eloquent than words.

"It is time for you to go now, darling. Courage, *chérisée,* for my sake." He pressed my hand lovingly before I slipped past the guard and out of the prisoners' ranks. For a while I stood in the middle of the vast empty street looking after Gleb and his comrades until I could no longer see them or hear the measured beat of their weary feet.

Two days later I sat with Olga Stepanovna and Zinaida Vasilievna on the curb outside the gates of the Ivanovsky monastery, not far from the Myasnitskaya, waiting for visiting hour. The venerable monastery had been turned into a concentration camp for political prisoners. Prosecutor Chidnov, a short man with sharp vindictive eyes, had informed us that our husbands were being held here for the time being. My impression of the man was less than reassuring. All the same, any misgivings my contact with Chidnov might have inspired were at least temporarily dispelled when somebody told me afterward that only prisoners whose cases were not considered hopeless and who were scheduled for an early interrogation were imprisoned in the Ivanovsky camp. In times like these, when secrecy shrouded every act of government, when subversion was rife and people lived day and night on the edge of disaster, rumors spread like wildfire and became an indispensable and often quite dependable source of information.

We had allowed ourselves plenty of time. It was only eleven now and the gates would not open until one. We wanted to be among the first to get in, but when we arrived the queue was already forming. As more mothers and wives and relatives and friends quietly joined the line, the end of it was soon out of sight around the corner of the monastery wall. Each of us carried a basket of food that was to last our men until Friday, the next visiting day.

At this time at least half the population of Moscow belonged to the vast throng of regular prison visitors. There were few who had not known in one way or another the inside of a Soviet prison or a concentration camp. Gaunt and in tattered clothes, their bodies trembling from anxiety and malnutrition, they stood there waiting, waiting to be allowed to extend to the loved one within, if only the a short hour, the warm supporting grasp of love and friendship. No sacrifice of time and strength and effort seemed to them too great to sustain the slender bond between those without and those within. For should it break, heaven help the prisoner!

Two days earlier, in the office behind the window bearing the letters S. K. F., I had found one of my countrymen. It had been a good visit with Mr. Hellman, with whom I could speak freely and who immediately offered to help me.

I had pulled from my hair the brown package with the remaining trinkets wrapped in the £100 note. He had suggested exchanging the note for gold rubles. They were not subject to the general inflation of the Soviet currency. Afterward, when I needed cash, he would gladly sell them for me at current rates, one by one.

So it happened that I was sitting there this morning on the dirty sidewalk outside Gleb's prison with our whole fortune banked upon my person, sewn securely into the hem of my corselet. Whatever happened now, I would be able to support the two of us until Gleb was released. After that, his wages would probably be far from sufficient to provide us with a decent living, but being a worker or a soldier would entitle him to rations. He who works eats. Specialists, men trained in some skills, were at this time at a premium, good military instructors like Gleb especially. There were rumors that war might soon break out between Russia and Poland. Such an event might well hasten Gleb's release. When he got out we would keep strictly out of politics. We would live and work like everybody else, like Nikolai Leonidovich and his father, insisting on nothing, going through the motions. For us, however difficult life might become, being together would make it endurable.

At last the gates opened and the long weary queue sprang to life. Two sour-faced unshaven guards admitted the visitors, searched their parcels, and, when no suspicions were aroused, let them pass into the monastery garden.

As I got through and looked up, I saw Gleb on the slight incline in front of the buildings. Catching sight of me, he came smiling to meet me. He put his arm around me and tenderly led me away from the crowd to a secluded spot by the high monastery wall, now no longer sequestering but shielding and protecting us. We sat down on a richly carved stone bench under the drooping branches of a venerable horse chestnut tree. Pyramids of sticky buds covered the tree and spread a faint fragrance. At our feet fat yellow spears of lily leaves pierced the black soil. In this peaceful place fear seemed to fall away.

At my next visit a week later Gleb had plenty of news to tell me. The promised interrogations of the Archangel prisoners had actually begun. Detailed questionnaires had been distributed and with cautious care Gleb had finally completed his. The need for officers in the army, he said, might well speed up the process. The happy prospect of his being set free played insistently in our minds. The newspapers, I told him, were full of the imminence of war, highly glorifying the opportunity to defend communism on the field of battle. Would this turn out to be the freedom-producing lucky break for us? A war? But as an instructor Gleb would of course not be sent on active duty.

Life in the Ivanovsky camp was quite tolerable; it was in fact both interesting and enlightening. In fantasy Gleb imagined himself being immersed in the actual life of a monk. He loved the old cells and the ancient flagstone-floored passages and dining halls. An atmosphere of high scholarship permeated the place, contrasting oddly with its present function, yet upheld by the type of prisoner segregated within its walls. Among them were educated and intellectual people. Some were socialists of moderate political conviction, old revolutionaries like Tolstoi, whose views on the methods and goals of the Revolution differed fundamentally from the Bolshevik ideas and who deplored the terror and the ruthless persecution of the intellectuals. All the prisoners were free to move in and out of the buildings and to associate with one another. Gleb had taken part in long conversations and discussions. He had set himself the task of studying political science and philosophy, with the goal of finding an intelligent solution to Russia's social ills. The monastery had a large library run by one of the monks, who still remained there—whether as a voluntary or involuntary prisoner Gleb did not know. He spent many hours each day studying in the library. He had also joined the bookbinding workshop. Working with books was one of his greatest interests, and mastering a book craft, he felt, might someday prove valuable.

Among the prisoners he had come across was one of his father's old friends, General Yuri Sasonov, an elderly gentleman with gray hair and a military bearing, whose only crime was being a general. He had been in this camp for fourteen months. He and Gleb had withdrawn into a corner to reminisce about happier days in Tsarskoe Selo. As children Gleb and his brothers had played with the general's daughter, Marya Yurievna. She lived in Moscow and could now look after the old man's most urgent needs.

We met them at the gates. Marya Yurievna was a pretty dark-eyed young woman whose freshness was already beginning to fade. Against her father's wishes—he had wanted her to marry an officer—she had chosen a *chinovnik,* a civil servant. Her husband now worked in the Narkomindyel, the Commissariat of the Interior. They lived in an apartment on the Nikitskaya, not far from the Myasnitskaya. Would I come home with them to see their baby?

On my next visit to Gleb I could tell him that I was now living in my own small room on the top floor of Myasnitskaya 18, facing the street. I had taken advantage of the Grigorievs' hospitality too long. So when Leonid Semyonovich had been able to arrange with the House Committee for me to have this room, I had moved in. I was now doing my own cooking on a small Primus stove, a priceless apparatus. There was only one drawback to the house: the plumbing was blocked solid. After the October Revolution, when the house was taken over by the proletariat, they had, through carelessness, plugged toilets and sinks to overflowing. And today, two years later, nothing had been done. So I had to run down four flights of stairs to fetch water from a tap and use the outdoor privies in the yard.

"Isn't it a piece of good luck—a place to go to when you come out, a home?" What comfort would it not be to live together in that little room!

Gleb was very pleased. How he longed for the day! Many of the prisoners had already been questioned and they were expecting to be released any day. Gleb had seen Prosecutor Chidnov. He was in the camp every day. The prisoners were being called in alphabetical order, and we figured Gleb's turn would come perhaps in a week or two at the latest.

I also told him that Mr. Hellman had brought me in contact with a Mrs. Linder, a Swedish Red Cross worker. She had just arrived from Samara (now Kuibyshev), where she had worked on the repatriation of German and Austrian prisoners of war. She was something of a heroine. Several months earlier she had broken her ankle and it had not been properly set. All the same, while the battles between the Bolsheviks and hordes of liberated Czechs raged, she had stuck to her post alone. At last she had been persuaded to leave. She had arrived in Moscow hobbling miserably, her face gaunt from suffering and overwork, accompanied by Else Lehmann, a German girl she had adopted. Hellman had found them a room not far from his office. It might be weeks before they could get their papers to continue home to Sweden. When visas were to be legally procured and passports officially stamped, Red officialdom almost stalled in its tracks. Mrs. Linder knew my family. She was a charming person, and the longer they stayed in Moscow, the better it was for me.

May Day 1920 broke upon Moscow with an orgy of revolutionary revelry. The streets were hung with bunting, and red banners floated on the gentle breezes of a perfect day. White sheets imprinted with rousing slogans in huge lettering were festooned upon the walls of all public buildings and strung across the streets. Since early morning squads of demonstrators had been marching through the streets from all corners of the city, converging upon Red Square, outside the walls of the Kremlin. As they marched past, bands playing, the "Internationale" reechoed with the beating of the drums.

Everyone who held a job was forced to take part in the demonstrations. For hours the people marched, all day they stood listening to their leaders, past masters of inflammatory revolutionary oratory, until many of them dropped. In their frantic enthusiasm, real or feigned, they shouted themselves hoarse, while some speechlessly drowned their antipathy in the revolutionary din. Nikolai Leonidovich returned home physically and emotionally exhausted.

On this day those of us who were saved from compulsory participation by unemployment stayed behind closed doors in our homes. For us the forced element in the uproarious celebration only accentuated the jarring discord. I wondered if the din reached Gleb in his secluded monastery garden.

A few days later Olga Stepanovna burst unexpectedly into my room while I was preparing Gleb's parcel for the next day's visit.

"Luisa, have you heard the latest?" she rasped, the faint odor of ether perceptibly on her breath, brown eyes dancing. "They have moved a bunch of them to the Pokrovsky camp—the Smirnovs and Boris, but not Gleb. He is still in the Ivanovsky."

I had awakened that morning with a headache and a dull ache in my legs. In fact, I felt ill. And now this! I feared and hated news of sudden changes, and Olga's announcement upset me. What did this mean? Why wasn't Gleb moved with the others? Was this good or bad? Would they now stop the interrogations? I sat down on the bed and began to cry.

"What's the matter, Luisa?" Olga sat down beside me. Suddenly her voice was full of tender solicitude. And it revealed to me a new side of her character, one of warm understanding and loyalty, usually kept concealed under the brash manner she so successfully assumed. Her sympathy only made me cry harder.

"Now, now, Luisa, you haven't heard all the news! Some of the men have been released and they brought a message to Zinaida Vasilievna from her husband. Buck up, girl, things aren't that bad! Soon they will all be released, you'll see!"

I managed to tell her that I was not feeling well, some kind of fever, legs aching, head aching.

"So that's it!" she said. "I'm going to take you right now to see a doctor. I know one not far from here. And then you go off to Chidnov and get special permission to visit Gleb today to tell him that you're not well. After that you go to bed for a few days and I'll come to see you. And if you have to stay in bed, I'll take care of Gleb's food parcel next week. Now let's get going!"

I felt too miserable to object. While Olga kept up a stream of gruff advice, she bustled about getting my parcel ready. She took my arm and led me down the stairs, out into the street.

The doctor was a swarthy undersized man who immediately subjected me to a thorough examination, plying me with questions. Had I been in contact with lice lately? When? For how long? Under what circumstances?

"Madame, you have contracted a mild form of fever," he said when he had finished. He did not mention the word typhus. "You are to go to bed and stay there until your temperature is back to normal. Light diet, of course, mostly fluids. No need for anxiety. Let me know if you need me again." I slipped him a thousand rubles. Satisfied, Olga Stepanovna now left me, saying she would be back that night to see how I was getting along.

Later that day I was shown into Chidnov's office at Lubyanka 2. He listened to my request with a bland half-mocking smile. To my surprise, he quickly wrote an order that I was to be admitted to the camp at once for a two-hour visit with my husband. Encouraged,

I ventured to ask about the prospects of Gleb's release, but he was noncommittal.

Tired and trembling slightly from excitement and exertion, I walked slowly the few blocks to the Ivanovsky camp. These two hours I would give myself completely to the bliss of being with Gleb. It was the fifteenth of May, a lovely spring day. Through a light-blue haze the sun shone softly. It was warm. The many trees growing inside the white-walled gardens, their tender green foliage spreading exquisite fragrance into the air, turned the crooked old street into a pleasantly parklike thoroughfare.

On this remarkable day even the guard at the gate regarded me with an amiable expression. When he had read Chidnov's note, he sent another guard to find Gleb. Within minutes Gleb came down the sloping path toward the gate, slightly perturbed to see me so unexpectedly.

"Lisa, *chérisée,* this is a surprise!" he exclaimed. "What's the matter, darling?" He looked into my face searchingly and his eyes clouded slightly. "Come to our bench under the chestnut tree and tell me all about it."

I reminded him that I had been a bit out of sorts at the last visit, and I told him the whole story. "Now we have two priceless hours together. Let's forget everything else!"

The monastery garden was enchantingly beautiful and peaceful and private. The chestnut tree stood in full bloom. The branches were laden with pyramids of fragrant white stars. Rays of sunlight penetrated between the new leaves and fell upon the path. The entire walled-in monastery court belonged to us two alone. Gently and with infinite tenderness Gleb began to make love to me. There was no aggressive crushing passion in his lovemaking. It was a finely tempered and delicately adjusted affirmation of devotion, a devotion severely tested and gloriously enduring.

The visit ended. Alone I walked slowly down toward the gate. I turned and saw him standing there tall in his khaki outfit, a figure framed within the fine old arches of the monastery. His hair lay sleek upon his head. A thoughtful man of quality and courage, he seemed at this moment supremely master of himself and his life. He waved to me and I waved to him. I walked through the gates filled with joy and pride that he was mine and I was his. And the heavy monastery gates closed creaking behind me.

I remember little of the following week. The high temperature often made me delirious. In clearer moments I felt only a gnawing ache of head and body. In a vain attempt to get back on my feet I devoured aspirin until my heart thumped against my breastbone, and with heavy feelings of premonition I worried despairingly over my inability to go to Gleb. Anastasia Denisovna trudged valiantly up the four steep flights of stairs to my room, bringing me food she thought I might be persuaded to eat. But the very sight of it made me sick and I could not touch it. Never mind, she said, she would be back again tomorrow.

Else Lehmann took over the responsibility of preparing Gleb's food parcels. Towheaded and placid, she went to the black market, ignoring the dangers of imminent arrest during surprise raids. She prepared dainty dishes for him, far tastier and better than I had cooked. For hours she stood in line to deliver them to him. With difficulty I wrote tiny notes of love and encouragement, which we hid inside the bread, telling him not to worry, that I would soon be able to come and see him, and for heaven's sake to take good care of himself. Back came his answers, tender, sweet, perturbed notes, ingeniously secreted in the empty basket.

"Darling, I am so worried about you! Do get well soon. Longing to see your face again. Interrogation going on, but at a slow pace, now at letter B. Wish so that I were free and able to take care of you. Do not try to get up and come to see me until you are well. . . ."

A second week passed, and a third. The next Monday Else came back from the camp with the parcel. She had not been able to deliver it. My head in a whirl, heart pounding from apprehension, I sat up.

"What's happened?"

"An escape," she explained. "Some got away, apparently, but most got caught as they tried to scale the wall. And all the prisoners have been moved to the Pokrovsky camp. No visiting or food parcels allowed. For a few days."

Terrible, worse than terrible! What was going to happen now? Olga Stepanovna had just told me the night before that her husband had been released and appointed instructor at the military school on the outskirts of Moscow. They were moving out there today. If only Gleb had been released before this crazy stupid dash for freedom at this most sensitive time! Now the interrogations would be interrupted, and heaven only knew what other reprisals and punishment would be imposed! What fools, what utter fools to risk their own chances of liberty, to risk the lives of both themselves and their fellow prisoners by such an irrational attempt!

Else tried her best to comfort me, and she succeeded temporarily. Tomorrow she would be back, and she would go to Pokrovsky camp and find out when parcels could be delivered again. She smiled, gently closed the door—and I was left with dread gnawing at my heart, numbing every reasonable thought.

The next day one of the released men brought another note from Gleb. It was full of encouraging news. Several of the men were expected to be released shortly. The Pokrovsky camp was not too bad, though not beautiful like the Ivanovsky. The rations were smaller, but working as a bookbinder, Gleb earned an extra half pound of bread a day. Best of all, they were again allowed to receive parcels on Thursdays and Sundays. Now he had only one desire, to know I had recovered and would come to him soon.

But the fever still lingered. My legs refused to support me when I tried to stand, and the temperature, down during the day, rose again at night. I tried to concentrate every thought on becoming strong enough to crawl, if need be, to the camp.

A few days later Anastasia Denisovna brought me another note from Gleb. "A man came with this," she said, and her eyes looked worried. "He guarantees safe delivery of your notes to your husband. Seems parcels and visits are again forbidden. Be careful Luisa Oskarovna," she warned, "don't trust him! But here is his address."

As I read the note, my heart sank. "Darling, if you are well again, I don't know. By now you probably know that parcels and visits are forbidden again. I am sending the note with this man, otherwise communication with you would be impossible. Everything here is the same, I have not yet been questioned, they are only at the letter D, and unless they do it out of turn, as they have with some, it will not be soon. It is hard to stay locked up like this without anything to do and without knowing anything about you. I need all my courage. Only one thought supports me—that you are close —waiting as I do for the day of our reunion. When—oh, when? I hate to see the best days of spring pass by without even being able to go outside. My darling, be strong and let us hope the days of separation will soon end, as happened last year when you came to

Archangel. Send your reply, and something to eat if you have it, with this man. If visits are not allowed on Sunday I will send you another message. Please give him a thousand rubles for me and be sure you make a list of all that you send me. There are rumors that all infantry officers will be sent to the Kochechovo camp, twelve miles outside Moscow. If true, it would be inconvenient for us. How I long to see you, my dearest! I kiss you a thousand times! Your own Gleb."

That night worrisome thoughts crowded in upon me. Sometimes they made me sit up in bed with heart pounding as I imagined the worst. A voiceless shout relieved the tension, discharged the pent-up fears, and momentarily calm returned. Why was he locked up inside the camp? If they were moved to that camp outside Moscow, interrogations would again be interrupted. Why, why? In any case, it appeared now that the best we could hope for was prolonged imprisonment. Incidents of "forgotten" prisoners were not uncommon, but as long as his life was spared, even that idea seemed tolerable. I would find out about this other camp and arrange to live close by. Others before me had followed wherever their husbands had been taken. Even Siberia could not frighten me. Supporting each other, sharing whatever life brought . . . I loved him so! And at last I fell into a troubled sleep.

Else had gone to the strange man with a note and a parcel for Gleb and I was waiting for her return.

When she came her face was strangely disturbed. She was pale and looked at me with eyes full of sympathy. She handed me back my note and parcel.

"They are all gone." She pronounced the words with difficulty. "Last night. The man thought they had been taken to the station."

An icy chill settled upon me. A frantic scream gathered in my throat. One single thought pounded endlessly in my mind:

"Those who are sent out of Moscow are lost—lost—lost!"

CHAPTER 22

A DESPERATE SCHEME

HOPE, strangely indomitable, refused to die. Now there was nothing to look forward to but months and months of imprisonment, perhaps years. But that thought brought immense relief from the awful fear of a sudden end.

I got out of bed shakily and reached for my clothes. "I must go!"

"No, no," Else protested mildly, trying to force me back into bed. "Where do you want to go?"

"To the man, the strange man! Come with me, Else, show me where he lives!"

Realizing she could not stop me, she helped me to dress. Again and again I had to sit down to rest. My gray dress hung on my body. My leather coat, held loosely with Gleb's shoulder strap to my shrunken waist, seemed inordinately heavy, and my tightly laced boots left an inch of space all around my shins.

Else took my arm and slowly we descended the steep stairway to the street. Some of my strength returned as we began walking. We spoke little, but Else's steady arm comforted me. My purpose—to find that man—interrupted the riotous race of my thoughts. The hope that this man would be able to provide an answer to the shocking riddle of Gleb's disappearance carried me through the streets.

It was the fifteenth of June, a beautiful summer evening. The setting sun broke into shafts of light slanting between the low houses, and the shadows obliterated the dust and the dirt on the angular streets. A whole month had elapsed since the day I had last seen Gleb.

"Where does he live, Else?" At our slow pace, the distance seemed endless.

"Not so far now. But you are getting tired. Let's sit down and rest for a while." We sat down together on the curb. I was clammy from weakness.

Presently, somewhere in the east end of Moscow, we arrived at a house of insignificant exterior. "Here we are!" Else said. The house was dark. Mounds of dust filled every corner of the dim winding stairs. Else knocked on a door. A woman with a morose expression admitted us to a dingy apartment and guided us to a narrow unaired parlor.

"Is Pavel Petrovich at home?" Else asked.

"Yes."

"Could we speak with him for a moment, please?"

As the woman left the room, she yelled, "Pavel Petrovich!" carelessly into the air.

A tufted drapery swayed and a man noiselessly appeared. Of slender build, he was below average height and his physical condition indicated that he was well fed. His features were sensuous, handsome. A shock of black hair overshadowed his white forehead, below which glistened a pair of shifty hazel eyes.

He smiled a courteous greeting to Else and bowed at me, mutely requesting an introduction. Else mentioned my name and he bowed again in acknowledgment. These perfect manners suddenly irritated me beyond endurance.

"Where is my husband?" I shot the question at him. Tears choked my throat and overflowed in deep-drawn uncontrollable sobs. "Have they killed him? Answer me, I must know!"

He lifted his hands as if to ward off my vehemence. "Madame must calm herself!" His oily voice was no doubt intended to convey sympathy. "All I know is that last night five hundred officers taken prisoner on the northern front were returned to Archangel for trial."

To Archangel! For trial! Slowly the full meaning of their having been returned to the place where their alleged crimes had been committed began to penetrate my understanding. What kind of justice could they expect there? What chance was there that the terms of the surrender would be even recognized? The fate of the tsar and his family passed through my mind.

He had said trial. Then they were still alive, there might still be time! So long as we knew them to be alive . . . Gleb would write! He would contrive to send a message to me, telling me where he was. But . . . "Why were the interrogations discontinued? Why were they sent away?" I asked. "Does this mean that the authorities will ignore the terms of the surrender?"

The man shrugged. "The evacuation of these prisoners came as a total surprise," he said. "I can only say that I have, believe me, the greatest sympathy for you and your husband."

The sentence lost him all credibility. I did not want his sympathy. My thoughts leaped to Gleb and his fellows. How shocking it must have been when they were suddenly ordered to line up with their belongings! And then the lonesome dreary march through the darkened streets without being able to tell their loved ones what was happening. Then to be herded aboard boxcars, locked in like cattle . . .

Abruptly the man sidled up to me and his eyes had a liquid shine. There was in his manner an almost imperceptible insinuation that put me on my guard.

In a low voice he said, "Why don't you appeal for help to the Swedish Red Cross?" He drew from his pocket a paper. "I have prepared a report on the Bolshevik terror. It must reach the outside world as soon as possible. It's a call for international intervention in the name of mercy to prevent further atrocities, to save the lives of your husband and of the thousands of other people who are languishing in Bolshevik prisons. Madame, you have no idea how many of these atrocities I have witnessed directly and indirectly." He injected a note of well-controlled emotion into his next words: "Would you not help, Luisa Oskarovna? You who are in contact with members of the Swedish Red Cross, would you not implore them to carry this important document across the border? They could do it safely. I count on you and I trust you."

In a flash I knew his secret. Anastasia Denisovna had warned me. As certainly as if he had said so, I knew that I was dealing with a Cheka *agent provocateur*. The thought that Gleb and I had been at the mercy of this man horrified me. He knew all about Gleb and me, where I lived, with whom I associated. What had Gleb, goaded by his anxiety for me, told him? Could he have jeopardized his own case or that of his comrades? What had I written in my notes to Gleb? But my certainty of the man's true identity restored my poise. I looked straight into his shifty eyes and told him that the Swedish Red Cross would never have anything to do with a project of this kind.

"Good-bye, Pavel Petrovich." And with newfound strength I left the room with Else following down the dark stairs and out into the dusty street. Once outside I shook violently, but the air was pure and we drew deep breaths.

Else took me directly to Mrs. Linder. She would not hear of my staying alone in my room that night. She and Else gave me supper and bedded me down on one of their own beds on the floor of their large sheet-partitioned room. They listened while I talked of my hopes and fears, my nerve-racking speculations on the fate of Gleb and his comrades. Tears never ceased to trickle down my cheeks, never stopped choking my voice. And my sleep that night was haunted by nightmares.

The next morning, after I returned to my room, Olga Stepanovna and Zinaida Vasilievna arrived. I was glad to see them, but they knew little more than I did. Apparently the Cheka agent had told me the truth about the prisoners' having been sent north; Olga's brother-in-law had confirmed it. The girls had been in contact with several of the other desperate wives. All were tormented by the same fears, premonitions, and misgivings, the same exasperating uncertainty.

Some people they knew had seen the party of prisoners being marched to the Nikolayevsky Station. The guards had not allowed anyone near the prisoners so they had not been able to speak to them. They had followed and they had seen them being locked into the boxcars, and the train had moved out of the station.

Olga left to see her brother-in-law and to gather more news. Still weak and shaky from the illness, I lay down and rested for a while. Else came with some food that Mrs. Linder thoughtfully had prepared for me. I ate it gratefully while Else sat beside me, and her presence was extraordinarily comforting.

In the early afternoon Olga Stepanovna breezed into my room. "Now, Luisa, you are not to worry, it won't help!" she said in her usual gruff way. "Now listen! The prisoners have just left Vologda, destination the concentration camp at Kholmogory. I have the number of the train—wait!" She rummaged in her purse and produced a piece of crumpled paper: "Here it is. Take it. You can have a telegram waiting for him at Kholmogory—just address it to that train number."

Kholmogory was a town on the river Dvina some distance from Archangel. The detailed accuracy of Olga's information never ceased to amaze me. I thanked her, but she had no time for that.

"Now you wire as I told you!" She pointed her finger at me. "We'll keep in touch with all the other wives. Someone is bound to get news from the men sooner or later. I'll be back tomorrow." She pushed open the door and with long strides walked down the passage to the stairs.

The possibility of getting in touch with Gleb was encouraging. A few doors down the Myasnitskaya, in a drab telegraph office rank with stale *makhorka* smoke, strewn with cigarette butts and the empty shells of chewed sunflower seeds, I wrote my message to Gleb. The fervent hope that it would eventually reach him to ease his mind banished from thought any speculation on the near insurmountable obstacles that lay in the way for the safe delivery of that naive message.

Days passed, days of harrowing suspense, days of hope lost and hope recovered. I was exhausted with thinking—thinking of what might already have happened to him and of what the future had in store. I waited for word that never came.

Then Zinaida Vasilievna received a postcard from her husband: "We are all safe at Kholmogory. Do not worry."

The message was shared by all of us and it seemed the sun had arisen upon a new day. Of course Gleb had sent a message to me also, only it had gone astray. It could have been lost in a hundred possible ways. That this one got through was a miracle. And it was wonderfully reassuring, for it constituted direct proof that our husbands were still alive.

From then on I ceased looking for messages from Gleb. Lying awake at night, wrestling with thoughts and fears, I reached a decision. I would go to Archangel, to Kholmogory. That was the only place for me to be, close to him, while he served his time in prison, however long that might be. Reunion was now a beautiful dream far off in the future. I envisioned years and years with him inside and me outside helping and supporting him, making life in captivity as bearable as possible. We were still young, and what had to be could also be endured!

Nina Aleksandrovna was still in Archangel and she would probably be able to help me find a place to stay. We would go to Kholmogory, it was not so far away, and perhaps I could stay there. What did time or anything else matter so long as Gleb was alive and I was near him? And I began my preparations for the long and hazardous journey.

Two weeks passed before I was ready to leave. Olga Stepanovna's brother-in-law provided me with a pass as an employee of the Commissariat of Communications on a special mission to Archangel. Planning what to take with me was the most difficult task. On this trip I would be thrown completely on my own, with few, if any, friends to consult and to help me. I would have to find my own way under entirely unknown, probably hostile conditions, in constant danger of arrest. It might take months for me to get myself tolerably well established, perhaps the whole coming winter in a climate of which I had, after all, only scant experience.

My clothing had to be warm and light, one change of underwear. Most important of all, I must take with me enough food for Gleb and myself to last for the first difficult weeks, at least. It must be nonperishable and highly nutritious. So I baked quantities of rusks made of eggs, milk, butter, and good flour bought on the black market. Together with canned foods added sparingly, they would make nourishing and palatable meals. Thus, I figured, the baggage would be light and easy to handle, for I would have to carry and protect it all by myself.

My friends said little, but they looked upon my decision with silent misgivings. They realized far better than I the risks involved in such a journey into the unknown. Mrs. Linder did not say much, she understood my need to act. She and Else got their papers for the continuation of their journey before I was ready to leave. When I came to say good-bye, she put a package of concentrated foods into my hand.

"Take this, my dear. I'll have no need for them. God bless you!" I realized that she did not think she would ever see me again.

The Grigorievs shook their heads. "Wouldn't it be better if you stayed here?" Nikolai Leonidovich hesitantly suggested. "Your husband will no d-doubt t-try to contact you here as soon as he can."

Mr. Hellman advised, "Stay where you are! The order to send them away originated here at the center. What they will do with them is decided here. You should try to find out who is responsible for these prisoners and get to see him. You would find out more, perhaps be able to—"

"I know, I know," I interrupted, "but it would take so long, and in the meantime Gleb might be killed!"

As the time for my departure approached, my friends' disapproval of my plans was not the reason why the preparations for the journey suddenly became oddly onerous. A curious embarrassing reluctance to carry out my intention possessed me, and I could not shake it. The very idea of the journey began to weigh on my mind like a heavy burden. Some part of me insisted that the whole project was utter foolishness. I began to imagine dreadful scenes—being robbed on the train, seizure and arrest, failure to reach my destination, failure to find Gleb, the damning revelation of my connections with counter-revolutionary activities. All this inspired me with a paralyzing presentiment, a cowardly conviction of the futility of my mission.

Olga Stepanovna came to say good-bye. "Wish you would give it up," she said. We sat on my narrow bed, the only seat in the room. My baggage, packed and ready, stood piled in the corner by the door.

Olga's voice was softer than usual and her manner less ebullient. Life for her and her husband at the military college was difficult. True, they were together, they could come and go as they pleased, and their everyday needs, food and shelter, were being adequately provided for by the Red Army. But every move they made was watched, every word they uttered and every person they associated with were noted. She said they both felt that Boris Pavlovich's skill as senior training instructor for the Red cadets and Olga's as nursing assistant to the medical officer were being used in somewhat the same way as domestic animals are used, the draft power of oxen, the milk drawn from the udder of the cow. Boris Pavlovich, high-strung and nervous, was finding his position and his work under the uncouth Communist commanders almost intolerable. Olga herself lived under the constant threat that, in spite of her efforts to ease her husband's tension, he would one day reach the end of his endurance.

She sat and talked of these things while her brown eyes rested quietly and sadly now on me, now on the opposite wall. Though little in life could really dismay her, today she was gravely concerned about their uncertain future. Gleb's optimistic ideas about life after prison came into my mind. With eager anticipation he had dreamed of the part he had thought himself willing to play in the new act of the Russian drama, for at last it would give him the chance to serve. Would he be better able than Kusnetsky, I wondered, to withstand the vicious political pressures of such a life?

The previous night I had had a strange dream so vivid I was still laboring under its influence, and I told her about it. I dreamed that Gleb and I were living in a small room on a top floor somewhere in Moscow. The doors to a balcony stood open and a light summer breeze gently rippled the sheer curtains. On the balcony was a long low object that had just been delivered to me as a gift. Thrown over it was a heavy silken cover the color of dead roses, edged with a rich tasseled fringe of dull gold. Gleb, just home from work, stood beside me. Consumed with curiosity, I was about to lift the corner of the cover when Gleb grasped me roughly by the arm and pushed me away.

"Don't touch that thing, Lisa!" he cried. "Can't you see, they have sent you a coffin!" And I awoke.

Olga said gravely, "You should not go, Luisa."

We sat for a long while, both deep in thought. Then she repeated with slow emphasis on every word, "You should not go, Luisa!" For a few minutes she remained sitting on the bed beside me, her slender hands folded in her lap. Then quickly she kissed me and left the room.

In the evening Mr. Hellman got me a rickety droshky to take me to the Nikolayevsky Station and we piled my baggage into it. He said good-bye. Alone and with a heavy heart I rode down the same dusty, gently sloping street I had struggled up on foot that evening almost two months ago when I arrived in Moscow. The same stark uninviting buildings passed in review with their empty shop windows, the same gray-faced belligerent crowd jostled past along the sidewalks, the same streetcars with swarms of people clustered at their entrances clanged their strident bells, insisting on the right of way. The hoofs of the horse clopped dully against the worn wooden paving blocks.

I found my place on the train. It began to fill with passengers. In the next compartment a woman loudly protested her right to a certain corner; a baby cried. Feet scraped incessantly against the dirty floor. Against some inexplicable repulsion I was forcing myself in the direction of Archangel. A sudden fright seized me and I clutched at the seat to prevent myself from dashing off the train. Why this incomprehensible feeling of doom? Courage ought to be my strongest support as I stood on the threshold of the most daring enterprise of my life.

Outside a bell clanged, the first warning of impending departure. A man in my compartment rushed out and presently returned with his battered kettle full of boiling water. His woman companion, a stiff black kerchief hiding most of her plain face, immediately made tea and poured it into two tin cups. Between steaming gulps of the weak brew the two of them chewed chunks of black bread. Through the din of imminent departure the second bell sounded fatefully in my ears.

Suddenly there were sounds of jostling outside in the passage. The next instant Olga Stepanovna stood in the open doorway of my compartment. Her black nurse's veil fell over her shoulders like widow's weeds and clung to her smooth forehead, leaving only a thin line of the white veil showing underneath. The oversized red cross on the breast of her black apron glowed with the color of blood. Never had she appeared so handsome. Her darting brown eyes fastened upon me.

She grasped my baggage. "Quick, Luisa, come on! Nina Aleksandrovna just arrived from Archangel. She's at our place. They are all dead!"

I was conscious of a second's shocking relief as if from some unbearable pressure. Blankly I followed her out, mute and unseeing. There was not a second to spare. The third bell clanged, and simultaneously, with a series of puffs and hisses from the laboring engine, the train began to roll past us out of the station.

CHAPTER 23

IN SEARCH OF EVIDENCE

IN an unremitting and indomitable process, life goes on. The healing of the wound, however deeply torn, begins the very instant it is inflicted. The energy and stamina required is actually of no account. The reaction is automatic, a mechanical device of balance disturbed, rebounding.

Three days passed after Olga took me off the train before I was able to pull myself out of the depth of despair. Recollection of those three days is hazy. There was the large room in the Kusnetsky apartment at the military college where Olga kept her three lost and desolate friends under her protecting wing: Nina Aleksandrovna, petite, emotional of a comeliness approaching that of a full-blown shower-drenched rose; Zinaida Vasilievna, too dainty and birdlike to be so badly hurt; and I, tear-stained and dazed. She put us to bed on low camp cots, side by side. She fed us as if we were frail invalids. She talked to us and tended us and kept us sane. Brown eyes darting, arms swinging in quick and decisive motion, Olga carried out her self-imposed task of big sister. And, aided by her strength and devotion, we gradually recovered enough marrow to continue.

Between sobs, tears dripping from her dark lashes, in gesture and voice unconsciously dramatic, Nina Aleksandrovna told us all she knew. A man, a Lett by the name of Kedrov, with a reputation for marked revolutionary zeal and hands stained by terrorist deeds, had been selected as the head of the Archangel Cheka in charge of the "liquidation" of the counterrevolution in the northern territories.

Nina told of the nightly searches and the ransacking of almost every house, of mad manhunts, of executions in cellars against bullet-spattered walls. She described the severe reprisals by the authorities in their frenzied attempts to subdue a population that for the most part had been only unfortunate pawns in a cruel game of civil war, interested in little else than being left to live their own lives in peace.

Kedrov himself, Nina said, hard and ruthless though he was, had taken no personal delight in the bloodbaths; he simply issued the orders. The purely sanguinary enjoyment was entirely the prerogative of his mistress and secretary, a she-devil beyond description. With sadistic satisfaction she wielded her silver-studded revolver on the black nights of mass executions, reserving for herself the privilege of dispatching the first victim. With her own dainty hands she performed the actual chore of liquidation. And it was on her instigation, Nina's informers had told her, that on the night of July 7–8 the party of 500 officers, our husbands among them, had been taken out of the camp at Kholmogory and mown down by machine-gun fire.

Thus Nina Aleksandrovna's story, most of it gathered at Cheka headquarters, where she had gone to plead for information about her husband. As flatly and ruthlessly as the deed itself had been done, they had told her the details.

As the first stunning effects of the story began gradually to subside, I felt for a straw on which to pin a desolate future. Death had brushed very close and I was left with a life yet to be lived. I asked Nina Aleksandrovna if she had any absolute proof that what they had told her was true. Did she see a list with their names? Was it not possible that some of them might have been sent to Siberia secretly?

Nina Aleksandrovna's large velvet eyes fastened upon me with the look of an ailing child being rudely aroused from a state of apathy.

"I have only the word of the man at the Cheka," she murmured.

"Then you don't know if it is true?" I persisted. "Why should these devils tell you the truth?"

"Don't say these things," she protested tearfully. "They were at Kholmogory, that I do know. Zinaida had this directly from her husband, and my husband also sent me a message from there. And now they are no longer there, that I also know. A reliable friend—

not the Cheka—told me, and I trust him. I know I can trust him," she insisted.

"Did they give you any of Aleksandr Dmitrievich's belongings?" I went on. Now tears were pouring down our faces; tears came so easily, one could not stop them from falling. "Do you know where they are buried?"

Nina Aleksandrovna stared at me. Her lips trembled. It was cruel of me to suggest hope to her again. "No," she said at length. "No, I don't know, but I am convinced they were all killed." Her words were drowned in a deep sob. Full of fear, her tear-drenched eyes rejected every thought of hope.

For me, hope was imperative. I could not go on without it. Give me hope, and I shall survive! Nothing that Nina had told us contained absolute proof that Gleb had been killed. I refused to believe it without conclusive proof. It had happened, many times, that men in a desperate attempt to survive had dropped a split second before the shots rang out, and thus escaped. Some had even allowed themselves to be buried and then, when all was quiet, had dug themselves out of the mass grave and crawled into hiding. Legendary stuff? Some of it, yes. But some did survive, lived like savages in the forest until they were finally rescued by local people with enough guts and humanity to risk saving a fellow human being. And thus some, after years of absence, eventually returned home. Why could it not happen again? Gleb had endurance, infinite patience; he was tough. And without making clear in my mind what an escape would have cost him in hardship and mental anguish, without recognizing limitations, at this moment I burned with the thought that someday perhaps he would come back.

Emotionally exhausted, I searched in vain for a sentence, words to express to my friends my profound appreciation for the wonderful comradeship we had shared, to tell Olga something of how grateful I was for all she had done. I wanted to make our leave-taking meaningful and memorable. But I found none. And in the late afternoon I could only kiss them a wordless good-bye.

An hour later I found myself once again trudging wearily up the Myasnitskaya, loaded down with my baggage. When Anastasia Denisovna opened the door, her only greeting was a sigh of relief; she asked no questions. The unexpected return of someone believed lost was in those days just as common as someone's disappearance forever. Later, at the supper table, with an equal lack of emotion, the Grigoriev family listened to the tale I had to tell them about Gleb. When I finished, they informed me with their usual casual kindness that the small room on the fourth floor still stood empty.

At this epoch in Russian history, Communist leaders and workers were being invited from outside the Soviet Union to observe firsthand the infant Communist experiment. Welcomed by *Pravda* with fanfares and with red carpets actually spread before their feet, the visitors were put up in the elegant suites of the former luxury hotels, now pragmatically named Soviet House No. 1, 2, and so on. They spent most of their time touring model schools, nurseries, hospitals, and factories under the supervision of well-instructed guides. It would not be entirely fair to accuse the hosts of creating these model circuits overnight by a supreme effort, purely for show, to deflect attention from the squalor and want that was obvious even to the most carefully shielded visitor. In part, at least, they embodied something of the great revolutionaries' visions, now being gradually put into practice and shown not without some justifiable pride.

A delegation of British Communists and unionists was the first to arrive. It was followed by others, a group of Finnish workers among them. One day Mr. Hellman told me about the arrival of a Swedish delegation. Through them, he pointed out, I might have a good chance of discovering my husband's fate. No doubt I could with their help gain access to some influential person in the Kremlin.

Early the next morning I called up Kata Dahlström, one of the delegates, a woman well known in Sweden for her vividly red views and militant attitude. A voice speaking in halting Russian answered the telephone. I told her my name and asked for an interview at some suitable hour that day.

"Certainly, come up any time. No, let me see, I have a conference at the Kremlin this morning. Three o'clock this afternoon? How would that be?" I said it would be fine. "All right. Then you will meet the others too," she concluded. Obviously, it never dawned on her that the request could come from one of vastly different political color.

With heart pounding, I appeared at the hotel at the set time. I felt like a bee gone astray, entering a strange hive. I walked into the lounge, but there was no one to direct me. A few people came and went, guests evidently, men absorbed in their own thoughts and plans, one or two women in severely tailored suits, all with red ribbons pinned in their lapels. I mounted the stairs and at the top of the first flight saw an open hall. A young man in trim blue uniform, a revolver tucked into the holster at his belt, sat behind a desk writing. I took him for the Cerberus guarding the entrance to this distinguished Communist guesthouse, and I was right. He looked up at me inquiringly.

I told him I had an appointment with Comrade Dahlström, the Swedish delegate.

"Your passport, *tovarishch!*" he demanded harshly.

The request was a shock. The only passport I had was the document issued by the former Russian consul in Stockholm before my journey to Archangel. Not daring to leave it behind in my room, I always carried it with me. To show it would reveal the whole story of my counterrevolutionary connections. But the man's insolence suddenly set fire to my temper. I whipped out the condemning paper.

The man rose from his seat, momentarily speechless.

"This!" he cried, disdainfully flicking with the back of his hand my double-eagled becrowned document. "This is no Book of Labor. This is glaring counterrevolutionary evidence! Where are your Soviet credentials?"

This was the first time I had heard of the Book of Labor, the individual identification without which no one could legitimately exist in the Soviet Union.

"I have no other credentials."

"You are a damned bourgeoise," he snapped. "You should be arrested!"

Where my courage and detachment came from at this moment, I have no idea. The threat did not touch me at all.

"Call up Comrade Dahlström at once, tell her I am here!" I ordered. And coming a bit closer to him: "If anything should happen to me—she knows who I am. . . ."

He seized the receiver and called her number. When I heard her answering, I snatched the receiver out of his hand. Speaking in Swedish: "Mrs. Kirilina, Miss Dahlström. I'm having a bit of trouble. The man down here won't let me pass. . . ." I hung up, and we stood glaring at one another for half a minute.

Steps came rippling down the stairs and a diminutive woman in a simple brown suit stopped on the bottom step. She surveyed the situation. Her fresh young face was keenly alert.

"I am Elin Linderoth," she announced in Swedish. "Mrs. Kirilina, you are to come up at once. Comrade Dahlström is waiting for you."

"He won't let me pass," I said with a sly look at the enraged receptionist.

Elin Linderoth took a few steps toward him, the color in her cheeks mounting, her small fists knotted at her sides. "The comrade has come to see me," she said with emphasis in broken Russian.

"But she is an enemy of the Revolution!" the man said. "She has got no credentials."

"I will have no interference with my friends," she quickly interrupted. "You understand? You are not to stop her when she comes. I personally guarantee her loyalty."

With these words she turned on her heel, and I had only a second to recover my offending passport and throw my antagonist a look of triumph. She took my hand and we ran upstairs as fast as she had come down.

Kata Dahlström received me with warm friendliness, a bit surprisingly, as she had no idea who I was or what I wanted. A formless woman in a styleless gray woolen dress, her gray hair standing on end around her plain face, she gave the impression of having a total disregard for method and order. She spoke nervously, constantly interrupting herself, as if her brain formulated ideas more quickly than her tongue could put them into words. For years she had been considered one of Sweden's most radical socialists. She had spent a lifetime propounding the rights of the worker and she had been an untiring champion of the underprivileged. Because of her militant attitude and her distinctive face and figure, the caricaturists had pounced upon her as a favorite subject for malicious ridicule, but she met all their attacks with unruffled indifference. In her present association with prominent international Communists and socialists she was accepted as the undisputed dean; both her intelligence and her whims were highly respected. The distinction of culture and wit belonged to her naturally and wrapped the whole of her shapeless and untidy person in impressive dignity.

The friendly atmosphere that met me when I entered the room gave me an immediate sense of confidence, and I felt no hesitation in relating to these people surrounding Kata Dahlström, fierce revolutionaries though they were, the full story about Gleb and his disappearance. Frankly and in plain words I told them exactly what had happened. My story was received with remarkable sympathy, and Kata Dahlström promised that she would arrange an interview for me with Comrade Leon Trotsky.

The staging of this portentous meeting required several days. Meanwhile, I spent much time in the company of Elin Linderoth and her husband. Tall, lean, with a friendly pleasant expression in his gray eyes, he was a convinced socialist. Despite differences in temperament, outlook, and background, we found ourselves drifting into a friendship based on mutual sympathy and tolerance. Elin often drew me into long discussions on socialist ideology. Ever since Miss Palmquist's well-meaning but ill-contrived attempt at Svensksund to introduce me to socialism, its idealism had appealed to me and lingered at the back of my mind. Now Elin explained the fundamental ideas of the Revolution as envisioned by prominent socialists, such as Maksim Gorki—its reasons and justifications. With ardent enthusiasm she spoke of the single unseverable society of equality and equity, as opposed to the "divided society," which she considered ultimately doomed. At the same time she drew deft comparisons between the theories of social democracy and those of pure communism, the latter now being put into practice in the Soviet Union. And in so doing, she subtly emphasized the difference between the ruthless dictatorship of the latter and the balanced moderation contained in the principles of the former. It amazed me to find so many similarities between Elin's political creed and the ideas Gleb had discussed with me and which he had regarded as practical and acceptable for his wholehearted participation in the rebuilding of Russian society.

Yet, though I had to agree with many of Elin's arguments, I could never agree with her excuses for the executions and atrocities committed in the holy name of the People's Revolution. What was to her an occasional necessity during violent political upheavals was to me totally intolerable. No goal, I told her, could be considered either idealistic or desirable that trampled souls and crushed spirits in the process of attaining its fulfillment. I refused to concede that the Revolution, merely by squelching all resistance in blood, could indeed be called victorious. But in the passion of our disagreement I failed to realize that the very same castigation could often with equal reason be leveled at the political opponents of communism. I forgot that passion, not reason, usually fires the defense of clashing political ideas.

Elin insisted on my accompanying the Swedish delegation on its tours through the factories and other institutions it visited. She felt I should see for myself the great social reforms that were actually being accomplished. So I went, and I saw factories, schoolrooms, and nurseries that were so polished and well set up that they had obviously been prepared for the benefit of the visitors. Children drilled in revolutionary parades sang the "Internationale" with gusto, as other children before them had sung "God Save the Tsar." Workers cleanly attired and glowing with well-being impressed us with their zealous revolutionary activities, all of which appeared to me overemphasized but to my companions gave convincing proof of the Revolution's signal success. And it was only natural that it should be so. Had they been acquainted with the overwhelming contrasts I had seen, the crowds of people at the stations and in the trains, the mobs at the marketplaces, the degrading filth and feculence of the prisons, and beyond all this if they had known the anguish of fear and insecurity that was the lot of almost every citizen of Soviet Russia, they might have judged what they saw slightly differently. And yet . . .

A few days later Kata Dahlström informed me that she had been unable to arrange an interview with Trotsky, but that Anatoli Lunacharsky, commissar of education, had promised to see me and do what he could for me. Mr. Linderoth was to escort me to the Kremlin the next morning at eleven sharp.

Like beams radiating from the sun, the main streets of Moscow run in all directions from the Kremlin, the center. Asiatic, Tatar in design, raised by the toil of serfs, its diagonal turreted brick walls, their color mellowed through the centuries, contain the emblems and the relics of Russia's historical past. Within, the former Imperial Palace with its white facade and the tall slender Tower of Ivan the Terrible vie for room with several churches, their golden onion domes on sunny days exploding with suns of their own. Symbols of love and piety, these churches within this bastion contrast strangely with the historical actualities of Russia's dark ages, past and present.

With my escort, whose identity opened all doors, I walked through the Red Gate past the helmeted guards. Rounded cobblestones worn uneven by uncounted footsteps covered the courtyard. We slipped into the palace through a back entrance and mounted a flight of stairs. In a spacious anteroom outside tall closed doors we stood waiting.

Softly the doors opened and a dark, plain-faced woman motioned to me. The vast room I entered was dimmed by heavy draperies. A few soft chairs and an enormous desk stacked with orderly piles of papers were the only furniture. Behind the desk sat Lunacharsky. A face of sharp intelligence confronted me. The pointed goatee streaked with gray, the well-shaped open forehead accentuated by its receding hairline belonged to a man of culture and refinement. The look of sympathetic interest in the dark eyes took away some of my nervousness.

Lunacharsky rose and greeted me courteously. He motioned to me to be seated and asked me to state my mission. His voice was soft and urbane. When I had finished, he looked at me sharply.

"These events are unfortunate," he said, "but under the present circumstances I am afraid unavoidable. I regret your distress and that I cannot do very much for you. However, I shall write a letter to Comrade Menzhinsky, who is, as you know, the chief of the Moscow Cheka. I shall ask him to give your case special consideration. As a former White officer, your husband comes under Menzhinsky's jurisdiction."

He began dictating the letter to his secretary. When it had been typed he read it carefully, then folded it into an envelope that he left unsealed. He rose and with a few courteous words handed it to me. The secretary ushered me out into the anteroom.

With the precious letter clasped in my hand, I crossed Red Square and went through the Ivorsky Arch and up the wide avenue past the Bolshoi Theater to Lubyanka Square. Spacious as Russia herself, the wide thoroughfares were ample enough not to appear crowded even though many people were out hurrying past me on this sunny and warm afternoon. Crossing the square, I stood before the tall former apartment building that now housed the dreaded Moscow Cheka. I was breathless from nervousness. Within minutes I would know Gleb's fate with certainty.

At the wicket in the entrance hall I presented my letter of introduction. The soldier, cap nonchalantly pushed back, was duly impressed by the signature.

"So you want to see Comrade Menzhinsky?" he said gruffly as I quickly recovered the letter.

He spoke over the telephone at his elbow and I heard Lunacharsky's name mentioned.

"Here, Ivan," he shouted. "To Comrade Menzhinsky!"

My guide took me upstairs through a maze of bare passages and rooms. No broom had reached into the corners where the light husks of sunflower seeds had whirled away to gather in piles with the dust. Finally we stopped before tall ornate doors. My guide knocked and I was ushered inside.

The room was narrow and deep. At the far end huge windows rounded at the top opened upon the square. A man stood in one of them looking out, his long thin hands clasped behind his back. Menzhinsky turned slowly and I faced a cadaverous-looking man with sharply outlined facial bones and a hard mouth above a dapper pointed beard. His eyes were black as night against the pallor of his skin, yet seemed fired with the unholy light of fanaticism. With a nervous movement he took the letter I held out to him.

"What is your errand?" he asked coldly. His piercing glance and icy manner intimidated me. I felt my self-control slipping.

"It is about my husband, Gleb Nikolayevich Kirilin," I began, trying to keep my voice steady. "He was among a large group of Archangel officers taken prisoner at Sumskiy Posad. They were brought to Moscow, to the Ivanovsky camp.

Menzhinsky remained silent, merciless, and I continued, swallowing to check the tears: "He was transferred to the Pokrovsky camp and on the night of June sixteenth he and about five hundred of the other prisoners disappeared. I have been told they were deported to Kholmogory. Please . . . can you . . . Where is he?"

I stopped. Menzhinsky had moved slowly around to the desk. He stood there examining his long fingernails. In front of him lay Lunacharsky's letter.

"Why should I tell you?" he finally asked.

"Because I am his wife—because I must find him—and I must know what happened to him!"

A burst of mirthless laughter broke from his thin lips.

"What, madame, if I cannot tell you?" he taunted with mocking suavity.

"But you must know," I insisted, hardly noticing the sarcasm of his words. "You have the list of the prisoners, you must be able to tell me what has happened to him. He is in your power. You have released some of these prisoners. The terms of the surrender guaranteed that they would all eventually be released."

Menzhinsky's eyes narrowed and his voice was impatient when he spoke again:

"This serves you nothing, madame." He began pacing to and fro. Suddenly he stopped in front of me and every word was sharp and distinct: "Men like your husband are malicious counterrevolutionaries!"

I stood rooted to the floor. Tears poured down my cheeks, choked me.

"I beg of you, please, tell me—" A knock on the door interrupted me. Menzhinsky walked across the room to the doors and with a gesture of affected elegance flung them open. Those outside came in, and he motioned them to the far end of the room. Then, bowing blandly, he indicated the open doors.

Frantically, my mind in a whirl, I searched for words to make this man tell me the truth. "Please tell me, what have you done—"

"I bid you good day!" Menzhinsky bowed again and I felt myself, in effect, pushed out of the room.

It was all over . . . so abruptly. Somehow I reached the street. For one awful moment I had stood locked in contest with the man who held the secret of Gleb's fate . . . and I had lost.

CHAPTER 24

PETROGRAD—LENINGRAD

I had learned nothing. But Menzhinsky had been conspicuously evasive. Perhaps there were reasons, perhaps Gleb was still alive. General unrest, combined with pressures from abroad, might well force the Bolsheviks to suppress new excesses, at least temporarily. Their hold on power was precarious and the foreign party members were quite critical of a great many of the conditions they had accidentally discovered in the Soviet Union. Moreover, the authorities were constantly being faced with gigantic problems in their efforts to reorganize the whole economic structure of a continent, to feed the starving and placate the discontented. The favor of the masses is fickle, and their power is overwhelming unless they are kept strictly cowed into submission. Gleb might still be alive! And I must wait for another chance to find out. And if he was alive, I must wait for him to come back to me.

But not here in Moscow. I would wait in Leningrad with Gleb's sister, Marie. Gleb and I had planned this, if the worse came to the worst. He would know that I would go to her. And if he did not come back, Marie and I would go in search of him.

Having reached this decision, I could not leave Moscow fast enough. The Linderoths arranged for me to travel to Leningrad in comfort and security as an international delegate. Thus, in a first-class coach and in the same sleeping compartment with three Communist officials, I traveled in complete safety.

On a drizzly November morning I walked out of the station into Gleb's beloved city. The air, the streets were shrouded in dull gray humidity, but I had become so inured to the gray monotony of the Soviet environment that it did not greatly disturb me. As I found myself in surroundings easily recognized from his vivid descriptions, always dramatically colored with his intense nostalgia, Gleb's presence seemed very close.

A shaggy *isvostchik,* huge in his voluminous coachman's robes, pulled his gaunt horse to a stop in front of me.

"Where can I take you, *barenya*?" he asked genially, leaning down from his high perch. I looked at him in surprise. I had not thought of taking a droshky, but the man's kindly voice addressing me by the intimate second-person pronoun, calling me *barenya,* that word of simple Russian courtesy I had not heard for a long time, filled me with warmth. So we settled on a suitable fare and drove off to Marie's address.

Many of the wooden blocks with which the streets were originally paved to soften the noise of the traffic had rotted, leaving potholes and making our progress very bumpy. The streets were almost empty and the few people about in the former proud Russian capital looked ragged and more resigned than the people in Moscow.

As the vehicle swung slowly into the Nevsky Prospekt the marvelous dimensions of the city swept away all other impressions. What generosity of outline! What great open distances! Surely the majestic plan of this city, built upon millions of pilings driven deep into the marshy lands around the broad mouth of the river Neva, crisscrossed by natural channels and manmade canals, vividly reflected the largess of its famous builder, Peter the Great.

We crossed the Fontanka Bridge, guarded at each end by a pair of mighty prancing horses cast in bronze. On the left stretched the long yellow facade of the palace formerly occupied by Russia's most beloved tsarina in her retirement, Maria Feodorovna, of Danish birth and the sister of Britain's Queen Alexandra. It seemed lifeless and abandoned.

The Gostinaya Dvor with its curving arcades of once-famous boutiques, now empty and shuttered, lay brooding with an air of heavy nostalgia. At its far end a gigantic bust of a revolutionary hero mocked the sad remains of Peter's city. Daringly cut in hard gray granite, it stood on its still unfinished pedestal, a symbol of stark realism and the new order.

My friendly coachman turned off the Nevsky onto a short street well hidden behind the towering dome of the Kazansky Cathedral. Before a low two-story house we came to a halt.

There was a Soviet dining room on the ground floor. The janitor, an aged man, directed me across a cobblestoned courtyard. I climbed a flight of well-scrubbed stairs and knocked at a door. And in the dimly lit hallway I met Gleb's sister.

Marie's resemblance to her brother was striking. Of elegant build, she had the same features, the small head, the steady gray eyes, the sensitive mouth. Too soon this eighteen-year-old girl had been torn away from the security of her childhood home and thrown into the harsh world of social upheaval. The impact had been severe. The nervous way she spoke and the restless movements of her hands betrayed the emotional shock she had suffered. And this underlined the fundamental difference between brother and sister.

Marie, I soon learned, had acquired none of Gleb's serenity, nor the calm detachment with which he had absorbed change and sought its natural and logical explanation. One could probably not expect this. Instead she had mentally enclosed herself in a shiny armor of immunity against tears and sorrow. She had made up her mind that she had done with suffering. She would no longer allow anything to touch her. She had built between herself and disaster an impenetrable wall. And the effort had left her slightly tremulous and breathless.

It was therefore natural that Gleb's fate should not touch her poignantly. To her his disappearance meant only that the long-expected end of her family was now a fact. Gleb had left her, and in the course of the two years since he went away she had become quite accustomed to the thought. She had seen the same thing happening to so many of her friends. Most of their families had now been dissolved. Her youth bade her to live entirely independently from the past, with new goals, new ties, new dreams, and fresh longings.

A year passed.

I kept in close contact with several of the wives of Gleb's comrades. New rumors continued to arise, keeping us constantly on edge and our hopes tormentingly alive. Whispers reached us of an isolated concentration camp at the Solovietsky Monastery on a bleak island in the White Sea, where political prisoners considered particularly dangerous were being held. Might not the Kholmogory prisoners have been sent there? If so, a message would come through sooner or later. Then someone heard of trains full of prisoners near Murmansk and of dark columns of men marching by night somewhere in the north. Perhaps some of our men might be among them. Frantically we grasped at every rumor. But each one melted away like mists before the morning sun, leaving nothing but this weird uncertainty that begot and sustained hope.

Early in 1921 a revolt broke out among the naval units at the fortress of Kronstadt, just outside Leningrad in the Gulf of Finland. At the same time there were wild rumors of riots in the factories, of spreading unrest and mass movements of troops. Against the rapidly deteriorating conditions and the hungry people's cries for bread, the Kronstadt cannon roared in protest. Once again our hopes soared. We listened tense, half unbelieving, yet hoping against hope for a favorable outcome of the revolt, filled with fervid visions of the downfall of the Bolsheviks and the immediate release of all political prisoners.

One day a man with a familiar face passed me on the Nevsky Prospekt. To my surprise he turned and, not looking at me, walked beside me just long enough to whisper quickly, "Luisa Oskarovna!"

He strode ahead of me, then slowed so that I was soon abreast of him again.

"Dmitri Grigorievich!" I recognized him with a shock—Gleb's fellow officer who had given me his pair of spare breeches on that first day out of Archangel. The last time I had seen him had been at the Ivanovsky camp. Had he escaped from Kholmogory?

"Careful, I am being followed. Where do you live?"

"Oldenburg Children's Hospital, Ligovka, second floor, first door left," I said without turning my head, and continued walking. The next instant he was gone.

I hurried back to the hospital where I had been working ever since I arrived in Leningrad. Was I to hear and know at last? Dmitri Grigorievich was obviously desperate for a place to hide. Nowhere would he be safer than at the hospital. My room was easily accessible and separate from the living quarters of the rest of the staff. I waited for him.

At dusk a soft knock on my door announced his arrival. Quickly and silently he slipped inside. No one had seen him.

I asked, "Where have you come from?" and for an instant I could hardly breathe.

"Moscow. I was released there." My heart dropped like a stone.

I prepared some food—all I had to offer—and set it on the table. The work gave me time to recover. For many hours we sat undisturbed and talked in low whispers about Archangel, about the mad adventure, and all that had happened since then.

"And then I was set free," he concluded, "and ever since I have been living in hell. To be a prisoner, or to be free under constant surveillance—which is worse, I don't know! A prisoner enjoys a certain security." He gave a short laugh. "I have been hounded from place to place, hardly daring to visit friends for fear of causing them trouble. They are after me now," he shrugged his shoulders lightly, "but who cares! Perhaps I'll be able to lose them. . . . But this, Luisa Oskarovna, is a blessed respite." An engaging, almost confident smile flitted across his face.

His clean-cut features, the reckless glint in his eye brought a warm vision of Gleb alive before me. Proud, always courageous, this man as I knew him and Gleb as I remembered him that last time, standing erect in the old monastery garden, seemed to me the prototypes of Russia's fair beleaguered youth at bay. Pour out the wine, comrades, God only knows what the future will bring!

We sat for a while in silence. From the other end of the corridor came a child's cry. The soft footsteps of the night nurse passed my door. She had nothing for the child—no extra blankets, no food, not even enough bandages to change the dressing on an aching wound. She had nothing but water and her own soft hands and gentle voice. The baby's cries stopped.

Suddenly on the wind we heard the thunder of the cannon at Kronstadt. We sat listening tensely.

"Tonight, Luisa Oskarovna, the situation is critical. Tonight the outcome will be decided."

At midnight Dmitri Grigorievich stole away. I never saw him again.

After he had gone, I sat for a long time and listened to the guns. Gradually the booming detonations diminished. Finally they stopped.

The next morning the news reached us that the Kronstadt revolt had been successfully crushed by the ancient ruse of the Trojan horse.

I walked alone slowly through the narrow streets of the Petrogradskaya Starana. On the Troitsky Bridge I stood leaning against the parapet, looking out over the broad slow-flowing river Neva. To the right the squat jagged walls of the Peter and Paul Fortress mirrored themselves in the quiet waters. Suddenly a puff of white woolly smoke mushroomed from the wall of the fortress and the noon-hour gun boomed. A split second later its echo resounded against the dark-red walls of the Winter Palace and the long line of palatial former foreign embassies and luxurious homes strung along the Nabersynaya.

The thought of security in a free land beyond the closed borders played in my mind. To sit once again at a well-appointed table and eat one's fill, to dress once more in fine clothes, to speak one's mind without fear, to be able to visit friends without risk of being caught in a dragnet of persecution after the unfortunate friend was arrested seemed blessings beyond ordinary imagination.

Yet how could I, in all sincerity, wish myself away from all that Gleb had lived for and loved with the most intense feelings of belonging and passion? Strange how Russia had gradually become part of my own life and being, this land, this people, this culture that were his very essence. Give me only a week of soft living outside, and I would break my heart to come back to this air, these sights, the wide perspectives, the smells, the insecurity, the hunger, the despair—to Russia!

EPILOGUE

AFTER more than two years of fruitless searching and waiting, of hope slowly waning, I crossed the Siestra Rieka one day and never went back. In time I came to another country on the other side of the earth. And because the new land was in possession of immense space and magnificent diversified solitudes, I felt that I could bear to live there.

But before I left, I had come to know Russia from the White to the Black seas, from the Baltic to the Siberian taiga. I had lived with her people during the devastating famine of the years 1921 to 1924, caused by a combination of revolutionary aftermath and crop failures. I joined the Swedish Red Cross Expedition attached to the Nansen Mission, an organization created by the famed Norwegian explorer, and which together with the generous Hoover American Relief Administration had come to the aid of the Russian people. As a relief delegate I worked in a large outlying district on the Volga steppes near Kuibyshev inhabited by the Mordovians, witnessed how death and in some cases cannibalism gradually gave way before the restoring effects of food. I lived with these people, saw their mute suffering, and realized their immense powers of resilience. I went into their huts and found their dying children abandoned without hope among the rags in a corner, and with the help of local nurses, special diets, and treatment restored some of them to life.

Later, as a delegate of the European Student Relief, also of the Nansen Mission, I lived with the Cossack people of the Novocherkassk and Rostov-on-Don region, listened to their undying dreams, and learned that in spite of their reputation for ruthless cruelty and reckless bravery, a warm gentleness was part of their character. And so this work and the travels linked with it afforded me unique opportunities to learn about Russia and to understand better the nature of her people.

Ten years after Gleb's disappearance, in the home of a friend who lived in an obscure northern town of the new country, I came by chance across a book titled *The Red Terror in Russia* by Sergey Petrovich Melgounov, a historian of note whose political views placed him among the active Mensheviks, the Russian Social Democratic party. My friend gave me the book.

Up to this time, I had avoided books about Russia, for they were either barefaced propaganda for or against her, or simply untruthful because of ignorance. The truth about Russia, I felt, was profound, intangible, and elusive. To sense the reasons for her greatness and the reality of her ignominy one must either be born of her or have come under her tormenting and fascinating spell long enough to have felt her heart beat.

This book contained stark facts, amply documented, about the earlier deeds of the Red terrorists. It revealed unspeakable horrors, the most repulsive perversities; and the author's heartstruck protests against the brutality of his people's abuse penetrated every sentence and paragraph.

It spoke of Archangel as the "City of the Dead" and of Kholmogory as the "Camp of Death" where thousands of prisoners, "the flower of Russian youth, had been slain. And it goes on: "All through that summer [1920] the town fairly groaned under the terrorist scourge; and though I lack figures to check the exact number of persons slaughtered there, at least I know that 800 [*sic*] ex-officers were put to death—officers whom the late Miller administration had authorized to proceed to London by way of the Mourmansk railway whilst the members of the administration crossed to Mourmansk on icebreakers. All of them were seized by the Bolshevists en route . . ."

At last, at long last, the historical fact lay before me.

That night my lamp burned its oil to the last drop while I lived my life with Gleb and with Russia over again. The information Nina Aleksandrovna had been able to gather with heartsickening effort had been essentially correct. That night when Olga Stepanovna had taken me off the train at the very last minute, Gleb was dead. His wish had been fulfilled. He had shared the destiny of his comrades to the last. He had shirked nothing, for he had realized that the cruel twist of fate they had been dealt was, in essence, as inevitable as the power that had directed their brothers' hands against them had been incontestable.

"I wish I could see things more clearly. Perhaps I never shall—for I must live in consequence with the fundamentally true traditions of my fathers and my training and principles," he had said once.

The balance of life required a readjustment. The force of this imperative was to be measured only against the force of its opposition. That Gleb's life became part of its bloody price was uncontrollable fate. But the utter wastefulness of these historic deeds, apart from their stark criminality, was and is irreparable.

Somewhere in the vast lands of the Russian north, Gleb is now one with his native soil. With the dawn came the light—and the thought lost its edge. He had borne the burden of his brief individual life willingly and loyally in accordance with the pattern of the whole. He had accepted the bitter penalty exacted for the sins of generations simply as a privilege of adjustment—nothing but this—to seek the balance and to perceive the rhythm.

ABOUT THE AUTHOR

Louise Lawrence is the author of several books, including The Lovely and the Wild, *which won the Burroughs Medal in 1969. She lives in a house she and her husband built in the country some two hundred miles north of Toronto.*

LAKE COUNTY PUBLIC LIBRARY
3 3113 02809 2601